On Islam

and

Shi'ism

Ahmad Kasravi
1890-1946

Ahmad Kasravi

On Islam

and

Shi'ism

Translated from the Persian by

M. R. Ghanoonparvar

With an Introductory Essay and
Bibliographical Note by

M. A. Jazayery

Mazdâ Publishers

1990

Library of Congress Cataloging-in-Publication Data

Kasravi, Ahmad, 1890 or 91-1946.
  On Islam and Shi'ism / Ahmad Kasravi; translated
from the Persian by M. R. Ghanoonparvar; with an
introductory essay and bibliographical note by
M. A. Jazayery.
  p. cm.
  Includes bibliographical references.
  ISBN:0-939214-39-3
  1. Islam–20th century. 2. Shi'ah. I. Title.
BP163.k38 1990   90-5897
297–dc20   CIP

Mazdâ Publishers   1990

CONTENTS

Translator's Foreword

Ahmad Kasravi (1890-1946) is without a doubt one of the most prolific writers of twentieth-century Iran, with broad interests as a reformer and thinker in virtually all aspects of his society. He published on a variety of subjects, including history, geography, social criticism, literature and philology. Consistently, in virtually all his works, Kasravi challenges the conventions of his time and what he sees as decadent ideas, superstitions and the varied other ills of the society. As one of the most controversial figures in modern Iran, he has attracted the attention of both supporters and detractors. Nowhere are his controversial ideas more evident than in his writings on religion and Islam in general and Shi'ism in particular. The English-speaking world has come to know Kasravi primarily through secondary sources, either in essays written about him or through passing references to his various ideas and endeavors in books concerning Iranian intellectual history. The present volume is the first translation of two of Kasravi's works, *Dar Piramun-e Eslam* [On Islam] and *Shi'igari* [Shi'ism].

Ahmad Kasravi was born in 1890 in the city of Tabriz to a religious family. Although his father was not himself a cleric, he nurtured the hope that one of his sons would continue in the vocation of Kasravi's paternal grandfather, who was a clergyman. He, therefore, named every son "Mir Ahmad," after their grandfather. Much to the dismay of Kasravi's father, three of his sons died in their early years. As Ahmad Kasravi writes in his memoirs, he was the fourth son of his father to be named after his grandfather, and expected to carry out his father's hopes.

At the age of six, Kasravi began his education in a traditional school (*maktab*). Following the death of his father when he was thirteen years old, Kasravi spent more than two years in a carpet-weaving factory, to help support his family. He then entered a seminary to become a cleric, as his father had wished. In fact, he began preaching at the age of twenty. However, with his refusal to conform to the conventional forms of preaching and dress, he soon became a target of criticism. Disillusioned, he abandoned this pursuit.

With his knowledge of Arabic and the Koran, Kasravi then was exposed to new, Western ideas and sciences through Arabic language publications. He became interested in and began reading on a variety of subjects, including calculus, geometry, algebra, astronomy and physics. In the meantime, Kasravi had become interested and involved in the Constitutional movement. Following his disagreements with some of the political groups in Tabriz, he went to Tehran, where he worked in the Ministry of Education and the Justice Department. Later, he worked in the Justice Department in Tabriz and Khuzestan, and afterwards, was appointed to various judiciary positions in Tehran.

Towards the end of his life, Kasravi devoted his time primarily to writing and advocating his reformist ideas. Kasravi was at times praised for his scholarly work on history and language, but he was also attacked for his views on religion and literature. For example, his condemnation of major Iranian poets as advocates of wine drinking and carefree living, which he deemed detrimental to the society, aroused the anger of the literati. At the same time, he wrote a number of works advocating his own beliefs, which gained him some following.

Kasravi has been a controversial figure in Iran for the most part because of his work on religion in general and Shi'ism, Baha'ism and Sufism in particular. In the context of Shi'ism, Kasravi dared to directly attack the Shi'ite clergy, which angered religious groups and eventually led to his assassination by a fanatical group called the "Feda'iyan-e Eslam" in 1946.

In addition to his native Azarbaijani Turkish and Persian, Kasravi was fluent in Arabic and knowledgeable in other languages, including English and Armenian. His linguistic interests extended to undertaking reforms in Persian language, reintroducing a number of older words or new coinages into Persian to replace foreign lexical borrowings, and he used them persistently in his own writings. Perhaps for this reason, his "*zaban-e pak*" or "pure language" is not always readily comprehensible to the average Iranian reader. Because of his lexical and syntactic usage, Kasravi's language is at times ambiguous and his style idiosyncratic. An attempt has been made in the present translation to preserve some of these features, even at times at the expense of clarity and lucidity in English. It must also be kept in mind that most of Kasravi's polemic writings, including the texts used for this volume, were initially talks given to his followers and then, often hurriedly, transcribed and published. In other words, the original Persian texts were not thoroughly edited and annotated by Kasravi, which may not have seemed necessary at the time, as they were addressed to an audience already familiar with the ongoing debates between Kasravi and the clergy. The present English text follows the Persian without editorial changes. Certain terms that are used by Kasravi with particular meanings have been transliterated and explained either in brackets or in the Notes following the second text.

Two versions exist of *Dar Piramun-e Eslam*, one was published in 1943/44 (Tehran: Peyman) and the other, a later, apparently revised version of the original text. The earlier version was used as an initial draft for the present translation. However, because of the extent of the discrepancies between the two texts in regards to both additions and omissions, the present translation is based on the fourth printing of the revised version (Tehran: Paydar Bookstore, 1963).

Shi'ism appears in Persian in a popular version entitled *Shi'igari* (1943/44) and an expanded version (1944/45) entitled *Bekhanand va Davari Konand* [Let Them Read and Judge]. The present translation is based on the latter edition.

On Islam precedes *Shi'ism* in the present volume, even though it was written at a later date, and Kasravi makes references in *On Islam* to *Shi'ism*, since it is a more general discussion of the subject. It is hoped that this order will place Kasravi's discussion of Shi'ism in a broader context. The translations are followed by notes, numbered separately for each text, at the end of the volume. Kasravi's own footnotes have also been included and indicated as such in the notes. A selected list of Kasravi's works, which appears in the 1963 edition of *Dar Piramun Eslam*, is included at the end of the volume. *Let Them Read and Judge* contains several pictures either of historical personalities or various Shi'ite practices. They have not been included in the present book.

In the course of several years since this project began, I have benefitted on various occasions from conversations with M. A. Jazayery, who has had a life-long interest in and knowledge of the works and ideas of Ahmad Kasravi. He has shared his thoughts with me most generously, for which I am grateful. In fact, together we read and compared the original and the English translation of the first dozen or so pages of *On Islam*, which I feel eventually helped me re-edit the tone and style of the present rendition. I would also like to express my appreciation to the Center for Middle Eastern and North African Studies at the University of Michigan in Ann Arbor for the opportunity to spend a year as a Rockefeller Fellow conducting research and writing on another project in Persian literature, which also made it possible for me to add the finishing touches to the present work.

M. R. Ghanoonparvar
Ann Arbor, Michigan
February 1989

Kasravi, Iconoclastic Thinker of Twentieth-Century Iran

by

Mohammad Ali Jazayery
The University of Texas at Austin

> *"When society requires to be rebuilt,*
> *there is no use in attempting to*
> *rebuild it on the old plans."*
>
> *John Stuart Mill*

I

Beginning about the year 1800 there developed in Iran a feeling that Iranians were a backward nation. The feeling resulted from military and political defeats, social and economic problems, and an increasing awareness of the outside world, i.e., Europe. This feeling led to a search for causes and remedies. There was a wide range of diagnoses and proposed remedies. The latter included: a strong army; higher education; modern schools, increased literacy, universal education; European-style law; constitutional monarchy; the republican form of

1

government; improving the economic conditions; wholesale adoption of Western material culture and way of life (modernization/Westernization); getting rid of religion; strengthening religion; communism.

Some suggested more specific remedies, e.g., founding factories, building railroads, publishing newspapers, importing large numbers of European immigrants and, in the area of religion, strict adherence to Koranic teachings, revival of Islam, reforming Islam.[1]

Varying degrees of thought and energy were devoted to the items in the preceding lists, and some specific actions were taken. When the Constitutional Revolution (begun in 1905) changed the system of government from absolute monarchy to constitutional monarchy, a general feeling of optimism--indeed of euphoria--enveloped the country. Yet neither the new governmental structure, nor any of the other specific actions taken before and after the Revolution changed much beyond the surface appearances of Iranian life. Despotism returned less than two decades after the Revolution. Foreign influence (political as well as economic) did not cease.

It was against this background that Kasravi's movement began: He attempted to identify the root-causes of Iran's problems and to propose specific solutions, within an all-encompassing ideology consistent with a particular world view which he had developed.

II

Kasravi lived a relatively short life--less than fifty six years. It was, however, a very eventful one, and even a mere listing of the facts, with enough explanations to make the list meaningful, would take several pages. In what follows, I shall mention only the more important highlights. Those interested in a fuller biography can consult his autobiography and other sources, some of which will be mentioned in this essay.[2]

Ahmad Kasravi was born in 1890 in Tabriz, the seat of the Turkish-speaking northwestern province of Azerbaijan in Iran, in a middle-class family. He received a religious education in Tabriz, studied the modern natural sciences on his own, and (as an adult) learned English at the American missionary school.

He was educated to become a Shi'i clergyman. However, he soon began to question the clergy's behavior--their hypocrisy, demagoguery, and greed; their abuse of religion; their obsession with the distant past and disinterest in contemporary problems; their disregard for the welfare of their flock; their divisive influence, which created and

2

encouraged sectarianism; and, of most immediate concern, the violently hostile response of most of them to the Constitutional Revolution. His unorthodox sermons and liberal activities, intensified after the Russian forces occupied Tabriz, added to his already well-known open-minded and liberal views on religion, attracted increasingly intense hostility from religious leaders. Mutual disillusionment was complete, and he left the profession. He was off and on excommunicated by several other clergymen.

Three major events--one sociopolitical; the second, personal--religious; and the third, cosmological--occurred within a five-or six-year period in Kasravi's early life which left a lasting impact on him, and, indeed, very likely determined the course of his life.

The sociopolitical event was the Constitutional Revolution. It began in 1905 in Tehran, but soon Tabriz became its center, saving it from the Royalists and their Czarist Russian supporters. The concepts of liberty, law, and popular government appealed to him, and he used the pulpit to incite the people in its favor. He was particularly impressed by the people's army, the *Mojahedin*, who fought the shah's forces as well as the occupying Russian soldiers. "This event was one of the most influential in my life," he said many years later in his autobiography. The reason: "the dastardly acts of many cabinet ministers and others," and "on the other hand, the resistance of a group of Iranians against an iron-fisted government such as Czarist Russia." [3] His love of democracy grew stronger with time. In fact, he considered his own movement, as far as its Iranian phase was considered, a continuation of the Constitutional Revolution.

The second influential event in Kasravi's life, which was personal and religious in nature, occurred in 1910-1911, when he memorized the Koran: In order to remember what he was memorizing, he felt he had to focus on the *actual* meaning of the verses (as against the meanings given by interpreters, commentators etc.). This caused "the first jolt to my ideas and beliefs." [4]

The cosmological event was the appearance of Halley's Comet in 1911, and his discovery that its periodic appearance had been correctly predicted by the scientific method. He embarked upon a program of studying the natural sciences on his own. The first book he read was on Astronomy. "I was pleased and happy to see that science had come to follow such a clear path in Europe." [5] His acquaintance with science, though limited, instilled in him a respect for the scientific method. In fact, a clear feature of his later thinking on religion was the strong belief that religion should be compatible with science. A side-effect of his interest in natural science was his decision to learn English, since Persian and other Middle Eastern languages were still rather poor in scientific publications. However, English was more helpful to him in his research in history and linguistics, since he did not pursue the sciences.

He moved to Tehran in 1921, where he joined the Ministry of Justice, which sent him all over the country, generally as a trouble-shooter. His last provincial assignment, as the head of the Department of Justice for the southwestern province of Khuzistan, was fraught with political problems caused by the presence of the Iranian Arab chieftain Shaykh Khazal. The Shaykh, though an Iranian citizen, and an appoint-ee of the Iranian government, was acting virtually as an independent ruler. Kasravi was assigned to that post not only because of his proven competence, but also because of his proficiency in Arabic. Kasravi clashed not only with the Shaykh, but also with the army officers head-ing the army sent from Tehran to restore control over the region. (The commanding officer was one Fazlollah Zahedi, who some years later became prime minister after the overthrow of Mosaddeq.) At the behest of the Ministry of War, the Ministry of Justice recalled Kasravi to Tehran.

Another important position he held was as Chief Judge of the Courts of First Instance for the District of Tehran. It was in this post that, in a suit brought by a group of peasants against Reza Shah's royal court, involving some land, he found for the peasants--unprecedented in Iran. He soon lost his judgeship.

He then opened a law practice, which he kept until shortly before his death, when his license was revoked for no express reason. As a lawyer, he was involved in the two most celebrated trials of this (or any) century in Iran, serving as council for the defence. The first was the 1938 trial, in a kangaroo court, of the "Fifty-Three", a group of young intellectuals arrested on charges relating to communism. (The name refers to the number of those originally arrested, and is still used, even though five of them were released, and only 48 tried.) With three exceptions, they were all condemned. [6] In the second trial in 1942, a group of police officials were tried for the torture and murder of politi-cal prisoners during Reza Shah's reign (1925-1941).

Kasravi's career also included some high-school and university teaching. At the University of Tehran, when a new law established professorial ranks, Kasravi was denied a professorship because he refused to retract his criticism of some classical Persian poets.

Throughout these years, Kasravi was engaged in scholarly research. In fact, he was one of a small group of young Iranian scholars who dominated the scholarly scene in the 1920s and 1930s, using Western research methods. Others included Said Nafisi, Abbas Eqbal, Mojtaba Minovi, M.T. Bahar, and S. Rezazadeh Shafaq. Kasravi's major specialty was history, in which he soon gained an international reputa-tion. His masterpiece is his seven-volume history of Iran's Constitutional Revolution (now available in a two-volume edition). He also published in linguistics. And he was an early advocate of Persian language reform, which (unlike others) he approached methodically, and on which he published extensively.

III

In the early 1930s, Kasravi began a new career as a social thinker. From then until his death, he studied Iran's social problems in detail, and suggested solutions for them. In broader terms, he also discussed Middle Eastern and world problems. In time, he developed a comprehensive ideology covering all aspects of society and culture. This was his central concern during this period, but he did not give up his scholarship. In fact, his major scholarly work, of more than 2400 pages (in the original edition), the history of the Constitutional Revolution, was written during these years, as were numerous articles on Persian grammar and on language reform, as well as other subjects.

Kasravi first presented his social views in a two-volume book, *Ayin* ('Creed'), in 1933-34. This was the first critical study in Iran of Westernization/modernization/industrialization, written at a time when Westernization was extremely popular in the country, and was being promoted by the government.

In December 1933 he launched the monthly journal *Peyman* (forthrightly during its first six months), of which he was the owner, editor, and almost sole writer. It ceased publication in 1942 after Volume 7, No. 9. During these nine years, this journal was the major vehicle for developing and disseminating his ideas. The journal format allowed him to discuss the same topics more than once, modifying, explaining, clarifying, answering questions and criticisms. Many of the books that he published after 1933 had their beginnings in *Peyman*, in some cases updated, and in a few cases reprints of its longer articles.

On August 25, 1941, during the second World War, Iran was occupied by the British and Soviet forces (later joined by Americans); and three weeks later Reza Shah Pahlavi abdicated and went into exile, succeeded by his son, Mohammad Reza Shah. Foreign occupation, and the expulsion of the powerful monarch, threw the country into utter chaos. The people, after years of believing their country to be invincible, were stunned by the ignominious defeat. However, one essentially positive side-effect of these events was the restoration (in varying degrees), for a brief time, of constitutional freedoms, including freedom of assembly and organized political activity.

5

On October 11, 1941, Kasravi gave a public lecture, entitled "What is to be done today?", in which he analyzed the recent events; cautioned against excesses; rejected the almost universally expressed belief that the former king bore sole responsibility for all the problems of the country; and warned that, unless something was done, despotism would return in a few years. He also briefly presented some of his views on the problems of the country and their solutions.

A number of people in various cities, having read the text of the lecture in *Peyman*, contacted Kasravi, suggesting the need for some kind of collective action. Some of them reprinted the lecture as a book.[7] Thus it was that the *Bahamad-e Azadegan* [8] was organized in late 1941 or early 1942. The nucleus of this ideologically-based political party consisted of a small number of people who, through reading Kasravi's writings, had in effect formed an informal group during 1933-1941, when political organizations were prohibited by the government.

The party grew gradually and became increasingly more active and aggressive, with branches in all major cities as well as a few smaller ones. The membership was never large, but it was very active and had many sympathizers. From the beginning, the fate of Kasravi and that of his party were intertwined. The bolder and more open they became, the more violent and persistent became the opposition. But they stood their ground on all fronts: against the religious and educational estab-lishments, against the government, and against personal and institution-al attacks. They were subjected to mobbings, knifings, imprisonment, dismissals from government jobs, denials of promotions. They were attacked in the Parliament and on the government-run Radio Tehran (as well as Radio Delhi). Numerous anti-Kasravi complaints, some bearing hundreds of signatures, were instigated by the Shi'ite clergy. These complaints took the form of telegrams to newspapers and government authorities, or of widely circulated communiques. Appeals were made to the Shah. Some newspapers published hostile articles.

The daily newspaper *Parcham*, edited by Kasravi, and the offi-cial organ of the Azadegan, began publication on January 23, 1942, and ceased publication after the December 8 issue, when all newspaper licenses were cancelled. A fortnightly edition began in March 1943, but its publication was suppressed six months later. This edition was in scope a combination of *Peyman* and the daily *Parcham*, dealing with both more general topics and current issues. Next began a weekly edition in March 1944, which was suppressed after seven issues. In March 1945, another monthly journal was begun. It had no specific title: each issue was given the name of the month in which it was pub-lished; e.g., *Farvardin- Mah-e 1324* ('the month of Farvardin 1324'). I believe this device was thought up by Kasravi the lawyer because such a publication would not be a journal, and therefore not subject to any licensing requirements. They were collectively referred to as *Daftarha-ye Mahaneh* ('Monthly Notebooks'). Plans were under way for publishing a daily paper but fell through as a result of Kasravi's assassination.

By March 11, 1946, Kasravi had published some eighty volumes of books of varying length, as well as hundreds of journal articles, and newspaper editorials and columns. Both the publications and his weekly lectures covered a wide cultural range, including religion in general, Islam, Shi'ism, Bahaism, Sufism, philosophy, economics, education, law, government, literature, women, *Kharabatism* (represented by Omar Khayyam's teachings), *Batenism* (the ideas of the Bateni sect, stressing the "inner" meaning of the Koran, later extended to literature, especially poetry, rejecting literal meanings in favor of symbolic interpretation), materialism, etc. His writings covered both general topics and current issues, the latter represented by newspaper editorials and columns as well as books on the Azerbaijan autonomy movement and on the United Nations (then just organized). His views on these and other subjects were iconoclastic. Hardly any cultural sacred cow was spared his severe and sometimes cutting whip.

In short, Kasravi analyzed Iranian society and its cultural institutions, found fault with most of them, expressed his objections to them, and offered a new system to replace the existing one. Reaction was strong in all quarters, but the most vocal and violent reaction came from religionists. Of the dozen books written about Kasravi in Persian, nine were written by clergymen attacking his detailed criticisms of the Shi'i sect of Islam. Perhaps the most interesting response by the religious element, especially in the light of the events since then, is represented by one of Rouhollah Khomeyni's first major books, *Revelation of Secrets*, published in 1943, a detailed attack on Kasravi's religious views on Shi'ism.

IV

Since the nineteenth century Iranian intellectuals, and by extension the Iranian society as a whole, like others in the Middle East, have been struggling with three broad concerns: modernization (almost always equated with Westernization), nationalism, and religion. Nationalism has been, on the one hand, a consequence of modernization and, on the other, its promoter. The Western powers' colonial designs have provided an additional impulse. The place of religion in this triad is the most complex. It has, as in the Middle East in general, helped fight

7

colonialism, and thus encourage nationalism (as it is now doing in Latin America). On the other hand, Islamic doctrine is more than slightly inimical to nationalism (and the concept of nation-state), and opposes secular government (a basic tenet of modern Western life), which is closely attached to nationalism. The Shi'i concept of society and government is clearly even more decidedly opposed to nationalism and secular government. This contradiction and conflict first created open--and in a sense public--debate during the Constitutional Revolution, and has come into prominent focus since the Islamic Revolution.

The leaders of the earlier Revolution thought they had resolved the conflict, presumably to the advantage of secularism, nationalism, and democracy. But they were mistaken, suffering from a false sense of security, as the Islamic Revolution made abundantly clear. What went wrong? To my knowledge, Kasravi was the only person who seriously attempted to find an answer to the question. First, however, it may be useful to make a quick comparison between the two Revolutions, in the context of the present discussion.

In the Constitutional Revolution, the secular elite co-opted the religious leaders--or some of them, to overthrow absolute monarchy--and then cast them aside (more or less). In the Islamic Revolution, the religious leaders used the secular elite, even the supposedly sophisticated leftists--and, upon overthrowing the regime, cast them aside, by rather drastic methods.

In fact, the two Revolutions, despite differences in leadership, motivation, international circumstances, and methods, in the end came to share certain important features, as reflected in the constitutions they produced. In both, Twelver Shi'ism is the state religion. Both require all laws passed by the Parliament to be verified, by a committee of clergymen, as being compatible with Islam, or else be declared null and void. Both recognize only those religious minorities recognized by Islam.[9] In both systems slander to Islam (but not to other religions, including, I believe, the recognized ones) is a punishable offence.

An important difference between the two regimes is that the government entrusted with enforcing the old constitution did not seriously enforce the articles dealing with religion (except for minority representation in the Parliament). The government set up under the new constitution clearly goes in the opposite direction. This retrogression is the more interesting and significant because it has occurred after seven decades during which religion was thought to be losing its hold--as a result of the former regime's supposedly anti-religious policies; of secular and expanded education and higher percentage of literacy; of greater spread of the natural sciences; and of more extensive exposure to Western culture, material and nonmaterial--all factors assumed to weaken religion and religious sentiment.

What accounts for this retrogression? What happened to the Constitutional Revolution, which introduced democracy, which, supposedly, lasted over 70 years (1906-1979)? Liberal-minded Iranian intellectuals had placed all of their hopes for their country in that Revolution. But the Revolution was soon derailed, and despotism returned; as did religious fanaticism, with a vengeance. In fact, something new appeared: "Islamic" government, which had at best been a very vague wish, with no structure, in very few minds. Many would say (and have said) that democracy had failed. This was said even before the Islamic Revolution. The question is: Did it? And if so, why? Kasravi, himself one of those intellectuals, and a witness to the Constitutional Revolution, sought answers to these questions: not glib answers, but answers based on careful research, and making use of insights from history and psychology. He concluded that there *was* failure. However, the failure was not the failure of *democracy*. Rather, it was the result of the failure of the leaders of the Revolution, and those who followed them, to understand that democracy could not long survive in a society whose most cherished cultural institutions, most of all its majority religion, are strongly antipathetic to democracy. For democracy to be, or to become, viable in such a society, those institutions have to be shaken to their very foundations; and new foundations laid. That is why Kasravi considered his own movement a continuation of the Constitutional Revolution. And that is why his ideology was so radical, and so comprehensive. It is to that ideology that we now turn. The intention in what follows is to provide a very short introduction to the subject, on which the best sources of information are Kasravi's own writings.

V

Kasravi's ideology, and his approach to analyzing the social and political problems of Iran (and to offering solutions), was based on certain premises and principles. An understanding of some of these at the outset is important.

The most important premise, basic to all Kasravi's teachings, and one that he discussed repeatedly, is the primacy of ideas as determinants of human action: a person's ideas, beliefs, dictate his behavior. He often summarized this premise in the statement: "The source of man's ideas is his brain; and the brain is ruled by the ideas that are in it."[10]

Another premise is that Iran's social ills (and political problems) are all interrelated. You cannot solve them separately.[11] For example, you cannot successfully fight despotism without fighting religious super-stitions, fatalism, certain parts of classical Persian poetry, and so on.

A third premise is that Iran's problems are not of recent origin. They are of long standing, accumulated during what he called Iran's "Dark Ages" (from the time of the Seljuq dynasty to the latter part of the Qajar period, approximately 1040-1850).[12]

Kasravi also addressed certain very common assumptions held by Iranians about their country's problems. Perhaps the most widely held of these is that Iran's problems are the result of external circum-stances, particularly foreign intervention into Iran's internal affairs. Kasravi, however, believed that those problems "are not the result of political defeat or temporary circumstances. They are, *more* than any-thing else (emphasis added), the result of the ills of the nation itself. Nor can loud clamor or rioting remedy them. Instead, each person must try to become good himself. On the other hand, the sources of these ills are the divisive and conflicting ideas which have taken root in the nation. We must eradicate these."[13] Kasravi was of course aware of problems created by foreign powers, perhaps more so than most, because of his research in recent Iranian history. However, he believed that foreigners take advantage of Iranian weaknesses. When, during the Second World War, some Iranians said that Iran's lot would improve after the War, he said: "A people will not benefit from the good things of the world as long as they are not good themselves... A nation may derive some benefit from circumstances, but the gain can be no more than temporary, and, ultimately, they cannot reap any results."[14]

Many people assumed that the important thing is to gain power; that with political/military power, all necessary reforms can be brought about. To them, Kasravi said on one occasion: "Suppose the Ministry of War or the administration placed the armies of Tehran under your control. Tell us what 'reform' you can make. One of the problems of Iran is the existence of religious factionalism.... tell us how you will solve this. Will you send soldiers [to the various religious groups] to obtain a 'pledge' from all of them to give up their religions? Can this happen?...."[15]

A third assumption has been that Iran's problems can be solved by joining some European movement or ideology. Kasravi felt that thoughtless adopting of a foreign ideology would not solve any prob-lems. Iran's problems are different and should be carefully studied and appropriate solutions found. He would not exclude anything European (or Western) that would meet the Iranian conditions, however. He certainly fully embraced the idea of democracy, for example.[16]

Kasravi also addressed the question of the procedure for putting his ideology (or any ideology) into effect. To those who criticized him because, they said, all he was doing was talk, he said: "All movements in the world have been born of words: words have been spoken, truths have been elucidated; intention to act has been born in people's hearts; ways of executing the plan have been recognized; a group of people, one in thought and in purpose, have joined hands and made progress."[17] In other words: (a) identify the problems and the solutions; (b) disseminate your findings widely, creating a movement; (c) form a party; (d) when the movement reaches the right strength, and the party the right size, move to take power (by parliamentary procedures, or revolution, or a combination of both). This passage, in effect, summarizes his plan of action, for he was interested in action and practical results, not in theory. An implication of this premise is the need for paving the way to power by preparing the people first. He strongly believed that creating a small intellectual elite, leaving the masses behind, would not produce the desired results. Involvement of the people must be broad and active.[18]

VI

Reference has been made to the establishment of the Bahamad-e Azadegan, following the publication of the text of Kasravi's October 11, 1941 lecture. Based primarily on this text that party drew up the "Sixteen Objectives of the Azadegan," as follows:

1. Supporting representative government and the Constitution, and resisting the return of despotism.
2. Spreading the meaning of representative government among the nation and preparing the people for it.
3. Overseeing the enforcement of the laws and protesting any violation of law that occurs.
4. Advocating the pursuit of clear policies.
5. Preventing unwarranted imitations of European parties.
6. Clarifying people's minds about what true wealth is; about the fact that its source consists of land, water, air, and sunshine; and about the need for appreciating these things.
7. Changing the conditions of commerce to its true meaning, and making it conform with the interests of the nation and the country.

8. Attempting to develop science and industry, and ensuring that, as far as possible, the country's industrial needs are met in the country itself.

9. Developing agriculture, making it the basis of life, and endeavoring to make villages larger and flourishing, and reducing the differences between them and the cities.

10. Preventing economic parasitism in whatever form, and making sure that each person's economic share is based on his merit and labor.

11. Fighting against divisiveness in beliefs, and working for unity in ideas and ideals.

12. Working to increase the population, and to make marriage compulsory and simple.

13. Trying to make clothing and implements used in life simple.

14. Making efforts to expand and develop public health, and fighting diseases.

15. Changing the structure and laws of the justice system, and simplifying judging.

16. Making elementary education compulsory, changing the school curricula, and eliminating harmful and useless teachings. [19]

The items on this list, which seem to have been compiled somewhat hastily, are not equal in significance or complexity. Furthermore, the degree of relevance of some items may have changed in the intervening 48 years. Still, it shows concern for all aspects of life - material, intellectual, and political. Almost one-third (items 1-4, 5,15) concern government, clearly the democratic kind. One-fourth (6, 7, 9, 10) deal with economics. One-fifth (5, 6, 8, 11, 16) address educational concerns. The rest (12-14) concern personal life.

The four years after these objectives were set were full and extremely active for Kasravi and the Azadegan. The party became more structured and better organized. In Tehran, its meetings were held at Kasravi's home; and a very small office was rented for the newspaper. By late 1945 these arrangements were quite inadequate. A building was rented to house the party headquarters and the modest printing facilities owned by a small company funded by several party members (with one floor used as the Kasravi family home). Branches (none with more than two or three dozen members) started in many cities. There were, in addition, some sympathizers who for various reasons did not officially join the party, however. Dozens of books were published, as well as a newspaper and journals (mentioned earlier).

By now Kasravi apparently felt the time had come for the party to become gradually involved in practical politics. On March 29, 1945 (exactly a month before the first attempt on his life), he started a new series of lectures by announcing: "In these endeavors which we have undertaken, one of our tasks will be to take control of the affairs of the country. This is one of our objectives; and beginning this year (i.e. the new Iranian year begun on March 21, 1945) we must take steps in that direction, and prepare ourselves...It is our obligation to try to attain to that position." [20] The text of the lecture series was published as a book, entitled *On the Road to Politics*, published in June or July 1945. After a brief reference to the efforts of several political leaders who, despite their good intentions, had not identified the basic causes of Iran's decline, Kasravi began with his concept of what Iranians needed to do to ensure a good future for themselves, and an honorable status among other nations. He then briefly outlined the major problems that had created obstacles in the way of making such a future possible. Put another way, he explained the obstacles to realizing the sixteen objectives the party had set for itself in 1941, and enumerated above.

"The Iranians," Kasravi believed, "should base their future life on three principles: first, working to reform the nation, and to get rid of all forms of ignorance and of (social) ills; second, taking charge of the affairs of their country, and showing good will towards Russia and Britain (then the two major powers capable of influencing Iran's destiny), treating them equally; third, taking an interest in the betterment of the world, fighting against evil, and collaborating in this field with other people of good will in the world. It is these three things that I call 'the three principles of politics'." [21]

Of the three principles, or objectives, of politics, the first, solving the long-standing deep-rooted internal problems, was considered by Kasravi to be the most important, the most basic. These can be summarized as follows: (1) religious, and the other older harmful teachings; (2) materialistic philosophy; and other harmful ideas recently imported from Europe; (3) linguistic factionalism; (4) nomadic life-style; (5) the high degree of illiteracy, and low development of science and technology; (6) the disastrous educational system; (7) bad laws and the ineffective administrative system; (8) misconceptions about economic principles; (9) the sad state of agriculture and rural life; (10) the inadequate public health system. He considered the first two items (ideological problems) to be the very basis of the miseries of the Iranian people. [22]

Before *On the Road to Politics* the many writings of Kasravi and the various other publications of the Azadegan had been covering numerous topics, elucidating their stated objectives and discussing the obstacles to achieving those objectives and ways of overcoming them. After that book, publications on those general topics continued, with two types of emphases added: A number of the new books dealt more directly with the problems the party was having with the government, using a confrontational tone; or dealt with specific political problems facing the country as a result of the Azerbaijan autonomy demands of the *Ferqe-ye Demokrat-e Azerbaijan*.

Another publication emphasis was a novelty, and reflected Kasravi's and the Azadegan's belief that any movement such as theirs should involve the masses; and the masses in Iran were illiterate, in general politically uninterested, and ideologically unprepared. Furthermore, the attempts at involving them had to be honest, not demagogic. The idea was not just to recruit large numbers of people for membership by making lavish promises or by concealing the party's true intentions and unpopular ideology. For this purpose, beginning in August or September 1945, a number of pamphlets were published in which that ideology was explained in very simple language, in the form of dialogues in each of which at least one participant was a party member. Six of these were written by Kasravi, the last published in December 1945 or January 1946. Four more were written by other party members and published later, the last of them attempting to explain the democratic system of government.

VII

Kasravi gave a clear clue to his view of Iran's problems in a concise statement in early 1935. In an article on journalism, he said in part: "In Iran, before the Constitutinal Revolution, life had a solid foundation. Only one corner of this foundation needed to be destroyed and rebuilt; that was in the matter of despotic government, which had to be demolished, and replaced with representative government.

"Once this was done, the foundation of Iranian life would not have to be uprooted. If there are rotten cracks in it, or if it is necessary to wash away its dirty spots, and to apply a new paint and shine to its walls, these tasks would never require demolishing the foundation.

"Put simply: After the Constitutional Revolution we only needed to put an end to religious superstitions, find a remedy for the illiteracy of the masses, eradicate divisiveness and factionalism among the people, make people deeply attached to and interested in Iranianness -- and things of this kind which were necessary. And after the Revolution, wise people did undertake these tasks. But when the clamor of Europeanisation rose up and, as a result of it, you journalists appeared, all of those wishes and desires were left unfulfilled, and now you have taken the axe to the foundation of life in Iran." [23]

The statement was, in effect, an outline, in a general form, of the program that Kasravi had set for himslef, as far as Iran was concerned. He may, as time went on, have discovered that the task was more complex, the powerful opposition more unyielding than he would have wished.

Considering the preceding statement, it is not surprising that Kasravi's first venture into the ideological arena was a critique of Europeanization, or Westernization. This was the latest source of problems for Iran, at least in his opinion; and, furthermore, it made the older problems even more complicated. He discussed Westernization in the book *Ayin* ('Creed'), already mentioned, the first volume of which appeared in 1933.

The germ of virtually all the ideas he was to develop later can be seen in this and the second volume, but the theme is *Orupayigari* ('Europeanization'). [24] Iranian fascination with Europe and the West in general, begun in the nineteenth century, had greatly increased after the Constitutional Revolution. In fact, it was one of the well-known and influential leaders of the Revolution who had declared in January, 1920: "Outwardly and inwardly, in body and in spirit, Persia must become Europeanized". [25] By the 1930s many intellectuals shared in this sentiment, which now also expressed government policy, but Westernization was not yet at its height. *Ayin* is an analysis of the West's own problems. It questions much in European and American life: the control of machine over man, the extremes of wealth and poverty, the plight of the worker, the economic system, the status of women, the legal system, attitudes towards religion, etc. The book received considerable attention in Iran and abroad. It triggered a lively exchange in the Tehran newspaper *Shafaq-e Sorkh* between Kasravi, on the one hand, and journalist Dashti (later Parliament deputy, and still later senator) and Parliament Deputy Liqvani, and others, on the other. It was this book that led some to call Kasravi "Iran's Gandhi." Kasravi respected Gandhi but differed from him in certain basic ideas. For example, he advocated controlling machines, rather than abandoning them. The book is a warning to Iranians not to be blind to the dangers of indiscriminate acceptance of all things Western, material and spiritual. He returned to this topic again and again through the years.

Kasravi criticized the West's way of life, and attacked its colonial and imperialistic policies. His disapproval, however, was not absolute. He made an intereting distinction: In a newspaper editorial, written during the Second World War, having expressed his criticisms of the

15

West, he says, nevertheless, that Europeans are better off than Easterners both in material life and as citizens: "The Europeans have gone
astray, having lost the road that would lead them to tranquility and
happiness. But they are not so low in their ideas and so irrational as to
do nothing in such perilous times, waiting to see what happens, saying:
'the night is pregnant; who knows what it will give birth to at dawn' [a
common Persian saying]. The consequence of the Europeans' erroneous ideas is that they have made their life hard and agonizing, seldom
enjoying tranquility. But the consequence of the inferior thinking of the
Iranians and other Easterners is that they are subordinate underlings to
others, and live in shame and humiliation. These two conditions are
very different." [26]

What, according to Kasravi, should Iranians take from the West?
On one occasion, speaking about the time the Iranians came into contact with "powerful and magnificent Europe", he pointed out that neither those who advocated the new ideas from Europe, nor those who
opposed them, showed any discrimination in their judgment. He then
divided the new cultural elements into five categories:

> (1) democratic government, rule of law, love of coun-
> try and sacrifice for the nation, organization of [gov-
> ernmental] departments, methods of raising an army,
> and things of this kind.
> (2) modern sciences, such as geography, history, phys-
> ics, chemistry, astronomy, mathematics, and so on.
> (3) using weaving, knitting, agricultural and [other]
> industrial machines, and benefitting from various inven-
> tions.
> (4) fervor for Europeanization, boast of civilization,
> clamour about progress, forming [useless, often extrem-
> ist] parties, writing novels, and so on.
> (5) Materialistic philosophy and its harmful teachings,
> regarding life as a battle-field, and other extremist and
> absurd ideas.

"It is obvious," he concluded, "that the first three categories
have been good and useful; and even though we may have some criticisms, it does not mean that we consider the Iranians wrong in taking
them over. It is also obvious that the last two categories have been bad
and harmful, and we have discussed each in the appropriate place." [27]

Another topic mentioned in Kasravi's 1935 statement was factionalism, its damage to the Iranian society, and the need for fighting it.
The major types of factionalism he discussed are religious and linguistic.

He does not mention ethnic divisions as such; those divisions generally overlap with religious or linguistic divisions, or both. There are only two religious divisions not entering such overlapping relationships. The Zoroastrians and (perhaps to a slightly lesser extent) the Bahais, both groups following religions native to Iran, are Persian in language and ethnic background. Kasravi's approach to factionalism reflects a perspective different from that of those who treat the matter in the majority-minority framework. Generally, members of the majority simply want the minorities to give up what separates them from the majority; and the minorities do not wish to do so. Furthermore, relations are not always ideal among the various minorities. Kasravi approaches the question in terms of the nation as a whole. He virtually never uses the term "minority." He speaks of "various religions," listing the Shi'ites along with Christians, Bahais, etc. Similarly, speaking of linguistic factionalism, he lists Persian along with Turkish, Armenian, etc. Furthermore, he emphasizes that the blame for the problems that exist in the relations among the various groups should not be placed on one side, but on both: "What nation and country should an Armenian or an Assyrian (under the present conditions) serve, and how? Supposing he did serve: Would others trust him?" Because of these divisions, Kasravi points out, the various groups "have not intermarried, or socialized. They have been living in the same country, but have been strangers to each other. These are things that cannot be covered up. Now the situation should change, and sensitivity and kindness begin on both sides: They should intermarry, socialize. Rivalries and hatreds should disappear; the borders that have been created should be removed. In every way, they should mingle and live in close unity." [28] An important point here is that Kasravi criticized *all* of the existing religions, most comprehensively, in fact, the majority religion, presenting his concept of what true Religion is, and hoped that the various religious groups would sooner or later abandon those things that now keep them separate.

As for the linguistic divisions, Kasravi, himself a member of the Turkish language minority, found linguistic factionalism harmful to the entire nation, and advocated the universal use of Persian in Iran. It is interesting that this sentiment, though far from universally held, was shared by a number of major Iranian intellectual-political leaders of widely differing philosophies: leftist and rightist, communist and capitalist, liberal and conservative (S.H. Taqizadeh, T. Arani, Kh. Maleki, as well as Kasravi - all native speakers of Turkish). Actually all educated Iranians who have mother tongues other than Persian are bilingual in Persian and their own language; some are multilingual. It would seem that universal literacy, which Kasravi advocated, would reduce the seriousness of the problem, if not completely eliminate it.

VIII

A major cause of factionalism in Iran is religious division. In addition, Kasravi found each religion containing objectionable teachings not conducive to democratic life. Since the religion of the majority of the Iranians, and the state religion, is Shi'ism, he spent a considerable amount of time in a detailed analysis and critique of that religion.

Kasravi wrote extensively on Shi'ism. In January or February of 1944, he published a book in which he first gave a brief history of its early development. He then listed a series of thirteen "objections" to that religion, followed by a list of six harmful effects it had on its followers. There is some overlap between these two categories, and among the various items. The major points Kasravi made in this book and elsewhere may be summarized here. [29]

1. *The Question of Succession* . The schism that eventually led to the establishment of Shi'ism as a sect was on the question of succession to the prophet Mohammad, and thus represented a political movement. The Shi'ites believe that all his successors were chosen by God, from among Mohammad's family. Actually only one of these men, Ali, the prophet's cousin and son-in-law, served in that position, elected by the same method the caliphs preceding him had been elected. Kasravi's point, in brief is, first, that there is no proof for this claim; second, that at any rate we cannot turn back the clock; and third, that the question is (or was) a political one, and should not have been made such an important part of religion. He also refutes the often advanced claim that the movement was an Iranian anti-Arab one. The original persons and groups involved were Arabs, and it was some centuries before Shi'ism came to become a primarily Iranian phenomenon.

2. *The Imams*. The Shi'ites have such an exaggerated view of the imams that they have placed them above prophets, vesting them with supernatural powers even the prophet did not claim to have: The imams, to them, were chosen by God; knew all the sciences; and all the languages; predicted the future, including all scientific discoveries and inventions; and were the only ones who knew the meaning of the Koran and of religion. Kasravi cites verses from the Koran in which the prophet clearly says that he cannot perform miracles, and that he is a human being like others, except that he is a messenger from God. How can his descendants, the imams, then, have such supernatural powers?

3. *The Hidden Imam*. On this Kasravi raises several major points: (a) This imam is believed to have been the eleventh imam's son,

to have died in childhood, and not to have been seen by others. Since the eleventh imam lived among the people, how could the birth and life of a child of his be unknown to others? (b) "Imam" means "leader." How could a man lead if he is not there? (c) No one can live 1000 years or more. (d) Why would God need to keep a man in reserve for a thousand years, hidden, to bring him out some day? People save certain things for future use (for example, canned fruits) because they have to, limited as they are in what they can do. God is not so limited. (e) The Hidden Imam is supposed to make the world good by supernatural means. Kasravi said that this would violate God's own law: He can choose someone from among the people to guide them, whenever the need arises, as he has in the past. And that person accomplishes his task by natural means: talking to the people, fighting against harmful beliefs, and so on; as Mohammad, among others, did.

4. *Pilgrimage to the Shrines in various cities of Iran and Iraq.* He considers this idolatry, since the persons whose shrines are thus visited are credited with power of healing and solving other problems. And the belief that such pilgrimage washes off all sins can only encourage sin.

5. *The Commemoration of the Martyrs of Karbala, and its rituals: self-flagellation and excessive weeping.* Weeping over events of a thousand years ago is unreasonable, he believed. Why is "anyone who weeps, or causes others to weep, or pretends to weep guaranteed paradise" (according to a *hadith*), he asks. Self-flagellation, wounding one's own body, putting dust or clay on oneself, and so on, is nothing but savagery, barbarity. The Shi'ites, he points out, are so pre-occupied with the inequities and unjust treatment of the imams that they see no other inequity and injustice. It is as though the perpetrators of the inequities on the imams have taken all the seats, with no room for any new ones: they are still cursing them after a thousand years, but no one mentions Ghengiz Khan or Tamerlane, who shed so much blood centuries later.

6. *Disrespect to the Koran.* The Koran, he says, was a book to read, understand, and follow in order to achieve salvation. It has lost its effectiveness, however, because of the belief that no one but the imams can understand it. And it is subjected to interpretation to suit each person's preferences. Instead of following the Koran, and thereby achieving salvation, they have made it a tool for advancing their own purposes. He also objects to using the Koran as a fortune-teller's tool, to divine the future.

7. *Taqiya or dissimulation in religion.* Hiding one's religion is hypocrisy, he believes.

8. *The Clergy.* Kasravi questioned the legitimacy of their pro-

fession; there is no priesthood in Islam. He also pointed out that they had no legitimate right to collect money in the name of *Khoms*, *Zakat*, and *Sahm-e Emam* ('Imam's share') from the people. These, he said, were taxes which the Islamic government, when it existed, collected for government expenses, as specified in the Koran and elsewhere. Since there was no Islamic government there was no reason to collect them. When they said their function was teaching religion to the people, he said that they were not teaching them religion; they were reinforcing their harmful beliefs and superstitions; and that, at any rate, "teaching religion" was not specified as an item on which funds from those taxes could be spent.

9. *The Velayat-e Faqih*, sometimes translated as "Guardianship of the Jurisconsult," a subject that has gained special and timely relevance since the establishment of the Islamic Republic, and which can be simply explained as follows: The only true Ruler is God, in whose name his messenger, the prophet Mohammad, ruled, followed by twelve imams. The twelfth imam went into occultation in 874 A.D. , to return at a time determined by God. During his absence, all secular rulers are illegitimate; they are by definition, *ja'er* ('oppressors'); and *ghaseb* ('usurpers'); Moslems should not cooperate with them. The *fuqaha* (plural of *faqih*; a jurisconsult, authorized expert in Islamic jurisprudence) serve as the deputies, or representatives of the Hidden Imam, holding power in trust for him, as it were. They exercise *velayat* 'guardianship' over the believers. The concept was originally taken (as it still is by some) to refer to general religious matters, not to government. However, it gradually came to be related to government, but still in a general way, until Khomeini gave it a much more definite meaning and substance. In this form, it is written into the constitution of the Islamic Republic, under which the chief *faqih* could overrule all government bodies and individuals, elected or otherwise. (How this position will evolve, now that Khomeini is no longer occupying that position, remains to be seen.)

The Islamic Republic represents the first successful attempt at putting the theory underlying it into effect. There are, however, those within the Republic itself who question the use of the original concept as the basis of a governmental system.

Traditionally, the concept of *velayat-e faqih* has affected life, and particularly the relation between the people and their government, in two related ways. First, it has given the clergy the kind of power vis a vis the secular government far greater than might be considered commensurate with their number, because of the part religion has played in Iran.

Secondly, because all secular government is by definition illegitimate in this system of thought, the believers have been taught that helping such a government is assisting the "agents of tyranny," and is religiously unlawful. One should not work for the government, for example. If a soldier is killed in the service of government he cannot go to heaven. It is quite legitimate to cheat in taxes, and so on.

The concept of *velayat-e faqih* has existed for some time. However, it was seldom discussed beyond the theological circles, and even there not in great detail, and not openly. Neither the masses nor even the intellectuals either knew the term or the theory, though they were involved in its implications. It was Kasravi who brought up the subject openly for the first time. Even more significant, he took it beyond the theoretical realm, a topic for the experts: He made a public issue of it. Kasravi had on a number of occasions referred to this claim of the clergy, and questioned it, more or less in passing. However, beginning in November 1942, he used a different approach, using much more explicit language, and calling attention more clearly to the direct conflict between their claim and democracy, which gives the people the right to govern themselves.

In an article entitled "Message to the Mullahs of Tabriz", in the daily *Parcham* for November 2, 1942, he addressed a series of questions to them concerning their claim. [30] These questions, with modifications, were published several times before his assassination. After the first *Parcham* publication, they were addressed to the clergy in general, or to particular clergymen by name, on one occasion to the *Imam Jom'a* of Tehran, who was said to have expressed outrage at Kasravi's (and his party's) criticism of Shi'ism. Then, in January or February 1945, the newspaper *Keyhan*, one of the two dailies with the largest circulation in Iran, and perhaps the most influential, published the most recent version of the questions. Seyyed Nur-al-Din, a major clergyman in Shiraz, answered them. *Keyhan* published the answers and Kasravi's response.[31]

Kasravi's questions to the clergy, the exchange between him and the Shirazi clergymen, and the whole debate on the clergy's claim cannot be taken up here in our limited space, if we are to be fair to both sides. Put briefly and simply, Kasravi questioned the basis of the claim; the qualifications of the clergy to run a government; the adequacy of religious law (the *Sharia*,) which, however suitable originally, could not, he said, meet the needs of the much more complex world of the twentieth century. He also pointed out that the Iranians had made a revolution some forty years earlier to establish a democratic government, which was incompatible with the clergy's claim (and with Shi'ism in general), and asked them if they expected the people to give up that form of government in favor of the kind the clergy advocated. They, on their part, used theological arguments to validate their claim; said that their form of government was not incompatible with democracy. They also said that they did not have to actually take over the government themselves; they could fulfill their duty (or exercise their right) by overseeing (*nezarat*) the government, providing guidance, granting it permission (*ejazeh*) to do what it needed to do. Kasravi asked why, if the government had to do the work, they had to tell it how to do it.

The central feature of the debate, on the side of the clergy, was the use of theological argumentation, including Koranic verses and statements attributed to the imams and the Prophet. Such arguments were familiar to Kasravi, who commented on them, especially when presented by the other side. However, his arguments focused on the broader perspective of the superiority of democracy, on the right of the people to run their own affairs. A secondary argument was the anachronistic aspect of the clergy's proposed type of government.

The conflict between Shi'ism, or Islam, and democracy can in a way be summed up in the fate, in life and death, of Sheykh Fazlullah Nuri. First he joined the two major clergymen leading the Constitutional Revolution (Tabatabai and Behbahani). Then he turned against it, and was eventually hanged. His objections to democracy are very clear in this passage: "[If] the purpose of Constitutionalism were to preserve the Islamic commandments, why did they want to base it on equality and freedom, as each of these pernicious principles is the destroyer of the fundamental foundation of the Divine Law? The foundation of Islam is obedience, not freedom; and the basis of its commandments is the differentiation of collectivities and the assemblage of the different elements, and not on equality." Further he says:"If the purpose had been the execution of the Divine Law, they would not have demanded equality between Muslims and infidels, ..., and would not have designated 'equality' as the law of their land." Still further:"... Do you not know that ... freedom of the press and freedom of speech are opposed to the Divine Law?..." In fact,"... your oath by the Qur'an to support the Constitution [required of Parliament deputies] is indeed like your swearing by the Qur'an to oppose the Qur'an. ..."[32] Since the Islamic Revolution, Nuri has been rehabilitated, and is highly regarded in the official circles.

Kasravi at one point summed up his views on these issues thus:"That representative government has not taken root in Iran, and has fallen on such disgraceful days, that a nation of twenty million has become miserable and helpless, that the children of the Anglo-Saxons come here from across the ocean to run this country [referring to the war-time occupation of Iran]--there are many reasons, not one or two, for these conditions. But the greatest is Shi'ism itself, and this claim of the clergy.

22

"One of the great tasks that needs to be accomplished in Iran is to have the groundlessness of this claim made clear, and to have these sinister and poisonous ideas come out of people's hearts." [33]

The reaction of the religious element, including the clergy, to Kasravi's relentless criticism of Shi'ism was quite strong. It took several forms, including petitions to the authorities, accusations of various types, physical violence, as well as published responses. Among the latter, we have already mentioned the written debate between a Shirazi clergyman and Kasravi, on the question of the role of the clergy in government. In addition, a number of books were written, one of which has since acquired a special historical significance, especially because of its author.

In 1943, Ali Akbar Hakamizadeh, who knew Kasravi, and was at least partially sympathetic to certain of his views, published a book entitled *Secrets of a Thousand Years*, in which he addressed a series of questions to the clergy. Khomeini, a clergyman not yet the influential figure he became later, wrote a reply, *Revelation of Secrets*. The book is actually an attack on Kasravi, whom he does not mention by name, but by such phrases as "the adventurer from Tabriz." [34]

IX

Except for Shi'ism and Islam, the Bahai religion is the only one Kasravi discussed, though much less extensively. He refers to it as "superstition upon superstition," since it was based on a series of concepts that he considered irrational, ultimately originating in the Shi'i belief in the Hidden Imam. He also mentioned the fact that Seyyed Ali Mohammad, the founder of Babism, and considered the precursor of the founder of the Bahai religion, changed his story several times, first saying that he was only the *Bab* 'Gate' to the Hidden Imam, then to be that Imam himself, and finally founded a new religion altogether.

The Bab, as he has come to be known, said that new prophets will appear from time to time, to meet the changed conditions of the world. Thirteen years later, a man, Bahaullah, claimed to be a new prophet. Kasravi did not question the concept, as Moslems automatically do, believing that there will be no prophets after Mohammad. However, he asked how conditions could change so drastically in thirteen years as to require a new "dispensation." And he severely criticized Bahaullah for claiming to be God.

In general, Kasravi reproached the Bahai religion for what he considered its copy-cat nature: thoughtless imitation of other religions, particularly Shi'ism. Thus, it established its own new "Mecca;" it guaranteed the reward of a hundred martyrs for memorizing and reading a certain text; it exaggerated the status assigned to Bahaullah. And he asked why the founders of the Bahai religion, who lived in a Persian-speaking environment, wrote in Arabic (and, bad Arabic at that), apparently on the assumption that Arabic is the only language of revelation.

Finally, Kasravi believed that a new religion should fight the harmful beliefs and ideas that it encounters, and that the Bahai religion did not do that. Exhortation to goodness is not enough. Thus, praising religious unity, or forbidding war, will not do anything: Standing over some ruins and saying "This place must turn into a green and pleasant garden," will not make it so; nor will it help a sick person to tell him "sickness is forbidden." [35] The causes of religious disunity, war, and other problems facing mankind, should be identified and removed before these worthwhile objectives could be achieved. Problems exist not because people want to have them, but because their beliefs and behavior create them.

In Iran, many Moslems automatically assume that movements such as the Bahai movement are "the work of foreigners." Thus, there appeared in Tehran what purported to be the Persian translation of the memoirs of a Russian diplomat who had invented the new religion. Kasravi the historian examined the document, in an article, in which he refuted its claim, and also questioned the authenticity of the book. [36]

Religious tolerance has not been an outstanding feature of life in Iran. It is therefore interesting to know that, while criticizing the Bahai religion in no uncertain terms, Kasravi recognized their rights (which even the government did not) and even defended those rights. Thus, when in August 1944, anti-Bahai riots broke out in Shahrood, in eastern Iran, resulting in loss of Bahai life and property, the public (or the Shi'ite majority) was led to believe that the Bahais had been the real culprits. Even the coroner's report blamed the victims. Then a local clergy published a book on the incident. In December 1944, the Azadegan published an eyewitness account of the event by a party member who was a government employee. [37] In a brief note (either composed by Kasravi, or at least with his knowledge and approval), the party's editorial board said, in part: "No matter how guilty one might consider the Bahais, they are citizens of this country. If their actions disturb peace and order, the government must be watchful and punish them according to the law. If their beliefs are corrupt, the mullahs or others should write books and show the corruptness of their beliefs with reason (as we have done). What is absolutely inexcusable is inciting barbarous illiterate people, causing those savage acts." Again, "What [the coroner] has done in the Shahrood case, ignoring [those responsi-

24

ble for] the riot; and furthermore, considering the Bahais' proselytizing and convening of meetings, which are normal activities, as criminal acts, trying to show them as the cause of the riot, is unjust and definitely counter to the country's interests." In an additional note preceding the author's introduction, Kasravi says, "We have no animosity towards any group. We are the enemy of injustice and oppression, of evil and of meanness. We fight aberrant and ignorant beliefs and actions."

The reaction of Kasravi and the Azadegan would not bear special notice in certain parts of the world. What makes it noteworthy are the circumstances. To my knowledge, no public figure or group made serious (or any?) protest, at least publicly. The exception was Kasravi and his group, who were in trouble with the Shi'i religious element themselves, and who, furthermore, were themselves critical of the Bahai religion.

X

Kasravi's approach to Islam begins with two general assumptions. First, there are two Islams: True Islam, which was founded by Mohammad, and remained more or less in effect for several centuries; and what passes for Islam today, coming in many sects and forms. These two Islams have little of significance in common, and in some ways even contradict each other. The original Islam spread so far and so fast, and had such great success in the world, as a state and as a civilization. Today, on the other hand, Moslems all over the world are inferior in culture and subordinate to others. Secondly, even in its true form, Islam could not meet the needs of a much more complex world; nor should it be expected to.

Mohammad's Islam, broadly considered, had two components: the ideological and the political. The beliefs forming the ideological component have lost their force because of the development, among the Moslems, of certain ideas and philosophies, old and new.

As for Islam's political component, it has lost its relevance. Moslems long ago gave up the notion of a single Moslem "community," upon which Islam's political system was based. Moslems now live as separate nation-states. (Indeed, even Moslem Arabs, sharing a common language as well, now form several independent governments.) Islamic laws (fiqh) have been set aside, replaced with Western or Westernized laws. Any attempt to revive them could not succeed, since they would conflict with the intellectual, psychological, and general make-up of today's society.

25

Kasravi's opponents brought up several points, or "excuses" as he called them, in response to his observations. One was: "If the people are bad, how is that the fault of religion?" Kasravi's answer: "...The fault of religion is that it has lost its essence [*gowhar*]; that it has transformed into ten or more varieties; that it has changed from worshipping God to worshipping human beings; that it has come to be full of baseless superstitions and silly legends; that it has fallen away from the times and cannot guide the people; that it teaches its followers to pay no attention to life, and be pre-occupied with the dead; that it teaches people to be expecting some invisible man [i.e., the Hidden Imam]. What greater fault is there?" [38]

Another response was: "People do not practice the religion. If they do, everything will be set right." He said: "It is far better that they do not practice it;" and gave examples of what might happen if they did: aggravated sectarian conflict, greater emphasis on pilgrimage to various tombs, and so on. "What, except harm, can result from practicing a series of irrational baseless acts?" [39]

When Kasravi criticized some belief or practice common among the Moslems, some people would say, "This was not in the original [religion]." Kasravi's comment was: "What does the original religion have to do with you? You are nowhere near the original religion. *The religion of a people is that which they actually practice.* [emphasis added]. Religion is not clothes, of which one may get two suits: one to wear, and the other to keep in the closet." He then asked Moslems how they would react if Christians, Jews, Zoroastrians and others took the same position; for, after all, those parts of their religions which are objectionable did not exist in their original religions. [40]

Another concept, related to the "original Islam" argument was expressed by his opponents in the sentence, "We will return the religion to its original form" or "We will reform Islam." These ideas were not new, even in Kasravi's time. To begin with, he said, nobody has done anything but talk about doing these things. Secondly, he asked them if they knew what the original Islam was; and, if so, why had they abandoned it to begin with. [41]

As was to be expected, in this debate about Islam, Kasravi's opponents often invoked the Koran. Thus, when he criticized some belief or practice among the Moslems, some people would say that the criticism was not valid. "Our book," they would say, "is the Koran. Are such practices in the Koran?" To answer this, he sometimes used an analogy: what they were saying was like the comment by a robber who, having been criticized for what he does, says: "These things [i.e., robbery, etc.] are not [permitted] in the Constitution. Our country's book is the Constitution. Does it permit robbery or banditry?" Kasravi then, referring to a certain practice among the Shi'ites, said: "Somebody should tell them: If it is not in the Koran, why do you do it?' Somebody should tell them: It is not in the Koran, but it is in your traditions [*hadiths*]; it is in your fiqh books..." [42]

Some said, "We will put the Koran in front of us, accepting whatever it says, and rejecting whatever it does not say." Kasravi said: "But have you not had the Koran in front of you all along? Furthermore, you seem to forget that all the various sects base themselves on the Koran, and none of them considers itself outside the Koran." [43] Finally, Kasravi said that the Koran could not by itself solve problems, not even in Mohammad's time. Mohammad and his supporters had to do many other things, including taking armed action. [44]

Kasravi questioned the Moslems' insistence that the contents of the Koran will forever remain valid. Thus, he reminded them, it permits slavery; it does not advocate democracy; it assumes the earth to be flat, and so on. [45] He was equally critical of those who criticized the Koran on such grounds. Both groups were wrong because, he said, they were confused about the work of a prophet, and the purpose of the Koran. The essence of the Koran, he believed, is to be found in those verses which provide guidance in social behavior. It is in this area that a prophet's responsibility lies. On all other matters (science, history, etc.), he knows only what his contemporaries know. [46]

Kasravi made an interesting observation about the Koran which is general, going beyond particular questions such as those mentioned above. It concerns the ability of the Koran to exert influence on the world of today: When it appeared in seventh-century Arabia, making such a great impact, there was no other book there to read. Today, people read many other books, and thus are subject to influences from many sources. [47]

The Koran, in other words, has lost its effectiveness, and it is used by people for their own ends. Referring to those who insist they can find everything in the Koran, he said: "The Koran, in their hands, is 'the tree of a thousand-and-one fruits.' What they do with the Koran is like what is done by a man who has a tree in his house and pretends that it can bear any kind of fruit, and so he buys every fruit that is in season, ties it with a string to the tree, and shows it to the people." [48]

XI

Another major recipient of Kasravi's denunciation was classical Persian poetry, on which he wrote at some length, focusing on its sociopsychological effects. He criticized it for teaching such harmful doctrines as fatalism, Sufism, and nonchalance toward life; for excessive praise of wine and shameless talk of homosexuality; for encouragement of such despicable qualities as flattery, cowardice, and hypocrisy; for praising tyrant rulers; and so on. He felt that such writings were incompatible with a decent, honorable, democratic way of life. Such uncompromising criticism discredited the most beloved Persian poets, whom he mentioned by name: Sa'di, Hafez, Khayyam, Rumi, etc.

Kasravi's attacks on Persian poetry (at the time virtually the only branch of literature fully developed in Iran) was not received well by the educated elite. One result was a series of lectures, by University of Tehran Professors Nafisi and Shafaq and Parliament Deputy Owrang, arranged by the Tehran Literacy Society, then the most important body of litterateurs and scholars in iran. The Society then invited Kasravi to present his views in a lecture, which he did in July or August of 1935. According to Kasravi, the Society then, after some discussion, arrived at the conclusion that thenceforth Persian poets should no longer compose in the ghazal form and, otherwise write in six specified subject-matter areas. No published record of this decision seems to exist. It is true that not many ghazals have been written (or at least published) in recent decades, but whether the society's decision had anything to do with it is highly questionable.

The first part of Kasravi's lecture was published in *Peyman*. Prime Minister Mohammad Ali Foroughi, apparently having read it, ordered the police to stop the publication of the second part (which had already been printed and in the bindery). A year later, Kasravi convinced the new prime minister, Mahmood Jam, to remove the ban. Kasravi also lost his University of Tehran professorship because he rejected the condition set by Minister of Education Ali Asghar Hekmat that he retract his criticism of the Persian poets. He and his supporters were also attacked, without being named, on Radio Tehran. The head of the government's Propaganda Department in a speech broadcast on Radio Tehran, declared: "We must not permit those who oppose poets to gain power." [49]

XII

If Shi'ism and classical Persian poetry were the areas that bore the brunt of Kasravi's sometimes cutting criticism, they were also the areas in which his opponents were most sensitive, and most vociferous. Perhaps the following episode will illustrate the point, and also provide

28

a clear indication of Kasravi's driving motive.

In the latter part of 1944, when Prime Minister-designate Morteza-Qoli Bayat's proposed program for his administration was being discussed in the Parliament, Deputy Ali Dashti made the following statement during his remarks:

> All of those things which should curb people's passions have disappeared. I shall mention a small example, although it is from the field of literature. Those gentlemen who are familiar with literature know that Sa'di in Persian is similar to the Koran in the Arabic language; that is to say, it is a miracle of eloquence. Hafez, with that high-mindedness, is a source of honor and pride for Iran. In other words, if a nation had only Hafez, it could feel proud. Mowlavi has a book which is truly perhaps unique in its greatness in the world. Unfortunately, there is a group in Iran today that says these things should be burned. [50] This is a sign of rebellion.
>
> The Ja'fari religion [i.e. the Twelver school of Shi'ism] is the official religion, and the constitution has so specified it. And the number of followers of this religion is very large in the world. Now a group has appeared who write against this religion and publish certain things about it. All of these are signs of anarchy and chaos. We want to know if this spirit of insolence and rebellion that is abroad in everything-[for example,] a government employee is given a truckful of sugar to send to Mazandaran [province], but he takes it to the bazaar and sells it - should not be brought to an end." [51]

These remarks (except the comment on the selling of sugar) clearly referred to the Azadegan, Kasravi's party. In response, Kasravi published an open letter to Prime Minister Bayat, entitled *The Government Must Answer Us*, with copies to the newspapers, some members of Parliament, and cabinet ministers.

He begins by saying that, if the government wanted to involve itself in these matters, it should either listen to what the Azadegan had to say and respond to it, or else have the law handle the situation; and that the government had no other choice; it could not use force to stop the Azadegan.

Next, he very briefly repeats his criticism of those poets mentioned by Dashti. He mentions their preaching of fatalism, hedonism, and the like; their repeating of baseless stories of extravagant supernatural powers supposedly held by Sufis and others (such as walking on water; the bouncing back of the knives dug into the Sufi Bayazid to those who had stabbed him, without injuring Bayazid); their open admission of homosexual adventures; and so on. He asked Dashti whether these harmful teachings exist in the writings of those poets, and if so, whether he considers them harmful or not. Merely calling something "literature" or "philosophy," or whatever, would not do, he says.

The bulk of the open letter refers to Dashti's comment on Shi'ism. A few preliminary remarks are followed by what succinctly sums up his objections to that religion:

> "This religion is incompatible with reason; it is incompatible with the sciences; it is incompatible with history; it is incompatible with Islam itself; it is incompatible with life. Finally, it is incompatible with representative government (or democratic life) which we won with bloodshed and sacrifice.
>
> "We have a hundred objections to this religion. But the greatest problem is on this final point - its incompatibility with representative government. That is why I am bringing it up with you, Mr. Bayat, who are the head of the government. I am bringing it up and requesting that the government show us a way [to resolve the issue]. I request that it step in and untie this knot for us." [52]

This passage is followed by an explanation along the lines described earlier in this essay, including the questions addressed to the clergy, concluding thus: "The clergy think that the government can force us to stop saying what we are saying. The government should make them understand that it does not have that kind of power; furthermore, nothing but reason can counteract reason." [53]

Referring to the complaints made by the clergy to the Shah on many occasions-most recently in Qom while he had been visiting there, he addresses the Shah: "We suggest that Your Majesty give the same response to their complaint. Or better yet, have the clergy send representatives to a meeting to be held at the Royal Court, or the White Palace, to discuss these matters, resolving the issue once and for all" [54] At another point, addressing Bayat, he says: "The government should ask the mullahs for answers to our questions; and if it supports them, the government itself should answer us." [55] Further on, he refers to a

30

mullah's attacks on Kasravi's party from the pulpit in a major Tehran mosque in the presence of the Prime Minister and his cabinet; and repeats his suggestion, with some modification, to the Prime Minister: "If the government accepts our proposal, it should send these questions of ours to them [i.e., the clergy], asking for answers; or invite representatives of the Ulama [the clergy] of Najaf [in Iraq, then the major center of Shi'i leadership], Qom, and other cities, and convene a meeting under its own auspices." [56] Finally, expressing wonder as to Dashti's reason for referring to Kasravi's party in the Parliament, he concludes: "...[We] have given our answers to his comments; and made our position vis-a-vis the government and the Parliament clear. The government could have done no more than take us to court for a trial. We have now come to court of our own volition, and are voluntarily seeking judgment. We have said what we had to say, and now it is the government's turn to speak up. It is the government's turn to answer us." [57]

Two other points made by Kasravi in this letter are worth mentioning here. One of these he had made many times before. It concerns a contradiction in the clergy's behavior:

> It has been observed repeatedly that the same mullah who says 'money from the government is *haram* [i.e., is religiously untouchable],' and the government employees are [agents of tyranny]', if a burglar breaks into his house some night, in the morning will rush to the police station complaining and grumbling 'what kind of country is this?!' Why don't the policemen stop the thieves?!' - making such protestations not remembering that these are the same people that he calls 'agents of tyranny' and sends to hell; that he considers the salaries they receive *haram* and evil. [58]

Such contradictions, he says, are not surprising. Referring to the Ulama's inconsistency on this issue, he sums the situation up thus:

> In short, the Ulama themselves are confused. They have set out on a road, stayed on it, reached a dark area, and are stuck there; and in the meantime, are doing much great harm to this unlucky nation. [59]

The other point, perhaps made here for the first time, is: "...[many] of the mullahs (especially those in Najaf, Karbala, and Samarra) do not know what harm they are inflicting; and if they do, they do not know the extent of it..." [60] He believed that, in discussions at the

31

proposed meeting, they might come to realize the error of their ways. "It may well be that many Ulama would come to sympathize with popular government and democratic life, abandoning their obvious hostility."[61] Neither the government nor the Shah, nor the clergy, accepted Kasravi's proposal (which he made on several other occasions as well).

XIII

The most serious accusation against Kasravi and the Azadegan was that they were anti-Islamic; that, in fact, he was claiming to be a prophet. We have already referred to the ill-treatment they received at the hand of their opponents, who were numerous and powerful, and of the government. We have also seen how the government repeatedly stopped the publication of their newspaper and journals. Then thirteen of his books were banned by the government, which claimed that they were insulting to Islam.

Finally, at the instigation of the Speaker of Parliament, the Ministry of Education and the Ministry of Justice, Kasravi was charged in court with "slander of Islam," a legal offense under a law never before enforced. On March 11, 1946, during the last session of the preliminary hearings on these charges in the Palace of Justice in Tehran, he was assassinated in court. The assassination was the first by the *Fedaiyan-e Islam* ("Devotees of Islam"). Mohammad Taqi Haddadpur, a young party member and employee of the party's secretariat, who was accompanying Kasravi, was also killed. An earlier attempt on April 29, 1945 had injured Kasravi seriously, necessitating surgery, but had not been fatal. It had also led to the imprisonment of the two party members accompanying him, as well as two of the Fedaiyan would-be assassins. One of the latter was Navvab Safavi, the founder of the Fedaiyan, who was involved in later assassinations, and who is highly revered by the Islamic Republic.

The assassins, who, after the assassination, had left the scene, reportedly loudly declaring what they had done, were later tried. The results were announced on November 2, 1946: Two men were sentenced to three-year prison terms, as the actual assassins; another five, as their accomplices, to seven months and fifteen days (time already spent in jail awaiting trial). The two men appealed; an extensive campaign was launched by Navab Safavi and Shi'i clerics in Iran and Iraq in their behalf; and the appeals court acquitted them.[62]

The Azadegan continued their work after the assassination, and for several years (perhaps seven or eight) were very active. The organizational structure remained intact through these years. Public talks at their headquarters in Tehran continued on a weekly basis, as it did in the provinces. Their most important activity, however, was in publishing, mostly reprinting Kasravi's books. The *Monthly Notebooks* also continued, through March 1947. A newspaper, *Jahan-e Pak* began on July 13, 1946, first published twice a week, then three times. This was replaced by a weekly edition, from February 4, 1947 to May 19 of that year. Yearbooks were published from 1946 to 1950.

From the early 1950's organizational activity slowed down considerably. There were always small groups, and several individuals, however, that kept working for the cause, almost entirely through reprinting of Kasravi's works as well as a number of ephemeral pamphlets too numerous to list here. One of the useful series of publications consisted of reprinting in book form some of Kasravi's journal and newspaper articles, usually thematic anthologies. The editing of these works, however, is quite unprofessional, and typographical errors are not few.

XIV

Many of the issues discussed by Kasravi, including religion, are of universal relevance (whether or not one agrees with his views on any or all issues). This was intentional on his part. However, as he himself clearly stated at the outset, and often repeated afterward, he had to begin at home -- Iran, but also (though less directly) on the (Middle) East; hence, for example, the focus on Shi'ism, Islam, and Persian poetry. In fact, his analysis of the problems peculiar to Iran is the particular application of general premises and principles to be applied, if they are valid, to the world in general. As such even that analysis provides clues to the general principles.

As far as Iran specifically is concerned, Kasravi's vision of her future clearly focused on preparing the Iranians for democracy, to which he most often referred by the synonym "government of the people" (*sarreshteh-dari-ye tudeh*).

His unequivocal preference for democracy should have become clear by now. Perhaps his most explicit statement is the following: "Some people are surprised to see that we value representative government so much, and talk about it in our books, and advocate it. One should know that representative government is the best form of government. It is the ultimate product of thought of the human race." [63]

Another statement, referring specifically to Iran, appears in a series of editorials introducing his party, the Azadegan. He begins a discussion of the party's platform thus: "More than anything else we want to promote representative government. As we have said, representative government or the government of the people is the best form of government. We must try and *firmly establish* it in Iran, and *hold on* to it." (emphasis added). [64]

How was this objective to be achieved? Parts of the answer can be found in the preceding pages. The following observations will therefore be brief. [65]

Kasravi, speaking not only as a social thinker, but also as an expert in Iranian history, said: "From the beginning of Iran's history to the time of the Constitutional Revolution, no more important event occurred than the Constitutional Revolution." Yet the hopes and aspirations it raised were soon crushed. As Kasravi put it, the Revolution was left incomplete. He ascribed this to two reasons: the fact that the people were not prepared for it; and the intervention of foreigners. No comments will be made here on the latter, since, as we have seen earlier, the Iranians' own weaknesses made such intervention easy. (At any rate, both he and other historians of the Revolution have provided ample evidence of foreign involvement).

As for the unpreparedness of the people, he saw two reasons for it: their ignorance of the meaning of democracy; and the existence of two great obstacles.

On the first point, he considered it a disgrace that forty years after the Revolution, not one out of a thousand in Iran knew the meaning of democracy. "They will not appreciate something whose meaning they do not know. Indeed, one should say: they can not possess it." [66] In fact, one of his strong criticisms of the Ministry of Education was that it did not include anything in its various curricula, from elementary school through college, about democracy and related notions. Nor did it delete from its textbooks and courses those materials that were clearly incompatible with the new way of life supposedly brought in by the Revolution.

The two great obstacles to democracy were Shi'ism and classical Persian poetry. Enough has perhaps been said already about the problem of Shi'ism, both in general, and in the specific context which concerns us here, to make further elaboration unnecessary.

As for classical Persian poetry, it had through the centuries helped perpetuate despotism (and was continuing to do so) in various ways; for example, direct catering to despotism by praising tyrants, even men like Tamerlane, in highly exaggerated fashion; encouraging flattery, in fact, sycophancy, among the people; and advocating ideas in conflict

34

with democracy and conducive to promotion of despotism, such as fatalism, hypocrisy, cowardice, non-chalance toward life and so on. As a matter of fact, in this connection as elsewhere poetry has served to promote ideas from various cultural institutions, such as religion, since it is accessible to a greater number of people.

Kasravi and the Azadegan tried to help solve this problem, towards making democracy viable in Iran, in a number of ways. Kasravi's history of the Revolution which, among other things, showed how ordinary people, many uneducated and illiterate, had risen to the challenge, was almost the only instrument Kasravi used before the 1941 abdication of the dictatorial Reza Shah. There were also books and articles on democracy. The daily *Parcham* devoted editorials and other articles to the subject. Then there were booklets in very simple language for those with little or no education as mentioned earlier.

The Azadegan's efforts in this area took other forms as well. They were the first citizen group to adopt the anniversary of the issuance of the charter establishing representative government as an occasion for celebration, regularly and extensively. There were festive (and instructive) gatherings throughout the country. (In fact, the date officially used by the government to mark the occasion was and still is, off by one day, as Kasravi discovered during his research. The Azadegan celebrated the correct date.) When they had a newspaper, they put out lavish special issues on that day. And they were (and I think remained) the only group to exchange greeting cards (printed especially for the purpose) on the occasion every year.

XV

Kasravi felt that there was a need, in Iran and throughout the world, for a new social order, but saw many obstacles to the establishment of such an order: Much in the social structure had to be destroyed before a sturdy structure could be built on new solid foundations. He said so himself on many occasions, and his ideological writings reflect this dichotomy: On the one hand, he analyzed and criticized the existing social order, and the assumptions and ideas that underlie it (and that make drastic changes necessary). On the other, he put forth his own proposals for a new order. In the preceding pages I have focused on his objections to certain parts of the existing social order. Some very general indications -- no more than a hint or two -- to his concept of the future may be gleaned from those objections. Introducing his alternative social system, in a meaningful coherent fashion, must await another occasion. A few comments, however, will be offered on his concept of religion, in Iran the major source of beliefs and actions, and elsewhere in the world still playing an important role.

Kasravi's analysis of specific religions covered Shi'ism, Islam, and the Bahai religion only, with passing references to Christianity, Judaism and Zoroastrianism. [67] His general attitude towards these three religions were the same as that on Islam: They were all great religions, perfect in their genuine form but since suffering corruption; and they cannot meet the challenges posed by changed circumstances, nor should they be expected to.

Kasravi defines "religion" as "the way of life," or "the high-road of life." He uses these short definitions quite frequently, but on some occasions he gives more elaborate definitions. He does so in different contexts, and from different perspectives. Perhaps the most important of these perspectives is his premise on human nature. After developing this premise, he sometimes related his expanded definitions of religion to it.

By the early 1930s when Kasravi started his work, many Iranian intellectuals, having recently read about Darwin's theory of evolution, believed that man was just an advanced form of animal, representing no more than a quantitative change, or improvement. The phrase "survival of the fittest" and the word "egoism" appeared in print and in conversation with great frequency, justifying a "dog-eat-dog" attitude towards life. Kasravi, who granted the possibility that evolution was a valid theory (after originally rejecting it), proposed that, although man might have evolved out of animal, he had advanced considerably beyond it, not only physically, but in one other highly significant way: by developing a major behavioral feature peculiar to him, and not present in animals: whereas he shares one driving force with animals--egoism; he now has another force absent in animals: altruism. The Persian words he used to designate the sources of these two driving forces were: *jan* and *ravan*, each representing one of the two conflicting facets of human nature [*seresht*, or *gowhar* or *nahad*]: *jan*, the facet shared with animals, and *ravan*, which was unique to humans. It is the task of cultural institutions such as religion and education to strengthen man's *ravan*. Each of *jan* and *ravan* is responsible for certain characteristic traits in humans. One of those under *ravan* is the desire for truth and the natural ability to recognize it, when exposed to it, inherent in human beings, though sometimes weakened (most often as a result of overexposure to harmful teachings of the type mentioned earlier). Also associated with *ravan* is *kherad*, the faculty of recognizing true from untrue, right from wrong. These concepts were extremely important to Kasravi, who credited them with being responsible for the ultimate success of great social movements. Conversely, he blamed the problems of society on the weakening of *ravan* and *kherad* in people. [68]

He also suggested that religions represent instances of "mutation" in cultural evolution. This view, interestingly enough, is reminiscent of the view later expressed by the American anthropologist Kroeber that the monotheism of the so-called Abrahamic religions corresponds "more or less to mutations or series of mutations in organic nature." [69]

One of his longer definitions of religion is the following:

What is religion? Religion is people's knowing well the world and the laws [that govern] it; realizing the truths of life; becoming aware of the essence of humanness; and living according to reason.

It is recognizing the true meaning of everything-- professions, trade, commerce, agriculture, industry, marriage, national life, government, and things like these--and putting everything into practice in its true meaning.

It is trying to improve the world, and as far as possible, rid it of its defects.

It is for the *ravans* to be strong, the *jans* to be subordinate, and life to be according to the [dictates] of *ravan* and its demands.

It is for everyone, in his desires, and his actions, to be concerned for the welfare of all.

It is for human beings not to remain ignorant of the Creator and his purpose, and not to pursue their own worthless purposes. [70]

In contrast, Kasravi believes, the followers of religions today do not know religion in the same sense:

They consider religion to be: believing in a God high up over the universe, a prophet under him, a series of imams (or saints) below him; accepting [as true] heaven and hell, the scale, the *sarat* (or *chinvat*) bridge, and things of that kind; loving the prophet and the imams, and visiting their tombs, and not forgetting their life-stories and keeping those stories always alive, and to be 'a friend to their friends and an enemy to their enemies'--this is what they consider religion to be; and the result they expect from it is having a thriving

life in the other world, and going to heaven.
One should say: religion to them is a 'structure in the mind' and certain actions for the purpose of 'heaven-seeking'...

That is why, he says, whenever someone has tried to create a new religion, they have created a structure of that kind. [71]

Kasravi believed that religion should be compatible with reason [kherad]. He never appealed to iman, i.e., "faith" as used in religious discussion. To those who asked why, if kherad, or reason, was effective, there was need for religion at all, he said religion is a teacher presenting the various truths to the people, but they use their kherad to judge what it presents to them. This is similar to the situation of students in a classroom. They need a teacher, but they use their own faculties to understand him. [72]

He also commented on the need for the compatibility of religion with science, and the relationship between the two: "Religion and science each uses a different route, but they both follow the same objective: bringing the truths in the world to light; and [helping] people of the world enjoy welfare and happiness. Religion must accept what comes out of the sciences, except where it touches on the domain of religion and the scientists have made errors, in which case religion should correct the errors with solid reasons (equal to the reasons in the sciences)." [73] He made it clear however, that "not everything that is in books is science. We do not want for every fanciful notion or hyperbole that this or that person weaves in the name of science to become an obstacle on the way of religion. By science we mean that which results from experimentation, and is indisputable [rowshan]." [74]

Kasravi believed that progress, or advance, in the world occurs in two areas: Science and the way of life (or religion), and that the two should keep up together if the world is to see peace and contentment. In recent centuries, advances have occurred in the sciences, "which have broken down the religions but have not eliminated them. They have weakened them, but have not put them completely out of commission." [75] So, it was time for advances in the realm of religion to bring it up to par with science.

"Religion," he once said, "is a tree whose root is human perception [daryaft-e adami], and its fruit, the salvation and contentment of the people of the world."[76] And in a conversation with a person interested in science, he said, "religion is the language of nature. This sentence means that religion is those truths that are gained from this world itself...," just as Galileo, Copernicus, Newton and others made their discoveries from observing the world itself, he mentions by way of example. "The same is true of religion. Religion (in its higher meaning) is truths gained from the world itself with the help of thinking and reason [*kherad*]. The founder of a religion takes what he says from this world itself; his reasons are also from this world itself. This is what we mean when we say: religion is the language of nature." [77]

God, prophethood, and revelation, all exist in Kasravi's concept of religion; so does reference to "the other world." But his approach and his focus are not the usual ones.

As for God, there is no mention of him in Kasravi's short (and most commonly repeated) definitions of religion ("the way of life", etc.). When someone objected to religion because, he said, "the basis of religion is God," and that "we cannot acknowledge the existence of God," Kasravi's answer was: "We do not agree that the basis of religion is the belief in the Creator. To the Creator we know, it is immaterial whether people know him or not; and he is in fact greater than one could know." He then went on to define religion along the lines mentioned above, concluding with the statement that one should believe in the Creator (the word he almost always uses, in preference to God) because the world could not have come into existence by itself. [78] As a matter of fact, his proof of God is the familiar first-cause and design argument. Furthermore, his comments on God are always brief and uncomplicated. There were certain things, he believed, on which we cannot advance beyond a certain point in our thinking; and if we try, we will bang our heads into a wall. God is one such thing.

In fact, Kasravi's justification of religion, and the need for it, does not stem from a belief, or the need for a belief, in God. It stems from his concept of human nature, as already indicated.

Two concepts, related to each other, that come up in any discussion of religion are "prophets" and "revelation." Kasravi mentions both of these, though briefly and infrequently.

A prophet, to him, is a person -- very rare in history -- who appears from time to time, to provide guidance in social behavior, that is, "a way of life." He is a human being, and accomplishes his task through human means, by using reason. He is not divine; and cannot perform supernatural feats -- nor does he need to. Except in his task of guidance, for which he is the best equipped person of his time -- in terms of insights into problems and solutions - he is like all others. As to how one recognizes a "true" prophet from a "false" one, Kasravi almost dismisses the question as unnecessary, saying that the proof of the pudding is in the eating. You know a prophet the way you know a physician. A pretender will give himself away. A true prophet would not have to present his "credentials" before he does his work. He says what he has to say; people listen to him; argue with him if what he says is unclear, and so on. In fact, he later found the Persian word *peygh-ambar*, literally 'messenger,' as well as "prophet" and its cognates in various languages, objectionable because of their semantic connotations. Instead, he coined *bar-angikhteh*, the participial form of an archaic Persian verb meaning to 'impel,' to 'incite,' 'to move (someone to do something),' 'to provoke,' and so on. Other derivatives include *angizeh* 'cause, motive, motivation,' and *angizesh* 'incitement' etc., both words also used in Kasravi's style, especially the former. *Bar-angikhteh*, then, means something like 'moved or impelled' by something, in the present context presumably by God.

A better idea of Kasravi's notion of 'prophet' can be gained from his use of the word in various contexts. For example, in a discussion of the development of civilization through the millenia, he says that human beings started life in savagery, self-centeredness, and lack of concern for others until some individual or individuals appeared who showed people how to live peacefully together, to make institutions such as laws etc. Further on in the same article, referring to those societies who still lived the lowest type of life as in ancient times, he says that is because "such individuals (or in better words prophets) have not appeared among them" [79] He thus refers to the individuals responsible for major advances in civilization as "prophets." In a similar context elsewhere he uses the phrase..."a wise man (or in better words: a prophet)..." [80]

Another comment which throws even greater light on his concept of prophethood, and of the kind of person, in general, who might fit it refers to "those who always mention philosophers along with prophets, everywhere bringing their names in tandem with the prophets. Sometimes they quote the prophet of Islam as having said of Aristotle: 'He was a prophet, but the Greeks did not realize it.'

"This is another example that they do not know the meaning of prophethood, and have no idea of the task that a prophet should perform. If they had given this status to Solon, Lycurgus, Socrates and Voltaire, and other such sages [*danayan*], it would not have been much objectionable. For these people have at least taken some steps toward the truth, and each of them has taught people something. But Plato, Aristotle, Molla Sadra, Haji Molla Hadi (both Moslem philosophers), and the like have done no more than opening an endless desert of idle imagination in which they got lost themselves and cause millions of others to get lost..." [81]

Kasravi believed in revelation. However, while revelation is commonly considered as proof of the truth of a religion, in its entirety and in specifics, for him, it refers to motivation, to a driving force impelling its receiver to action.

In general religious usage, religious truth is divinely revealed to a person (a prophet), who then passes it on to others. These others, by whatever criteria -- including the observance of miracles (or hearing about them) -- accept that person as a genuine receiver of revelation, a true prophet. From then on they accept whatever has been revealed to him, on his say so. No further proof is needed. If anyone is in doubt on some revealed point, he assumes himself to be at fault. He might ask a more knowledgeable person (perhaps a professional theologian), and accept his answer, especially if the latter supports that answer by reference to the record of revealed truth (citing verses from the Koran, for example). If unconvinced by the answer, he will weaken in his religion, perhaps even leave it, or be excommunicated.

In Kasravi's thinking, revelation is of no concern to anyone but its receiver. It is the divine inspiration causing him to undertake a certain task; at times, at least, also to resolve specific questions of substance. But in conveying this substance to others, he uses normal methods of human reasoning. Kasravi's insistence that religion should be compatible with reason and science, both products of human faculties, is therefore consistent with his concept of revelation: one does not need to (and cannot) verify the genuineness of a claimant to prophethood in order to verify the truth of what he says. If anything, one might say, the reverse is the case. One, using his reason, verifies the truth, and then concludes that the person must be a prophet. But even this is not necessary, according to Kasravi. In fact, if a person puts forward such a claim, insisting on being accepted as a prophet, claiming to perform miracles and do other unnatural (and unnecessary) things popularly associated with prophethood, catering to the existing superstitions rather than fighting them, that in itself raises, or should raise, questions about him. This, for example, was one of the points he made about the founders of the Bahai religion. [82]

On the "other world," or the immortality of the soul, he says very little, and he does not seem to have solid proof. Most of the time he mentions these concepts, it is to tell people that they should think of this life and that happiness in the next world depends on how one lives in this one."...This world and that world are connected together, and there could be no good [life] in that world without [one's] being good in this world. Useless actions that give no benefit in this world, will be no more than causes for regret in the other world. That is what must be said about the next world. There is no need for more." [83]

Some people asked Kasravi why he used the word "religion" to designate his teachings. He said, on one occasion, that the purpose of his efforts was to see "Iranians rid themselves of ignorant beliefs and of the divisiveness which afflicted them;" to see "Easterners saved from this

41

backwardness and inferiority, and attain a free life;" and to see everyone, "Eastern or Western, abandon the conflicts and quarrels that exist and to embark on a rational path. ...If we say 'religion', these are what we mean." However, "we are not interested in names. If the name of religion has become degraded, you can call it whatever you want." [84] In another conversation he said, "we do not insist on giving our efforts and our way (*rah*) the name of 'religion.' We are more interested in results than in nomenclature. We are explaining certain truths and opening a high road for the life of the people of the world which can be called the 'high-road to salvation,' or 'clean life', or 'creed of reason,' or some such thing. If it is the name that drives scientists away, the solution is very easy." He then explains why he had been using the term "religion." First, in Iran most objectionable beliefs and practices existed in the name of religion, as did the factionalism in society. Nothing positive could be achieved until those problems were cleared up: "Until a pool is cleaned from quagmire, adding clean water will do no good." When there are so many differences and misconceptions on something, resolving the matter requires "clarifying things and extricating the truth."[85] Secondly, he said, despite the present state of the various religions, their founders had been after the same things he was advocating. He cites Jesus as an example, saying that it is clear even from the Gospels, compiled sometime after his death, that "Christ's objective was to make people do good things, encourage them to cooperate with each other, and kill their terrible egoism." [86]

Some people feel that Kasravi was too pre-occupied with religion. Indeed, his writings on religion, both in volume and in the amount of detail, used more of his time and energy than those on any other subject (with Persian poetry a distinct second). But his reasons were not theological, nor even general intellectual. Even this brief essay makes this clear. But, for his broad purpose, he had no choice, or so he felt:"Our task is not just to put religion in order. But until we put that in order, we cannot do anything else."[87]

XVI

At some point, rumors started to the effect that Kasravi claimed to be a prophet -- a very serious accusation in a primarily Moslem country. At first, he ignored the accusation. Later, he asked the accusers where he had made such a claim, indicating, in the process, that he questioned the popular notion about prophethood (angels, miracles, etc.), as we have seen.

42

Actually, Kasravi did not claim (or accept) any special privileges for himself. Once, when someone suggested that he call himself a *mosleh* ['reformer'] he said: "I need no name...You have made religion a game, and have set these formalities for it. There is no need for these kinds of things..." [88]

In fact, even before the question of prophethood came up, Kasravi expressed a dislike for titles or title-like phrases so common in Iran. In later years, he asked those sending articles for his daily *Parcham* (and by extension others) "to write my name just 'Kasravi.' The title 'philosopher' or 'great learned man' and the like, will not be a cause of pride for me. So far, my comrades have not given me a name, and I like my own name more than others." [89] The question more or less resolved itself, however.

The members of his movement spontaneously began to address him in letters, and to refer to him among themselves, as *Rahnema*, literally someone or something that shows 'a (or *the*) way.' It translates 'guide' in English, used to mean 'guide, guidebook, tour guide, telephone directory, traffic light, dissertation supervisor,' etc. It can also refer, as a general non-technical word, to intellectual and spiritual guides of mankind, such as philosophers, religious thinkers, etc., without specifically religious connotations. Against this background Kasravi, in a lecture on November 22, 1943, once again referring to the accusation that he claimed to be a prophet concluded his remarks as follows: "I loathe the name *peyghambar* [prophet]. This word was wrong to begin with, and people's understanding of its meaning is even more wrong. If I must have a name, I would choose the word '*rahnema*', which my comrades have been using for a long time. No one should call me by any other name."[90] I am inclined to think that an important reason for making this decision and announcing it publicly was to forestall other people's using the word *peyghamber* to refer to him. (Given the conditions in Iran, even some of his supporters might have used it, especially after his death.)

XVII

Those who adopted Kasravi's ideology gradually came to be referred to as *Pakdin*, and the ideology as *Pakdini*.[91] The word *pakdin* literally means a person whose religion is "clean(s)ed" (or who has a clean religion). It is a word which appears in Persian literature at least as far back as Ferdowsi's great tenth-century epic, *The Book of Kings*. It is, in Kasravi's usage, as much a descriptive term as a proper noun -- perhaps more so. It is not a new religion in any accepted sense of the term. It does not have the structural features one finds in the various religions. In a sense, when compared with them, *Pakdini* is definable by what it is not: no miracles, no sabbaths, no "pillars of the faith," no hierarchy, no heaven-and-hell, no pilgrimage, etc. etc. It refers to all the basic humanistic principles. Conversely, if existing religions are freed from their structural features and from their superstitions and formalistic accretions, reduced to their basic elements, they will (in Kasravi's thinking) lose their differences, and their followers become *Pakdin*. The term, furthermore, can bring together people from the various existing religions. Here lies a very important difference between Kasravi and other religious reformers. Each of the others tried to reform his own religion, keeping it separate from others. To Kasravi a major purpose of religion was to bring people together. He addressed all religionists. He sought to reform, not *a* religion, but Religion.

There is one other very interesting point on this question. On the very few occasions when he defines "*Pakdini*" the definition is the same as that he gives for "religion" in general, and that he believes applies to all religions in their original genuine form.

Finally, both Kasravi and his comrades generally referred to their ideology, that is, to Pakdini, as *rah*, which means 'road, way,' rather than as *din* 'religion.'

Relevant to this question is the question of why Kasravi used the word "religion" at all in reference to his ideology. We have seen that he was willing to have it replaced with "way of life," "living by reason," etc. Similarly, his concept of "prophet," basic in any religious discussion, is certainly in its most important implications, human in nature.

In the light of what has been said on his views on religion, it is not surprising that some people have referred to his ideology as "secular religion", on the face of it, at least, an internally inconsistent term. He reminds others of the Deists. Kasravi himself said that what he was advocating was "natural religion" sought by Voltaire and others. At least one scholar fully knowledgeable about Kasravi's thought has suggested "civil religion" to fit his notion of religion. [92]

XVIII

A few words might be said here about what has happened since the Islamic Revolution. During the first few months of the Islamic Republic, when censorship and other forms of governmental restrictions had not taken hold yet, a number of Kasravi's books were reprinted in Tehran. Soon a stop was put to this, however. Since then, on a number of occasions, known members of the Azadegan have been subjected to varying degrees of persecution and violence. Both Khomeini and others have attacked Kasravi publicly. (Interestingly enough, Khomeini, on at least one occasion, referred to him as a good historian, and a good writer, while attacking him for his religious views.)[93]

Kasravi's books continue to be reprinted outside of Iran by various publishers. In the absence of copyright protection, it is well-nigh impossible to keep track of these reprints, or of the number of editions, since the same book is sometimes published by more than one organization. His history of the Constitutional Revolution appears to be the only book that has continued to be published within Iran.

XIX

There is no time here to give a detailed analysis of what has happened to the Azadegan party during the past three or four decades, or to try to explain why it has not made progress. One major fact, however, can be mentioned: the tremendous and complex nature of their task. The Azadegan were fighting all segments of the establishment-- political, religious, literary-academic, educational, economic, in a highly traditional culture. No other group has done that. There was no "interest group", or economic class, or any other category of people, whose particular interest they were defending against others and on whom they could therefore count. They were, in a sense, fighting the very people--or at least their most cherished traditions--whose cause they were advancing. To make things more difficult, when they started, in 1941, political organizations were, for all practical purposes, something new in Iran, especially one based on ideology, and there was no collective experience to draw on. Furthermore, unlike most other parties, they neither had nor sought either financial backing or moral support of the Iranian government or of rich Iranians, or of foreign powers. Had Kasravi lived a few more years until the party was on a sounder organizational basis (and with a larger membership), things would very likely have been different. As it was, removal of Kasravi from the scene, occurring at a very sensitive juncture, at first made his fellow-party members more determined, and resulted in a burst of energetic activity. Gradually, however, things slowed down and, as far as structured activity is concerned, ultimately came to a standstill.

However, there is a difference between movements such as that of the Azadegan in the twentieth century and those of earlier eras that could save Kasravi's ideology from oblivion, and indeed perhaps cause it to ultimately gain the attention it deserves. At the very least, the printed word will keep alive an accurate record of the ideology as presented by its founder. That even in Iran the number of literate people continues to increase will help. If proper conditions should prevail, at some point in the future, other means of mass communication would also help.

Finally, developments within Iran itself might work in favor of the movement. The Islamic religious establishment, always criticizing the secular government and directly or indirectly seeking an "Islamic" government and a Shi'i society as the ideal solution for Iran's problems, has had its chance to show what it was talking about. Other groups, leftist and rightist, have also been tested.

There are, in fact, some signs of increased interest in Kasravi's ideas. Some visitors from Iran inform us that more people than before read Kasravi's writings, and find them more appealing than before. Outside of Iran, the same is true. His name appears with some frequency in letters to the editors of emigre Iranian press, and in some articles. Occasionally, an entire newspaper or journal article is devoted to him. Some references to him indicate misunderstandings, some serious, or based on a speaker's or writer's wishful thinking. But perhaps, on balance, his ideology will become better known, and judgments of it, favorable or unfavorable, will be based on accurate knowledge.

XX

Kasravi's ideological writings have received next to no attention by experts in Iranian affairs. Native scholars, and almost the entire political elite, have, in their search for explanations of what happens in their country, and for solutions to her problems, been looking outward. They think in terms of communism-capitalism issues, East and West labels, and so on. Or they look backward: primarily in terms of Islam, specially Shi'ism, favorably or otherwise, with or without grafting some features of Western life onto it. The Iranian masses, as well as almost all the members of the groups mentioned, have been seeing Iran's problems in terms of what might be called "visible", i.e., the immediate causes: for the most part, oppressive governments, sometimes of particular acts of oppression; and foreign powers' interference in Iran's internal affairs. Beyond that, one hears, or reads, about economic parasitism, dictatorship, religious "superstitions", "petit bourgeoisie," etc. Foreign experts, even when comfortably at home in Iranian culture and

Persian language sources, follow the same routes. By way of a clear example, we might mention the fact that the notion of "Islamic government", and the concept of *velayat-e faqih* that underlies it, caught everyone by surprise. The diagnoses made by these groups at best represent symptoms, or secondary or tertiary causes; and even to the extent that they are accurate they suggest only immediate and temporary solutions. We must look further and deeper. And here Kasravi may be of some help.

If some of us have been looking outward, and some, backward, Kasravi felt that we must first and foremost look inward. And we must look deeply and hard. Kasravi's ideological writings, which try to come to grips with these complex problems, have received next to no attention by the experts in Iranian affairs. I suggest it will be instructive for them to look into his ideology, and to do so with care and patience, not casually (as a few have done, to everybody's loss). It can, or might, supply a few answers; and suggest a few avenues of approach which have been neglected. He might not be right in everything, but he may have more than just embarked on the right track. What his ideology needs now, as it did forty years ago, is not blind acceptance on faith, or blind rejection on faith, or neglect, or praise. It needs to be studied, analyzed, taken apart, before a final evaluation is made, and any action, if necessary, is taken.

NOTES

1. The books and other writings by Fereidoun Adamiyyat and Homa Nateq are very useful for information on the intellectual developments in 19th century Iran, and the major figures involved.

2. Most of the information on Kasravi's life in the following pages is taken from his autobiography, which, however, goes through 1930 only. For the period after that, information can be found in his various books and articles too numerous to list here. For the period after late 1941, when his party, the Azadegan, in which I was actively involved, was founded, I have drawn on my own knowledge.

3. *Zendegani-ye Man* [My Life](Teheran:1323/1944), #15. The English translations in this essay are mine. I tend to be conservative at times, though I hope not overly literal. I omit all diacritics in my transliterations of Persian words.

4. Ibid, #13.

5. Ibid, #14.

6. For information on this trial see Ervand Abrahamian, *Iran Between Two Revolutions* (Princeton, NJ:1982),155-62.

7. *Emruz Cheh Bayad Kard?* [What Is To Be Done Today?](Tehran: 1320/1941).

8. *Bahamad* 'party' was coined by Kasravi to replace the common word *hezb*, partly because the latter had been discredited by the record of various political parties.

9. Actually only specified Christian groups, the Armenians and the Assyrians, are recognized.

10. See, for example, *Dadgah* [The Court of Law](Tehran:1323/1944), pp. 13-14.
   I use "Idea" generally to render Persian *andisheh*. Kasravi uses this to refer either to specific ideas or to attitudes.

11. *Dar Rah-e Siyasat* [On The Road to Politics] (Tehran:1324/1945), #27.

12. *Peyman* 7(1320/1941-42), p. 373.

13. Fortnightly *Parcham* (1322/1943), pp. 100-01. The phrase "loud clamor or rioting" here refers to the street riots by students and others on December 8, 1942, when, among other things, the House of Parliament was occupied by the rioters. One of the things the government did was to cancel all newspaper licenses.

14. Fortnightly *Parcham* (1322/1943), p. 313.

15. Ibid, p. 327.

16. *On The Road To Politics* (note 11 above), #39.

17. *On The Road To Politics*, #29.

18. See *What is To Be Done Today?* (note 7 above),4th edition.,(Tehran:1336/1957),pp.12-13.

19. This list appears on the cover of the text of the lecture (see note 7 above). A commentary on these objectives by Kasravi published in daily *Parcham*, 6 Aban-17 Azar,

1321?October 28-December 8,1942 covered the first five objectives only, since the paper was discontinued. Another party member, [Esma'il] Va'ezpur, wrote s ashort history of the party, its organization, and commentary on all sixteen objectives, in daily *Parcham*, 9 Tir-30 Meher, 1321/June 30-October 22, 1942.

20. *Farvardin Mah-e 1324*, pp. 9-10.

21. *On The Road To Politics*, #9. The word translated as "politics" in this title is *siyasat*, which however is broader in scope; it can mean"policy" and "diplomacy" as well. In this title, and much of the book itself, it covers all of these meanings.

22. Ibid, page 17. Those reading Kasravi's writings should keep in mind that he uses two Persian words when referring to specific religions:*din*, generally to mean "religion"; and *kish*, generally to mean a religious "sect" (for the common Arabic loanword *mazhab*). However, he also uses kish to mean "religion" when referring to the present decayed form of a genuine religion:In this context he in effect ignores the commonly observed distinction between "religion" and "sect"; in his view, any schism within a religion is pernicious and contradicts a major reason for religion, which is to unite people. In short, *kish* always has negative connotations.

23. *Peyman*, 2(1313/1935),p.169.

24. As Kasrvai himself pointed out in a footnote, by "Europe" he meant the entire West. Also according to him, an Arabic translation of the first volume of this work was published, as *al-Tariqa*, in Egypt soon after the Persian original appeared. However, I have been unable to obtain a copy. Jalal Al-e Ahmad, who published his *Gharbzadegi* in 1962 on Westernization, had at one point read Kasravi's writings, according to himself, although he does not mention Kasravi as his predecessor on this subject. Actually, the approaches of the two men are different, though the question cannot be discussed here. According to Kasravi, both volumes of *Ayin* were translated into English. See *Peyman* 1:12(15 *Ordibehesht* 1313/April 5, 1934),p. 34. There is no evidence, however, that an English translation was ever published.

25. S.H. Taghizadeh as quoted in E.G. Browne, *A History of Persia*, 4(Cambridge:1924, reprinted 1953),p. 486. Many years later, Mr. Taghizadeh stated publicly that he had changed his mind on this subject.

26. Daily *Parcham*, 19 *Mordad*, 1321/August 10, 1942.

27. See *Ma Cheh Mikhahim?* [What Do We Want?](Tehran: 1339/1950) (reprinted from a serial article published in 1319/1940),pp 33-34.

28. *On the Road to Politics*, #21. For one analysis of Kasrvai's view of factionalism, religious and otherwise, see Ervand Abrahamian, "Kasravi:The Integrative Nationalist of Iran," in *Middle Eastern Studies* 9(1973),pp 271-95.

29. What follows is based primarily on *Shi'igari*[Shi'ism](Tehran:1322/ 1943),actually on its slightly revised edition, entitled *Bekhanand va Davari Konand* [Let Them Read and Pass Judgment](Tehran:1944). There is also an Arabic version: *al-Tashayyu' wa-al-Shi'a* (Tehran: 1944).

30. Daily *Parcham*, 11 *Aban*,1321/November 2, 1942.

31. The version to which the Shirazi clergyman responded was that in *Dowlat be Ma Pasokh Dahad* [The Government Must Answer Us] (Tehran:1323/1945). The entire

exchange between the two men was reprinted (with some shortening) in *Ordibehesht Mah-e* 1324. More on this later.

32. From Nuri's *Kitab Tadhkirat al-Ghafil va Irshad al-Jahil* [Book of Admonition to the Heedless and Guidance for the Ignorant], translated and edited by Hamid Dabashi, in *Authority and Political Culture in Shi'isim*, ed. by Said Amir Arjomand (Albany: State University of New York Press, 1988), pp. 356-358. The complete translation appears on pp. 354-370. The Persian text originally appeared in Tehran in 1326/1908-9.

33. *Let them Read...* (note 29, above), p. 93.

34. A. A. Hakamizadeh,, *Asrar-e Hezar Saleh* [Secrets of a Thousand Years] (Tehran:1322/1943), and Rouhollah Khomeini, *Kashf al-Asrar* [Revelation of Secrets](Tehran?,1363 A.H.,lunar/1944?}. Apparently, the first edition of the latter was no more than 25 pages. This edition is 334 pages. According to one source, Khomeini wrote this book after some high-ranking clergymen ('*Ulama* and *Marjae*') in Qom who had read the Hakimzadeh book approached him to write a refutation to that book, since he was a recognized expert in the '*ulum-e 'aqliyyeh* (rational sciences). See Seyyed Hamid Rowhani (Ziyarati), *Barrasi va Tahlili az Nehzat-e Emam Khomeini* [An Inquiry into and an Analysis of Imam Khomeini's Movement] (Tehran:1360/1980), vol. 1, pp. 37-38.

Other books written by Shi'i authors in response to Kasravi include: Taqi Adibpur, *Tisheh bar Bonyad-e Kasravi* [An Ax to Kasravi's Foundation] (Shiraz?:1324/1945?); Nur al-Din Chahardehi, *Da'iyan-e Piyambari va Khodayi* [Claimants to Prophethood and Godhood] (Tehran:1366?/1987/);Mir-Abolfath Da'vati, *Dar Pasokh-e Kasraviyan* [In Answer to the Kasravists], 2nd ed. (two vols. in one), (no date, place, or publisher); Mahmud Razandi, *Chand So'al az Kasravi* [Some Questions from Kasravi] (Tehran: 1323/1945); Mehdi Seraj Ansari, *Nabard ba Bidini dar Bare-ye Kasravi va Kasravigari* [War Against Irreligiocity, On Kasravi and Kasravism], 2nd. ed., (Tabriz:1345/1966); and *Shi'eh Cheh Miguyand?* [What Does the Shi'i Say?], 3rd. ed., (Tabriz:1385 A.H., lunar/1966); Morteza Mahdavi, *Kajravigari, dar Pasokh-e Ahreman* [Kajravism, in Answer to the Devil], 2 vols.,(Tehran:1324/1945); Farhang Nakha'i *Kajraviha-ye Kasravi* [Kasravi's Abberations],vol.1 (Mashhad:1375 A.H., lunar?/1957?); Seyyed Nur al-Din Shirazi *Shekast-e Kasravi* [Kasravi's Defeat] (not seen by this author).

35. Kasravi's book on the Baha'i religion is *Baha'igari* [Baha'ism] (Tehran:1322/ 1943). The quotation is from page 59.

36. The Persian translation is entitled, *E'terafat-e Kinyaz Dalghurki* [Confessions of Kinyaz Dalgorouky]. The first edition is not available to me. I have seen what, though undated, must be the second or later edition. One of Kasravi's points had been that the original edition did not identify the Russian sources. This edition does refer to the source, though I have so far not been able to verify it. Even if such a source exists, and the translation is correct, the reliability of its content cannot be automatically assumed. At any rate, the point I have made above, Kasravi's objectively, will not be affected. Kasravi's comments appeared in fortnightly *Parcham* (1322/1943), pp. 169-177, 203-207, under the title "Aftab-e Haqayeq ya Dorugh-e Rosva" [The Sunlight of Truth or a Disgraceful Lie]. The first edition was going around as a chain letter. Kasravi's copy

bore the title "The Sunlight of Truth." The Russian diplomat in question appears to have been Prince N. S. Dolgorukii, Russian Minister in Tehran in 1889. The name is so listed in Nikki R. Keddie, *Religion and Rebellion in Iran* (London, 1966), p. 12 (footnote), and the index to that book. Several other English sources refer to him by his last name only. It is not clear where the first name *Kinyaz* of the Russian title originated.

37. The two books are:Sheykh Abdullah Shahrudi, *Dasa'es va Fetneh-angiziha-ye Baha'iha* [The Intrigues and Trouble-making of the Baha'is](Tehran:1324/1945); and Y. P., *Haqayeq-e Goftani: Dar Piramun-e Hadethe-ye Nangin-e Shahrud va Koshtar-e Baha'iyan be dast-e Shi'iyan* [The Truths that Need to be Told: Concerning the Disgraceful Incident at Shahrud, and the Massacre of the Baha'is by the Shi'is](Tehran:1324/1945). At this writing the first book is not available to me.

38. *What Do We Want?* (note 27, above), p. 169. In what follows, I use this and other sources generally in preference to *Dar Piramun-e Eslam* [On Islam](Tehran:1322/1943), which is extremely compact , summarizing ideas which he had developed in the above book and many other books and articles.

39. Ibid, pp. 169-70.

40. Ibid, pp. 174-5.

41. Ibid, pp. 183 ff.

42. *Porsesh va Pasokh* [Questions and Answers] 2nd.ed. (Tehran: 1325/1946),pp. 30-31.

43. *Peyman* 7(1321/1942), p. 603.

44. *What Do We Want?*, pp. 189-90.

45. *Dar Pasokh-e Badkhahan* [In Answer to the Antagonists] (Tehran:1340/1961),p. 19.

46. Fortnightly *Parcham* (1322/1943), pp. 159-61; *In Answer...* (footnote 45), p. 50.

47. *Peyman* 6 (1319/1940), pp. 702-03.

48. *In Answer ...*, pp. 24-25.

49. Kasravi's books on this subject are: *Dar Piramun-e Adabiyyat* [On Literature] (Tehran:1323/1944); and *Hafez Cheh Miguyad?* [What Does Hafez Say?](Tehran:1322/1943). His articles were collected in *Dar Piramun-e She'r va Sha'eri* [On Poetry and Poets] compiled by Mir Mehdi Mo'bed (Tehran:1335/1956). This collection, inadequately edited, also includes writings by several others. An attempt to summarize Kasravi's views on Persian poetry and the ensuing debate has been made in my "Ahmad Kasravi and the Controversy over Persian Poetry," in *The International Journal of Middle East Studies*, 4(1973), pp. 190-203; and 13(1981),pp. 311-327.

50. The reference is to the Jashn-e Ketabsuzan [Feast of Book Burning], which Kasrvai established, held on the first day of Winter (December 22), at which each party member burned (or otherwise destroyed) books he had collected through the years which he now considered harmful.

51. *Dowlat be-ma Pasokh Dahad* [The Government Must Answer Us] (Tehran:1323/1945), p.2. This booklet was published in June of 1945. Bayat had introduced his cabinet to the Parliament sometime between November 22-December 22, 1944. The Dashti remarks about the new cabinet, which included the reference to Kasravi, were apparently triggered by the Feast of Book Burning on December 22, 1944.

The comment on the "truckful of sugar" refers to the economic problems in the country caused by the war in general, and the Allied occupation of Iran in particular.

52. *The Government...*, pp. 10-11.

53. Ibid, p. 18.

54. Ibid, pp. 18-19.

55. Ibid, p. 20.

56. Ibid, p.24.

57. Ibid, p. 25.

58. Ibid. pp. 22-23.

59. Ibid., p. 23.

60. Ibid., p. 21.

61. Ibid., p. 24.

62. *Jahan-e Pak*, 12 *Aban* 1325/November 3, 1946; *Khandaniha* 16:3(6 Mehr 1334/September 29, 1955), pp. 34-35

63. *Mordad-Mah-e 1324* [August 1945](Tehran:1324/1945), p. 1.

64. Daily *Parcham*, 28 *Farvardin* 1321/April 7, 1942.

65. What follows is based almost exclusively on *What is...* (note 7, above).

66. *August 1945* (note 63 above), p. 3.

67. At the time of his death, Kasravi was working on several books, including "*Mardom-e Yahud*" [The Jewish People] which, if completed, would have provided us with information on his views on Judaism and Christianity in somewhat specific terms.

68. His book on this subject is *Dar Piramun-e Ravan* [Concerning *Ravan*](Tehran:1324/1945), though he discussed this in numerous other places. Kasravi in one place glosses ravan as 'soul', but whether they are full equivalents needs to be carefully studied.

69. Quoted in John C. Greene, *Darwin and the Modern World View* (New York:1963),p. 100.

70. *Varjavand Bonyad* [Sacred Foundation] vol.1 (Tehran:1322/1943), Part ii, #1. This book was to contain all of Kasravi's teachings more or less in their final form. Part I, dealing with the world in general, and II, on religion, appeared together. Part III, dealing with national life (political, economic, educational system, etc.), the longest and most detailed, appeared in 1323/1944. A projected final Part IV, dealing with family life was never published, though he might have been working on it.

71. Fortnightly *Parcham* (1322/1943), pp. 274-5. The *sarat* bridge, as believed by the Shi'ites, is a bridge between hell and heaven, which only those entitled to go to heaven can cross; others slip and fall into hell. *Sarat*, an Arabic word, actually means 'path'. In the sense used by the Shi'ites, it is apparently a distorted form of *chinvat* (or *chinvad*) a similar bridge in Zoroastrianism.

72. *Peyman* 7(1320/1941), p. 166.

73. *Khoda ba Mast* [God is With Us](Tehran:1322/1943), inside back cover.

74. *Peyman* 3(1315/1936), p. 645.

75. *Din va Jahan* [Religion and the World](Tehran:1323/1944),p. 15.

76. *Peyman* 3(1315/1936),p. 88.

77. *Questions...* (note 42, above), pp. 56-57.

78. *Peyman* 6 (1319/1940). pp. 74 ff.

79. *Peyman* 7(1320/1941), pp. 58-59.

80. *Piyam be Daneshmandan-e Orupa va Amrika* [Message to the Scientists of Europe and America](Tehran:1328/1949), a reprint of a series of articles under the same title originally appearing in daily *Parcham*. An inadequate English translation appeared in Tehran, in 1963.

81. *Rah-e Rastegari* [Road to Salvation], 3rd. ed.,(Tehran:1338/1959), pp 73-74. First published in 1316/1937.

82. His major statement on revelation appears in *Sacred Foundation* (note 70, above).

83. *Sacred Foundation*, II,#10-11; the quotation is from #11.

84. *Religion and...* (note 75, above), pp. 5-6.

85. *Questions and ...* (notes 42, above), pp. 18-19.

86. Ibid., pp. 20-21.

87. *Peyman* 3(1318/1939),p. 353.

88. *Questions and ...*, pp. 11-12.

89. *Parcham*, 19 *Shahrivar* 1321/September 10, 1942.

90. Weekly *Parcham*, #4(19 *Farvardin* 1323/April 18, 1944),p. 7.

91. Members of Kasravi's party in Iran are thus designated by two names interchangeably: *"Azadegan"* (used so far in this essay), and *"Pakdinan"* (plural form of *Pakdin*). There is a distinction, however. The latter term (or an appropriate equivalent in another language) can apply to anyone joining the movement anywhere, not just in Iran. *"Azadegan"* referred to the Iranian group as a political organization; it is the plural of *Azadeh*, meaning 'free', 'free-in-spirit', 'liberated from useless or harmful psychological and ideological encumbrances."

92. On Kasravi's own view see Peyman 7(1320/1941-42), p. 34. That Kasravi was "probably a deist" was proposed by Yahya Armajani, in "Islamic Literature in Post-War Iran," in *The World of Islam:Studies in Honor of P. K. Hitti*, ed. by J. Kritzick and R. Baily Winder (London:1959), pp. 272-282. Kasravi is discussed on pp. 280-281. Firuz Kazemzadeh refers to him as a "thorough secularist", in *Islam and the West*, ed. by Richard N. Frye ('S-Gravenhage:1957), p. 195. "Civil religion" was suggested by Professor A. Fathi of the University of Calgary (in private conversation).

93. Khomeini said:"Kasravi was a historian, and his historical knowledge was good. And he wrote well. However, he became conceited. He reached a point where he said that he was a prophet. He even abandoned all the prayers. He believed in the Koran. And he brought prophethood down to his own level. He could not reach high; he brought prophethood down." Khomeini made these comments during his commentary on the first chapter of the Koran, quoted in the airmail edition of weekly *Keyhan* (Tehran edition), for 8 Shahrivar 1368/August 30, 1989), p. 12.

BIBLIOGRAPHICAL NOTES

The following list of useful works only slightly overlaps with the items cited in the notes.

For a bibliography of Kasravi (as well as a few other pieces of information) one might begin with:

Katira'i, Mahmud, "Ketabshenasi-ye Kasravi" [Bibliography of Kasravi], *Farhang-e Iran-Zamin*, 18(1351/1976), pp. 361-98. It covers books only.

Other bibliographies will be found in the works by Jung, Paya, Ramyar, and Staley listed below. Some of the articles listed cite items not referred to elsewhere.

Persian Sources

I. Works by Kasravi

The best introduction to Kasravi's ideology can probably be provided by the two following books, both mentioned in the essay:

Ma Cheh Mikhahim? [What Do We Want?](Tehran:1339/1960, originally published in 1319/1940). It summarizes Kasravi's criticism of the existing social order, partly in historical context. This book should be read first, followed by:

Dar Rah-e Siyasat [On The Road to Politics], 2nd. ed.(Tehran:1324/1945). This is Kasravi's own last published summary of his ideas. It is shorter than the above; and it provides, in general outline form, some idea of his proposed solution to Iran's socio-political problems.

Kasravi's scholarly publications are well known and available fairly easily. His shorter works are now accessible in three collections:

Karvand-e Kasravi:Majmu'e-ye Haftad-o-Hasht Resaleh va Goftar az Ahmad Kasravi [A collection of Seventy-eight Monographs and Articles by Ahmad Kasravi], ed. by Yahya Zoka (Tehran:1352/1973).

Neveshteha-ye Kasravi dar Zamine-ye Zaban-e Farsi [Kasravi's Writings on the Persian Language], ed. by Hoseyn Yazdanian (Tehran:2537/1979). This is a much more complete collection in the area of language and linguistics than the above volume. A lengthy introduction by M. A. Jazayery summarizes Kasravi's work in this area.

Dar Piramun-e Tarikh [On History], ed. by Hoseyn Yazdanian (Tehran:2537/1978). This is a collection of Kasravi's writings on historiography, and on his history of the Iranian Constitutional Revolution.

II. Works By Others

Asil, H., *Seyri Dar Andishe-ye Siyasi-ye Kasravi* [A Survey of Kasravi's Political Thought] (Tehran:2536/1977).

Dastgheyb, 'A., *Naqd-e Asar-e Kasravi* [A Critique of Kasravi's Works](Tehran:1357/1978).

Nateq, N., *Sokhanani Chand dar-bare-ye Ahmad Kasravi* [Some Words Concerning Ahmad Kasravi], supplement to *Rahnema-ye Ketab* 20:11-12(Tehran:2536/1957).

Tabari, Ehsan, *Jame'e-ye Iran dar Dowran-e Reza Shah* [Iranian Society During the Reza Shah Period] (Stockholm:1356/1957).

Non-Persian Sources

Abrahamian, Ervand,"Kasravi:The Integrative Nationalist of Iran," *Middle Eastern Studies* 9(1973),271-95.

Aliyev, S.M., "Ahmad Kasravi Tabrizi's Life and Work During the 1920's and 1930's," Institut Vostokovedeniya (Oriental Institute), Moscow, *Kratkiye Soobshcheniya* 36(1959),77-85. (In Russian.)

_____ "The Relationship of Ahmad Kasravi to the Problem of Reform of the Modern Persian Language and Writing System," Institut Narodno Asil (Asian People's Institute),Moscow, *Kratkiye Soobshchenya* 30(1961),95-102. (In Russian.)

_____ *Ahmad Kasravi Tabrizi (1890-1946) as a Historian and a Social Figure.* Author's Abstract of Dissertation for a Doctorate Degree as a Candidate in Historical Sciences at M.V. Lomonosov Moscow State University Institute of Oriental Languages, 1961. (In Russian.)

Banani, Amin, "Ahmad Kasravi and the 'Purification' of Persian: A Study in National Motivation," in Ivo Banac, John C. Adkerman and Roman Szporluk, eds., *Nation and Ideology: Essays in Honor of Wayne S. Vucinich.* New York:Columbia University Press, 1981, pp. 463-79.

Fathi, Asghar, ed., *Women and the Family in Iran*, Leiden: E.J. Brill, 1985.

_____, "Kasravi's Views on Writers and Journalists: A Study in the Sociology of Modernization," *Iranian Studies* 19(1986),pp. 167-

82.(See *Iranian Studies* 19:3 for corrections.)

Jazayery, Mohammad Ali, "Ahmad Kasravi and the Controversy over Persian Poetry. 1. Kasravi's Analysis of Persian Poetry," *International Journal of Middle East Studies* 4(1973),190-203.

_____,"Kasravi, Ahmad," *Concise Encyclopaedia of the Middle East*,(Washington, D.C.: Public Affairs Press) 1975, p. 168.

_____,"Kasravi Tabrizi, Sayyid Ahmad," *Encyclopaedia of Islam*, new edition, vol. 4, pp. 732-733. Leiden: E.J. Brill, 1976.

_____,*Farhangestan:La Academia Irania de la Lengua*, traduccion y edicion de Oscar Vribe-Villegas. Mexico City: Universidad Nacional Autonoma de Mexico, 1979.

_____, "Ahmad Kasrvai and the Controversy over Persian Poetry. 2. The Debate on Persian Poetry Between Kasravi and His Opponents," *International Journal of Middle East Studies* 13 (1981), 311-327.

_____, "The Modernization of the Persian Vocabulary and Language Reform in Iran," *Language Reform: History and Future*, ed. Istvan Fodor and Claude Hagege. Hamburg:Busk Verlag, 1985, vol. 2, pp. 241-267.

_____, "Madjma' 'Ilmi:(ii), Iran," *Encyclopaedia of Islam*, New Edition, vol. 5, 1094-1099. Leiden: E.J. Brill, 1986.

Jung, Edeltrud, *Ahmad Kasrawi Ein Beitrag zur Ideengeschte Persiens im 20. Jahrhundert*. Inagural Dissertation. Philosophischen Fakultaten der Albert-Ludwigs-Universitat zu Freiburg i. Br., 1976.

Kazemi, Farhad, "The Shi'i Clergy and State in Iran: From the Safavids to the Pahlavis, " *Journal of the American Institute for the Study of Middle Eastern Civilizations* 1(1980), pp.34-52.

_____,ed., *Iranian Revolution in Perspective*, [*Iranian Studies*, 13:1-4(1980).]

_____,"The Fada'iyan-e Islam: Fanaticism, Politics and Terror," in Said Amir Arjomand, ed., *From Nationalism to Revolutionary Islam*, MacMillan, in association with St. Anthony's College, 1984, pp. 158-176.

Khomeini, Ayatollah Ruhollah, *Islamic Government* (New York: Manor Books, 1979).

Mottahedeh, Roy, *The Mantle of the Prophet: Religion and Politics in Iran*. New York: Simon and Schuster, 1985.

Paya, Huschang (Fruher Huschang Harzwilli), *Schadrawan Sayyed Ahmad Kasravi aus Tabriz als Denker und Sozialreformer des neuzeitlichen Iran*. Inagural Dissertaion. Fakultat fur Orientalistik und Altertumswissenschaft der Ruprecht-Karl-Universitat zu Heidelberg, 1978.

Ramazani, R. K.,"Intellectual Trends in the Politics and History of the Musaddiq Era," in James A. Bill and William Roger Louis, eds., *Musaddiq, Iranian Nationalism, and Oil*. Austin, Texas: University of Texas Press, 1988, pp. 307-328.

Ramyar, Minoo, *Sayyid Ahmad Kasravi: Historian, Language Reformer and Thinker*. Durham, England:University of Durham M. Litt. Thesis, 1968 (unpublished).

Regan, Carol, "Ahmad Kasravi's View on the Role of Women in Iranian Society as Expressed in *Our Sisters and Daughters*," in Asghar Fathi, ed., *Women and Family in Iran*. Leiden: E.J. Brill, 1985, pp. 60-76.

Sayyar, Jamshid, *The Welanschaung of Ahmad Kasravi*, translated from Russian into Bulgarian by Boris Bakarski, 1964.

Staley, Jr., William Converse, *The Intellectual Development of Ahmad Kasravi*, Princeton University Ph.D. dissertation, 1966(unpublished).

Vercellin, Giorgio, "Ahmad Kasravi et le lingue inventate". In *F.S. Bausani*, 181, pp. 379-384.

ON ISLAM

I have spoken many times on Islam. I would like to speak once again on this subject, and I hope that this will be the last time I do so. I am writing this in order to leave no room for excuses for anyone. As for those who will not accept what I have to say, I have nothing else to say. Let God be the judge.

INTRODUCTION

I: There Are Two Islams

First, we must realize that there are two Islams: One is the Islam which that noble Arab founded thirteen hundred fifty years ago,[1] which survived for centuries, and the other is the Islam which exists today, appearing in various forms, including Sunnism, Shi'ism, Esma'ilism, Aliollahism, Sheykhism, Karim-Khanism, and the like.[2] These two forms are both called Islam, but they are completely different; they are indeed contrary to one another for two reasons:

(1) Based on Research. We know about the original Islam and know well that it was different from the Islam that developed later. The former was a pure, iconoclastic religion, while the latter consists of a series of totally idolatrous and tainted sects.

(2) Based on Results. The original Islam organized the disunited and helpless Arab people into a single nation ruling half the world. The latter Islam disunites the nations and makes them weak and subservient. Today, Moslems are among the most degraded and abject people of the world, living under the rule of foreigners without considering their position as inferior. Here, it should be pointed out that a tree is judged by its fruit. One tree bears such a sweet fruit, and the other this bitter one. Can both be regarded as the same?

61

II: Nothing Remains Of The Original Islam

It must be said, frankly, that of the former Islam, nothing remains. There were two aspects to the religion established by the noble Arab: One was guidance in matters of belief, and the other, political organization. In other words, on the one hand, that noble man purified the people's beliefs, taught them to worship God, taught them monotheism and a series of truths about life. On the other hand, he founded a large state in the name of Islam, in which all Moslems lived together, followed one calif, practiced Islamic laws everywhere, paid *zakat* and *khoms* religious taxes and continuously fought the infidels, striving to advance Islam.

Today, all of this has been destroyed and eliminated. In regards to beliefs, today the minds of Moslems have been tainted with every kind of misguided belief. In addition to the worship of domes and the worship of the dead, which are variations of idolatry and have become extremely popular among Moslems, there exist other misguided beliefs, including the empty delusions of the Sufis, the fabrications of Greek philosophy, the false teachings of the Batenis, the nonsensical compositions of the Kharabatis, and the like.[3] Finally, in recent years, various false teachings of Europeans have also become popular and have added to all those misguided beliefs and practices. Today, Moslems know little of the truths of life. The grand clerics of al-Azhar University and the *mojtaheds* [religious jurists] of Najaf, not to mention the common people, have sunk into a deep, dark state of ignorance.

We have said elsewhere that religion consists of the loftiest of ideas. People with religious beliefs must be superior to irreligious people in life and must benefit from the world in regards to knowledge and perception, and also in terms of moral and ethical attitudes (as was true in the early centuries of Islam). But today, Moslems are inferior in every respect. The beliefs of Moslems today not only fail to help them progress, but indeed hinder their progress, and nations who want to advance must necessarily abandon Islam.

The Islamic political institutions have also completely broken down. Today, there is no state called Islam, because Moslems are divided among themselves, each group creating a country in the name of its own ethnic group. For instance, the Turks have a country in the name of their ethnic group; Iranians live only as Iranians; and the same is true of the Afghans. As for the Arabs themselves, not only do they live in the name of the Arab race, rather than in the name of Islam, they have more than twenty or thirty governments, each separate from the other. In Iraq, Egypt or Kuwait, native Jews or Christians or Arabs are considered compatriots. But an Iranian Moslem or a Palestinian Arab is regarded as a foreigner there. In Iran, the Armenians, Assyrians, Zoroastrians, and Jews are considered Iranians and equal to others; but a Moslem Arab from Iraq or Egypt is considered a foreigner.

The Islamic caliphate has long been dismantled. Even when it existed, it was a source of disgrace, because Moslems from India, Morocco and other places took up arms upon the order of European Christians and went to fight the calif. We have not forgotten that when the previous World War began,[4] when the Ottoman sultan held the title of calif, and the Ottomans also became involved, Islam was not effective enough to prevent the Moslems in India and Morocco from allying themselves with the enemy. But the reverse did happen: The enemies of Islam were able to separate the Moslem Arabs from the calif and force them to engage in hostility and war against his army. Such was the extent of the impotence and worthlessness of the caliphate. It was precisely for this reason that the Ottomans overthrew it and liberated themselves.

As for *feqh*, or Islamic laws, as we know, in most places they have been abandoned and replaced with European laws. The Arabs have themselves done so. In Iran, people engaged in armed rebellion, and under the leadership of the clerics, adopted French laws.

As regards fighting against the infidels, today Moslems are in such an inferior state that not only do all of them, with the exception of the Ottoman Turks, live as subjects of foreigners, but worse still, they do not consider their subjugation demeaning and have accepted it.

War (or *jehad*) was devised so that Moslems could liberate the people from their misguided beliefs and ignorance and to help them attain a better life. What could be the purpose of war or *jehad* at the present time, when Moslems suffer from their own ignorance and live an inferior life?

The unity of all Moslems, obedience to the califs (those endowed with authority) and fighting the infidels (*jehad*) were three strong foundations of Islam. Today, all three of these foundations have crumbled and are no longer relevant.

That is why we say that nothing remains of the earlier Islam.

CHAPTER 1

The Detrimental Consequences
of Islam

We are speaking of the Islam of today. Not only does this so-called Islam--an establishment run by the clerics--not do any good, it does a great deal of harm and is a source of misery. If we consider the East-erners' problems and their sense of helplessness to have three causes, one is this very establishment. Because of the constraints of time and space, I will confine myself to discussing a few major detrimental consequences of Islam.

I. This Islam Is The Source Of Misguided Ways And Ignorance

Moslems everywhere and of every sect have sunk into a state of misguided ignorance. If I were to enumerate their ignorant beliefs and practices, I would need to write a large book. Here, I will only briefly list some of them.

A. The first source of their devious ways is their lack of understand-ing of the true meaning of religion. Despite the interest they exhibit in religion, they are ignorant of its true meaning. Religion consists of "understanding the meaning of the world and life and living in accord-ance with the dictates of *kherad* [rational faculties]." They have not understood this. They consider religion as comprised of a series of baseless superstitions and harmful practices. To them, religion is something marginal to life.

For instance, as mentioned above, Moslems today divide themselves on the basis of ethnic group in most places and live according to European laws and customs. They study European sciences, which are not compatible with religious beliefs. They hang on to their religions and are still bound by them, because they think of religion as something separate from life, the result of which is happiness and salvation in the next world.

Even more interesting is the fact that there are still clerics in Najaf, Karbala, al-Azhar University, and in other places, who study *feqb* and write books on the subject without offering any reason whatsoever for doing so. Is this not a sign of their misguided ways and ignorance?

B. Understanding the Creator is basic to religion, but these people do not know Him. They have fabricated a god out of their own imagination, who sits up in Seventh Heaven, running the world through the angels, a god who, like a selfish, autocratic king, goes into a rage at the slightest disobedience on the part of the people, sending sickness, famine and earthquakes, but later, when the people turn to him and begin to plead and wail, his wrath subsides and he ends his punishment.

Such is the god that they imagine, a god who has created the world for the sake of a few, a god who bestows favors, accepts mediators, and speaks to the people through prayer beads and verses of the Koran (*estekbareb*).

C. *Kberad* [rational faculties] is the most valuable gift of God, and everyone must recognize and follow it. The truth is that the purpose of religion is to strengthen the rational faculties. Moslems neither recognize nor value them. Indeed, because their beliefs and practices are irrational, they are hostile towards rational faculties and minimize their value. They have frequently come and argued with us as to why we place so much importance on rational faculties. We have heard them say: "The rational faculties [*aql*] of different people differ."[5]

D. Prophethood is one of the bases of religion and is, indeed, one of the secrets of the universe. They do not know its correct meaning and maintain a number of groundless beliefs about it. In their opinion, when God chooses a person, Gabriel appears to that person and speaks to him. The barriers between him and God disappear and angels continually visit him. The prophet then announces his claim to the people and the people demand "miracles" from him in order to test him. If he is capable of performing them, they will accept him, and henceforth accept whatever he says. This is what they understand of prophethood--which is, it must be said, totally nonsensical.

The books of Moslems are full of stories of miracles attributed to the noble founder of Islam: He splits the moon in two; he ascends to Heaven to see God; he brings the sun up again after it has set; he makes a spring flow from his fingers; and he speaks to a lizard.

If you ask a Moslem the reason for believing Mohammad to be a true prophet, he will immediately respond: "He performed miracles; he split the moon; he had knowledge of the invisible." We respond, "We read in the Koran that whenever the Prophet was asked to perform miracles, he clearly stated his inability to do so, so how can you say that he performed miracles, and on what basis do you write all those stories in the books?" Here they are at a loss and have no answers.

E. As for the next world, they have filled their minds with nonsensical delusions about it: When a person dies, he comes to life again in the grave; two angels--one called Nakir and the other Monkar--firey clubs in hand, come to him and ask him certain questions in Arabic, such as, "Who is your God? Who is your prophet?" He must answer each question properly, otherwise the fiery clubs will descend upon his head. If he is a sinner, the grave will close in on him very tightly. On Resurrection Day, everyone will rise out of his grave and all will gather in a desert. God will sit on a throne, with prophets lined up on both sides. Sins and acts worthy of reward will be balanced on a scale. Each prophet will mediate for his "people." Then, people will have to cross the very thin, sharp "Bridge of *Serat*." One group will go to Paradise, and the other will fall to Hell.

F. In religion, if people understand God, they must also understand His laws (about how the world operates). Understanding God without understanding His laws is useless. However, Moslems are ignorant of God's laws. Here are some examples:

(1) This world operates systematically and everything is the result of something else; nothing can occur without a cause. But Moslems are forever seeking acts without causes, those which are contrary to the laws.

For instance, they treat illnesses with prayers; they consider their leaders to be capable of "miracles" or "wondrous acts"; they believe in the second coming of Christ, the reappearance of the Imam in Occultation, and the immortality of Elias, all of which are contrary to the laws of the universe. And if you object, they respond: "It is not outside the realm of God's power." These ignorant people do not know that God has established boundaries for His ability and laws for all His work, which do not allow everything which could be to be.

(2) This world is constantly progressing. Progress is a significant part of the laws of the universe, so that at any given time, other improvements occur. But, Moslems understand the reverse to be true. To them, the past is better than the present or the future. It is in the light

of this misconception that they fail to value their own time, always thinking about the past. This is one of the causes of their backwardness.

(3) It is the will of God that every once in a while a godly movement occurs, a righteous path is opened to the people of the world, and misguided beliefs and practices are eliminated. But, Moslems consider this process to have ended with Islam. In their ignorance, they perceive that the hands of God are tied, believing that even if millions of years go by, God will no longer concern Himself with the world.

(4) While they hold such beliefs about time and think as they do concerning religious movements, they expect that at the end of time, Jesus will descend from Heaven or Mahdi will appear and change the world. They do not understand the laws of nature and have fabricated such ignorant beliefs.

These were six areas in which Moslems are misguided. Each one of these is a separate, rooted, misguided belief, which is worse and more harmful than worshipping the idols of Lat and Hobal.[6]

These are the ignorant practices that can destroy the world and make the nations inferior. The purpose of religion, which human beings need, is to prevent such beliefs and practices.

These are the misguided beliefs in which most Moslems are entangled, and which comprise the ignorance of the sheikhs of al-Azhar University and the religious scholars of Najaf, in addition to the many other misguided beliefs in which the common people are entangled, or other false teachings and misguided beliefs, including Shi'ism, Batenism, Sufism, Kharabatism, Greek philosophy, Aliollahism, and Baha'ism, which are common in most Moslem countries, and each group claims one of these as its sect. In addition, in recent years, materialism has also come from Europe to the East and has become very common among Moslems. Today, most of the educated (clerics among them) are irreligious and materialistic. The only thing is that some of them openly display their irreligiosity; but many, despite their irreligiosity, will not let go of religion, living with weak beliefs in doubt and helplessness.

II: Moslems Submit To Subjugation

Worst of all is the degrading and abject state in which Moslems live. Today, Moslems everywhere, with the exception of Turkey, are under the control of Europeans and have submitted to this degradation, none of them even thinking about freedom. To put it more clearly, today, Moslems have given up the idea of having a country in the name of Islam and do not even hold such a hope in their hearts. Indeed, today, there is a contradiction between being a Moslem and loving freedom. Moslems, in every country, are divided into two groups. One group is made up of those who desire freedom for their country and the honor and dignity of their nation, and who strive towards this end. This group has turned away from religion. The other group consists of those who are devoted to religion (or pretend to be), but whose hearts are devoid of the desire for freedom, honor and dignity, and who are hostile to those who seek freedom.

Why is this so? Allow me to briefly retrace the history of this phenomenon. Fifty or sixty years ago, when European sciences and the new ideas of the Europeans spread among the Moslems, and in every country there appeared movements in the name of patriotism or representative government and the like, clerics or leaders of Islam everywhere found such ideas and movements incompatible with their establishment and everywhere expressed their hostility toward them. Consequently, a gulf was created between religiosity, on the one hand, and the desire for freedom and patriotism, on the other. In order to preserve their establishment, the clerics tried everywhere to make their followers (who are the religious people) abandon love of such things as country and nation, even to make them become hostile to such ideas. This is the history of that separation.

The truth is that in the world as it is, Islam is not suitable for a large free country called the Islamic world. Nor is it suitable for people in the countries which are populated by Moslems to retain that religion, operating their countries in accordance with its laws, and at the same time to be free. The political institutions of Islam were not meant for today's world. It is not possible to run a country with them. Those who understand and value the meaning of the freedom and independence of a country and whose sense of honor and dignity prevent them from submitting to the control of foreigners will inevitably turn away from religion. On the other hand, clerics and others who cannot or do not want to turn away from religion will have no choice but to give up such notions as freedom, independence, and patriotism. In order to be able to retain their religion, they happily accept subservience to foreigners.

If you examine the situation carefully, you will see that the ideals of Moslems (the practicing ones), wherever they are and no matter to what ethnic group they belong, consist of having their mosques respected, not having their way to Mecca blocked, having their domes (or, as they call them, their holy sites) remain intact, having respect shown to their Friday and Islamic holidays, having the Koran recited on the radio in the evening or morning, and occasionally having some European write in praise of Islam and its founder. It is just these few things that comprise the ideals of the religious Moslems. Under these few conditions, they

68

are all willing to be subservient to any government, European or Asian. This is so obvious that it requires no further elaboration.

III: Moslems Boast of Their Ignorant Beliefs and Practices

As we said, the beliefs held by Moslems today, which they consider religion (whether about God and the prophets or about life and the hereafter), are all false and all founded in ignorance. It is precisely these ignorant beliefs which keep them from progressing and which have caused them to become so wretched and degraded. On the other hand, as we shall see, the progress of time has left Islam and other religions behind. But Moslems themselves do not know this. Indeed, they are so ignorant that they boast of their ignorance, thinking of themselves as possessing salvation and hoping that Europeans will convert to Islam. They have heard that when Islam appeared, people converted to it in droves, and they assume that the same thing should happen now. They do not realize that neither Islam nor the times have remained the same. We have often seen that overzealous novice clerics entertain the futile wish of going to Europe to engage in the propagation of Islam. Some have often been heard to say in despair, "Why on earth do these Europeans not become Moslems?"

Many of them hope that sooner or later some powerful European leader will convert to Islam and will spread it far and wide. During the last World War, when the German Kaiser--purely in order to deceive the Moslems--pretended to support Islam, Moslems, smiling with delight, congratulated each other and everywhere displayed their support for Germany. Later, when Mussolini and Hitler appeared, they focussed their hopes on them. In the beginning of the present war, when the Germans were advancing rapidly, most Moslems everywhere engaged in "Hitler praising." Some were saying: "God has chosen him, and you will see that he will even become a Moslem."

One day, a merchant who had traveled to India and Russia came to me, and among other things, began to praise Hitler. He then added: "There is only one thing left, that is, for him to become a Moslem and bring Islam to the height of its glory." This was not something that deserved an answer from me. It deserved nothing but silence. However, he would not stop, continuing with even more nonsense. In an effort to stop him, I said: "How could Hitler bring Islam to the height of its glory?" He answered: "He has power. He is able to do anything." I saw that it was getting worse, so I just said: "Let us not continue this conversation."

If the readers will consider this response carefully, they will have an example of the extent of the ignorance of Moslems. Note how many erroneous beliefs are mixed together in this argument.

(1) Because he has heard of Hitler's gains in the war, he is attracted to him from this distance, placing irrational hopes on him, supposing him to be a man of God.

(2) He thinks that religion cannot spread except through force, and that is why he expects Hitler to help spread Islam.

(3) He finds no shortcomings in his own religion, which is full of misguided beliefs and practices, and hopes it will spread in Europe.

(4) He is totally ignorant of the problems which the sciences have created for Islam and other religions. When Moslem youths are educated and become acquainted with European sciences, they become irreligious. Yet, this person expects European scientists to convert to Islam.

(5) There have been movements in all Islamic countries where Islamic laws have been abandoned and, through revolution and bloodshed, European laws and ways of life have been introduced. Yet, this person wishes the Europeans to accept Islam and its laws and to use them among themselves.

On another occasion, a cleric said the same thing about Hitler, expressing the same hope for the spread of Islam through Hitler. I asked him: "Is the number of Moslems larger today, or was it larger at the dawn of Islam?" He answered: "It is a hundred times larger today than at that time." I said: "If this is true, why is it that they were able to make such conquests then, while today they are wretched and subservient to others?" He said: "Well, today, Islam is weak." I asked: "Why is it weak? Why were they strong at that time, with their small numbers, while today, despite their large numbers, they are weak? What is the secret?" He could not answer. I continued: "If you do not know the answers to these questions, you should remain silent rather than insisting on debating in ignorance." Then I said: "You may not know the secret of the Moslems' weakness despite their larger number, but we do. At that time, the source of Islam was clear. Moslems knew nothing but Islamic beliefs, were steadfast in them, made sacrifices, and, despite their small numbers, made many great conquests. But, today, the source of Islam is vague and obscure. Islamic beliefs have been polluted with hundreds of ignorant and misguided beliefs and practices, and Moslems are disunited and in disarray, not to mention the fact that their beliefs are weak. That is why, despite their numbers, they are incapable of doing anything and live under the control of others.

"Hence, the problem is with Islam itself, with the beliefs and the teachings themselves. Could Hitler solve this problem? Is this the kind of task he can accomplish?"

When I made these observations, he hung his head, rose to his feet and left. This was another example of the ignorance of the Moslems and the boasting of their misguided beliefs. Not only is this kind of boasting a sign of ignorance, but it has the harmful consequence of Moslems not realizing their problems and not searching for salvation. In their boastfulness, they forget their wretchedness and degradation.

IV: Moslems Resist Any Good Ideas and Any Salvation

Because of their certainty of the truth of their misguided beliefs and their reliance on the strength of those beliefs, Moslems resist any good ideas and any salvation, show hostility, and create obstacles.

In the past forty or fifty years, we have witnessed the Constitutional movement, or the government of the people, which is itself the result of world progress and the advancement of ideas. Moslems have opposed such movements in Iran, in the Ottoman Empire, and in other places to the point of bloodshed. They engaged in disruptive and deplorable actions when schools and colleges were established. They have opposed the establishment of offices for records and documents. They have refused to accept the use of the solar calendar. There have been countless actions such as these.

Worst of all is their reaction to the Pakdini movement.[7] Today, the world suffers from materialism, which destroys the roots of religion, belief in God, good deeds, uprightness, tranquility of life, and everything else. Materialistic philosophy, which has deep roots, considers the world nothing more than this tangible material system and does not believe in God, the soul, and the afterlife, or *kherad*, which are the bases of religion. It lowers human beings to the status of animals, considering them incapable of good deeds. It considers life a battle and the world a battle field. It teaches everyone to think of nothing but his own pleasure. We have raised the banner to fight this philosophy--the most powerful and frightening of all misguided philosophies the world has ever seen, one which is in every way incompatible with religion and its objectives--and we respond to it from every angle. However, we see that Moslems, instead of being pleased and supporting us, react with hostility and create all sorts of obstacles. Why? Because we do not say these things in the name of "Islam"; because these things are different from their irrational beliefs.

See what this religion has come to, whose followers fight the efforts made to eliminate irreligiosity, but allow themselves to be hostile and to create obstacles in their way.

Many readers may not be aware of the meaning of these observations and of our purpose in making them. I will state them more clearly.

Since the scientific movement began in Europe two or three hundred years ago, it has resulted in the failure of religions, for several reasons.

(1) The contradictions between the sciences and what is contained in religious books concerning the earth, the sky, the stars, and so on.

(2) The philosophy of materialism appeared because of the advancement in sciences and became widespread along with the sciences. Materialism is the enemy of religion; it is contrary to religion in every respect. This philosophy considers the world nothing more than a superficial, material system, placing human beings in the same category as animals, without the potential for improvement, and regards life as nothing more than a fight for survival among the living.

(3) As a result of the spread of sciences, ideas have progressed and human life has changed with the new inventions. That is why religions have become obsolete and the laws that they offer for life have become inferior.

The result of all this has been that religions have been defeated and devalued. The masses of the people have turned away from religion and those who did not (some ignorant old men and women) have become weak in their beliefs and have begun to doubt. The religious leaders realized that they were impotent and did not try to prevent the situation. Rather, they allowed this situation to happen and withdrew from it. It must be said, frankly, that religion became like "contraband." The religious people have not merely gone into a kind of hiding here and there, they actually pretend not to hear the hundreds of criticisms lodged against religious books and even the foundations of religion and do not respond to them. They do not pay attention to the contradictions that exist between religion and science.

Since a hundred years ago, this has been the situation with regard to Judaism, Christianity, Islam, and other religions. Their leaders are content that some organization--even one of wretchedness and degradation--has been established, one which is supported by old women and simpletons or tricksters and evil persons who profit from religion.

An examination of the issue reveals that most priests in Europe and many clerics in Asia are irreligious or weak in their beliefs, because they have read the books of the materialists or have listened to their statements. Since they are like impotent smugglers, despite their awareness that modern sciences are incompatible with their religious beliefs, and that the young people who study will become weak in their beliefs and even irreligious, priests, mollas, rabbis, and others, nevertheless, send their sons and daughters to schools and colleges to study those sciences.

In Europe, Nietzsche, Bakhner, and other standard-bearers have risen and written so many books on materialism and irreligion. Thus far, no response has been made by priests--a response, that is, which is of acceptable scientific value. In Asia, in Egypt, Shebli Shamil and Salameh Musa and others have published books which have shaken the foundations of theism and religion. The scholars of al-Azhar University and the clerics of Najaf have only pretended not to hear and have merely tried to preserve their own organization.

If a high-school student goes to al-Azhar University or Najaf or Karbala, which are considered religious centers, to engage in debates with religious scholars and clerics, he will receive no response to any criticism or question he may set forth. That is why I say that these religions have all become like contraband.

The wretchedness and worthlessness of religions reached a point that some reformists, like Marx, regarded them as harmful to the world and considered it an obligation to fight them. In the opinion of such reformists, religions are remnants of the human Age of Ignorance and a continuation of idol worshipping and superstition. They think that prophets were charlatans who took advantage of the people's ignorance and taught them a series of superstitious beliefs. As proof, these reformists state that in the present time, the age of sciences, no one can claim any longer to be a prophet, and no one mentions God and His having a hand in the affairs of the world.

Much has been said and written on the issue of religion and science having been at odds since ancient times, until, finally, science has triumphed and totally destroyed its rival.

In Iran, much has been written on the issue of Europe being a place for science and learning, while Asia always gives rise to "religion, superstition, and delusions." Religion has become so debased that some people, in order to avoid being considered ignorant, openly proclaim to be irreligious. Separation and incompatibility between religion and science have reached the extent that no one would even suppose that "religion and science could coexist, both pursuing the same ends."

In short, at such a time when religion has been so debased, by the will of God, we raised the standards, stood up against materialism, and responded strongly to each one of its false teachings. We clarified a series of very important truths and showed that religion itself is a system superior to science. Thus, we honored the pure name of the Creator and silenced the unenlightened. For more than ten years, we have been working in this vein and, with the help of God, we have overcome all the misguided beliefs and practices. But what can be said when we see that Moslems--those helpless and ignorant people--instead of being pleased with our efforts and victories, are displeased, and the clerics engage in all sorts of hostility. What we have done is in accordance with the will of God, and what they do is motivated by their ignorance and misguided beliefs.

As we said, they do not understand religion in the sense that we are saying and do not seek the same end as we do. In their opinion, religion is a system by which to show the glory and place of the Prophet of Islam and his family.

They recite such quotes as, "Had it not been for you, We would not have created the heavens and the earth," and the Shi'ites add that "Had it not been for Ali, We would not have created you." In their opinion, God created the world for the sake of the Prophet of Islam, Imam Ali ebn Abitaleb, and their family. And religion functions merely for the purpose of making them and their status known, as well as for mourning them and visiting their shrines, the reward for which will be nothing more than their mediation on the Day of Resurrection and going to Paradise.

That is why in their minds, no matter what happens to Islam, it will remain eternal, it will not be harmed by the ignorant and misguided beliefs and practices which have found their way into religion, and they have no fear of the wretchedness and degradation of the Moslems.

The question is whether religion is for the sake of the people or the people are for the sake of religion. We say that religion is for the sake of the people. But they do not accept this and consider the people to be for the sake of religion. We say that religion should show the highway of life to the people, make them aware of the useful truths of the world and prevent them from being misguided and disunited. That is why we say that religion, which has lost its essence and has been mingled with misguided beliefs and ignorance, can be considered as having been destroyed. But they say that religion is for the purpose of acquainting the people with those "revered" by God--that is, the Prophet of Islam and his family--and their status, to have the people accept them, always repeat their names, demonstrate love and fondness for them, keep their stories alive without allowing them to get old, and make their domes places of worship to which they will make pilgrimages from far and near. For them, this and only this is religion and its end.

But I have been digressing. The hostility of the Moslems toward the correct path to salvation is itself one of the great detriments of this establishment they call Islam. Furthermore, the behavior of the Moslems is the result of their religious beliefs, not merely a passing whim: Let the world be as it may, they should not allow this tainted establishment to be eliminated and the myth of God's love for those He reveres be disrupted.

V: Politicians Have Made a Tool for
Themselves of This Establishment

Another detriment of this establishment they call Islam is that powerful governments who wish to conquer the world and have set their eyes
on the impotent and helpless Islamic masses have made of this establishment a tool for the advancement of their objectives.

It is imperative to speak at length on this subject (in fact, to say
everything there is to say on the subject would require a separate
book); however, since time does not permit me, I will try to be brief.

These governments, which do not stop at using cannons, guns and
tanks for the advancement of their policies, but follow every path and
employ every means to do so, are well aware that various sects that exist
under the name of Islam create great problems for Moslems and on the
whole afford these governments several distinct advantages:

(1) They create disunity rather than unity and alliances and instigate
conflicts and hostility among the people.

(2) They degrade ideas, greatly hindering Moslems from living in full
equality with Europeans.

(3) European sciences and certain beneficial movements which have
appeared among the Europeans (such as constitutionalism and patriotism), and which have also reached the East, became ineffectual as a
result of coming in contact and being incompatible with these sects.

Because these governments are well aware of this, they support
many of these sects, and in doing so, they reap much benefit; which is
to say that since the followers of these sects and their leaders find such
governments supportive of their sects, they are inclined to rally behind
them and willingly submit to being subservient. (We have frequently
witnessed in Iran that whenever foreigners have set foot in this country,
the clerics and their followers engage in joyful celebrations.)

It is with this idea in mind that Europeans give a free reign to these
sects wherever they are, value their leaders, and support them both
openly and secretly. In addition, Orientalists, a group of political
government employees, continually write and publish books about
these sects. In the guise of nonpartisan research and historical assess-
ment, they strive to stabilize the foundations of each sect, as we have
seen them do in regards to other misguided beliefs, including Sufism
and Kharabatism, writing books in support of these ideas.

For instance, in regards to Sufis, they try to show that Sufis have
been profound thinkers pursuing certain truths; whereas, we know for a
fact that the substance of Sufi ideology has consisted mostly of fabrica-

tions. Hence, their teachings are like deadly poison for the people at a time such as ours. More surprisingly, Europeans have based their lives on hard work and self-sacrifice, and we witness how they struggle, how they fight their wars against each other, and in order to gain superiority over others, how they have thousands even hundreds of thousands of their young people killed without remorse. But, in regards to the Easterners, they praise Sufism or Kharabatism, which are based on the degradation of the world, carelessness about life, idleness and laziness, or they show their support for sects the consequences of which are nothing but backwardness in life. From this point, you can deduce their hidden motives.

The same is also true of Islam. In truth, this establishment called Islam serves the interests of greedy expansionist governments at every turn. Besides, as we said, religious Moslems are prepared to live subservient to any government, and only wish to be free in their religion (or better said, their own sects). That is why when Mussolini rose to power in Italy and wished to take over some Islamic countries, we saw that he pretended to be a supporter of Islam. One could say that he was practicing to be a shepherd of these scattered flocks. Also, the Japanese government, which for many years desired to take over Burma, Java, Indochina, and India, displayed its support for Islam, practicing to be a shepherd.

Although there were many Moslems in Japan, the motives of the Japanese government were purely political. It would be impossible for Japan to have an Islamic government one day.

VI: This Islam Degrades the Name of God

The greatest detriment of this establishment called Islam (and also other religions and sects) is that it degrades the pure name of God. Such religions and sects offer a series of unfounded ideas and useless instructions--which neither conform to science nor benefit life--in the name of "religion" or the "path of God," providing the irreligious and unenlightened an opportunity for criticism.

Today, the important question is whether or not God truly concerns Himself with this world and shows a path to the people. Obviously, since science is founded on materialism, they have not accepted such questions and scientists have dismissed them as irrelevant.

As we said, today, the masses of the people are irreligious and do not submit to the belief in the existence of God, let alone accept His guidance. But we have spoken much in this regard and have provided solid

76

responses to these materialist scientists. We have shown that every so often a divine movement must appear and a new highway open to life.[8] But this highway must not only conform to the rational faculties and science, it must also be above science and act as a teacher to the rational faculties. It must teach the people the laws of life and be a source of comfort to the people and the prosperity of the world. Such a valuable system can be called "the path of God" or "religion." If religion comes from God, it must be comprised of ideas higher than those of the people.

How can the teachings of sects--most of which oppose the sciences and the rational faculties, are incompatible with life and, on the whole, consist of empty and pedestrian ideas and futile and irrational instructions--be called religion? How could this wretched contraband establishment deserve to carry the name of God?

Will calling such teachings religion not turn the people away from religion? Could ascribing such ideas to God result in anything but the destruction of His pure name?

These are the great detriments of this establishment, known as Islam in name only, which we have briefly enumerated. These are the detriments which emanate from each sect and are common to all of them. However, some sects have other exclusive detriments. For instance, the Shi'ite sect, which is the Islam of the Iranians, has particularly detrimental attributes, the enumeration of which would be lengthy in itself.[9] In this sect, ignorance has reached such a level that the sect considers government, as it exists and should be, as "illegitimate" and prohibits the payment of taxes and service in the military without realizing the ultimate consequences. On the other hand, they give money in the name of religious taxes [*zakat* and *mal-e emam*] to the clerics, who have absolutely no responsibility in this world. According to the beliefs of this sect, anyone who makes a pilgrimage to Karbala, Najaf or Mashhad or sheds tears in religious mourning ceremonies will be absolved of all sins, which is why most of the religious people commit price-hiking, hoarding and violations of the law, and have no regard for their country. In fact, some of them are thieves, tyrants, and swindlers, who, relying on making a pilgrimage to Karbala or holding religious mourning ceremonies, live unabashedly and with peace of mind. Of this kind of detriment, much can be found in this sect.

CHAPTER 2

Excuses Made by Moslems

When these detriments are enumerated, Moslems have particular excuses which they present one after another. In other words, they offer a justification, and when you respond to it, they present another, until the have presented all the excuses one by one. During these few years, we have tested these justifications well. Hence, we will mention them one by one and respond to each.

I: Why Blame Religion for the Wickedness of the People?

We have frequently witnessed that when we speak of the helplessness of the Moslems or of their disunity and misguided beliefs and practices, they respond: Why blame religion for the wickedness of the people? This is their first excuse.

We say, people have always been wicked and the very purpose of religion is to turn wickedness into goodness. The fact that a religion is unable to make its followers good and unite them shows that it has deteriorated. When Islam appeared, the Arab people were irreligious idol worshippers with many bad qualities. Islam taught them theism and turned them away from evil. This is what a religion must be--not a religion in name only, with its followers flailing in misguided beliefs, ignorance, and evil.

The detriments that we have enumerated in this book stem for the most part from the religion itself. It is from the religion itself that various sects have appeared and disunity has been created among its followers. It is the religion itself which has become filled with misguided beliefs and ignorance, and which fills the minds of its followers with degenerate and unfounded beliefs. It is the religion itself whose time has passed and which is incompatible with today's life. Hence, its followers will either have to preserve it and renounce freedom and dignity, or they will have to abandon it in order to attain freedom and dignity. It is the religion itself which contains empty and worthless teachings concerning both God and the next world, as well as life and the benefits of happiness and tranquility. And, finally, it is the religion itself which forces its followers to oppose the correct path to salvation and to be hostile to any effort in this regard which is not carried out in the name of their religion.

Supposing that Moslems awaken, want to become good and avoid the evil practices that we have recounted, what can they do? Could it be anything else but giving up the sects that they follow under the name of Islam? Could they follow any other path?

In this regard, the truth is that Moslems do not know the impurities in their religion, because they are so confused. They are not aware that their religion has lost its essence, and that its time has passed. Every group follows a sect of misguided beliefs and ignorance and is helpless and backward vis-a-vis the advancements of the age. The followers of every group continually think in terms of pure Islam and its time, unwittingly considering themselves followers of Islam and imagining that they live during its time.

And then, because they do not understand the meaning of religion, they imagine that since religion was initially pure and had a strong foundation, later on, no matter in what condition it has become and no matter what impurities have polluted it, no harm could come to it.

Indeed, the religion whose purpose is to show the glory and grandeur of a few people and from which no other benefit is expected would not be harmed, no matter what condition befalls it. Those individuals have accomplished their task and assumed their status, and the impurities that have come to religion do not affect them.

In order to clarify these statements, I will give some examples. Sufism is one of the deep-rooted and greatly misguided beliefs to have appeared in Islam. We have often seen that because we have criticized Sufism, some people have been angered to respond: "What does Sufism have to do with Islam? Sufism comes from Rome and opposes Islam."

We ask: Which Islam are you talking about? Which Islam do you have in mind when you ask, "What does Sufism have to do with Islam?" If you mean the initial Islam, that is not what we are talking about. You, too, are strangers to it and do not know it. If you have in mind today's Islam, this Islam is closely tied to Sufism. Even if the seed of Sufism comes from Rome, it has taken root and grown branches and leaves in the Islamic world. The place where it grew was the Islamic world and thousands and hundreds of thousands of Moslems have always been and still are Sufis. The leaders of Sufism have always talked about the Koran and used its verses to support their beliefs. The false teachings of the Sufis are so widespread among Moslems that rarely can you find anyone who has not been affected by them.

The same is true of Kharabatism. This aberration, whose founders were Khayyam and Hafez, is not only totally different from Islam, but it is contrary to it. Nevertheless, it is commingled with today's Islam and its false teachings have found a place in the people's hearts and minds. See how weak a religion has become that it accepts and commingles with beliefs that are nothing but irreligion.

We have seen that for fifty years, when Orientalists begin to make a ruckus about Khayyam, masses of Moslems turn to his poetry, which is all comprised of false teachings. His quatrains have been translated into Turkish and Arabic as well and spread among Moslems.

These are some examples of the impurities of the Moslems' beliefs. Nonetheless, when a religion has been so polluted and is commingled with misguided beliefs and ignorance, is there room for anyone to say that "people are wicked, why blame religion?"

All else aside, today in Iran, we witness one kind of ignorance from the followers of Islam which we would not have believed if we had heard it of the African savages. To Shi'ites, the government (or the administration of the affairs of the nation) is the right of the Invisible Imam, and in his absence, the *mojtahed*s [religious jurists] (particularly the *mojtahed*s of Najaf) are his deputies. That is why every Shi'ite must pledge allegiance to one *mojtahed* and obey him exclusively. He must pay him *zakat* and *mal-e emam* (which are Islamic taxes). On the other hand, he should consider the king or the government of the country *"ja'er"* [oppressive, i.e., illegitimate], consider the payment of taxes, military service or any kind of support for the government as sinful and engage in hostility towards it, to the best of his ability. But at the same time, the Najaf religious scholars live outside the country without accountability to anyone. Undoubtedly, if people were to gather and call them to come and take charge of the government, they would refuse. But these same *mojtahed*s recognize the government as being responsible for the affairs of the country, and their followers, too, expect solutions to any problems to come from the government. For example, if one of them is robbed one night, the next morning he will hurry to the police precinct and begin to make a scene.

See how ignorant and degenerate they are and how tyrannical

80

and shameless they are in their beliefs. Their leaders go to some corner outside the country and say: Do not pay taxes to the government which establishes administrative offices and runs the country, the government that employs an army, police, and gendarmes, but pay us, who do and will do nothing for you and are not accountable for anything.

At a time when nations are engaged in the fiercest of battles and every group puts its life and property at the disposal of the government, what could be the condition of such a group with such beliefs? Could it have any fate other than wretchedness and misfortune?

Finally, we should realize that this obvious ignorance and these misguided beliefs have not been thought up by the people, but are the foundations of the Shi'ite sect itself.

Those who say, Why blame religion for the wickedness of the people? must be reminded of these and similar matters. They must be reminded that today's Islam consists of such beliefs.

II: People Do Not Follow Religion

This is another excuse. When they are unable to respond to you, as if having heard nothing, suddenly, they say, "People do not practice their religion; if they would, everything would be fine."

We say, This is not true. Moslems practice all their beliefs (all that can be practiced): They perform prayers; they fast; they read the Koran; they build Mosques; they go on pilgrimage to every town where domes are built; they pay *khoms* and *zakat* [religious taxes]; and they make pilgrimages to Mecca. They have forgotten all else, have given up all glory, and merely follow these practices.

In these years of war and hardship, we have seen that Moslems have not given up going to Mecca, and suffer every kind of hardship to get there.

Last year the government of Iran had warned Iranians against going to Mecca. But we saw that they did not heed this warning and as it became known later, six thousand people had suffered much hardship to get to Mecca secretly and illegally.

In Iran, Shi'ites follow their beliefs in holding religious mourning ceremonies, crack their heads, practice chest beating [*sinehzani*] and self-flagellation with chains [*zanjirzani*], and they take their dead out of the grave to be sent to Qom and Iraq. They disgrace themselves before foreigners, but do not stop such practices. Hajis and Mashhadis, who, in accordance with the teachings of their sect, consider the government to be a "usurper," are hostile towards the government, despite the fact that they need it. And as best they can, they evade paying taxes or letting their children go into military service. They have no respect for the laws and are proud to break them.

They do all of this in accordance with their religious instructions. How, then, could one say, "The people do not practice their religion"?

Since European sciences have spread, groups of Moslems everywhere have turned away from religion and refuse to follow its instructions. This in itself shows that religion is weak and what we say is true. This in itself indicates that religion has lost its power and cannot survive misguided beliefs. In any case, failure to practice religious instructions cannot be an excuse for you, because others who practice them are worse and more corrupt than those who do not, and the detriments that we have enumerated are the result of believing in religion and following its instructions.

It is astonishing that when we tell them about the ignorant and misguided beliefs of their sects and of the evil from which Moslems suffer, they pretend not to understand and say: "People do not follow the instructions; otherwise, all would be fine." This they say without understanding that it cannot be an answer to our criticism. They do not understand that because those ignorant and misguided beliefs are a part of their sect and within themselves, the more people follow them, the worse the results will be and the greater the harm.

We know some will say: What we want are those instructions in religion which concern truthfulness and good deeds. These are the instructions that we wish people to follow and it is from these instructions that we seek results.

I respond: Is religion the only source of such instructions? The religion that you profess and call Islam is comprised of various sects, which are founded on other things. As we explained, there are several grossly ignorant beliefs at the basis of the present Islam, in addition to other kinds of ignorance, which are unique to every sect. If you want the people to practice religion, obviously, they will practice these ignorant beliefs before anything else (as they do now).

And then, can life operate only through truthfulness and good deeds? Are other instructions and knowledge not required? What results could be achieved from truthfulness and good deeds by people who consider the dead to have a hand in the operations of the world; who imagine God to be an easily offended, autocratic king up in the sky; who, without understanding the laws of God, consider the past ages of the world better than the future; and who await the descent of Jesus or the appearance of Mahdi to bring good to the world--people whose minds are so polluted with such degenerate ignorance? Even if Moslems are truthful and do good deeds, they are like subservient, miserable slaves who are truthful and do good deeds among themselves, but gain nothing else.

Finally, I ask: Why do Moslems not practice truthfulness and good deeds? Why do they not believe in such practices? If you do not know the reason, we do. In this establishment called Islam, no importance is placed on truthfulness and good deeds. And today, Moslems concern themselves very little with such things. Rather, in this Islam, in every sect of it, there are ideas which have made such things as truthfulness obsolete.

When religion is merely for the sake of obtaining Heaven, and then only by performing prayers, fasting, and going to Mecca or Karbala, what need is there for truthfulness and good deeds?

Let me state it more clearly. Today, Moslems do not want religion for the purpose of improving their lives and bringing dignity to the nations. Therefore, of what value to them are such notions as truthfulness? Instead, they think of religion as an establishment which Moslems must preserve by submitting to any kind of degradation and humiliation. As we have said, they do not want religion for the sake of the people, they want the people for the sake of religion.

One day, I was conversing with a cleric, recounting for him the ignorant and misguided beliefs of the Moslems, and telling him that these practices are the source of the misfortune of the nations. The cleric used this statement as an excuse and responded: "They are not responsible. People do not practice them." I said: How could they practice them? Several paths have appeared in this religion. Which one should they follow and which one should they practice? He said: "Everyone should practice what he believes." I responded: They do so. Everyone practices what he believes. But this cannot be religion. The purpose of religion is to free people from disunity and set them all on one path. If everyone practiced whatever he thought and whatever he wished, what need would there be for religion? Then, how could you object to the ignorant idol worshipers of Africa? Why do you call them infidels? Do they not consist of groups, each of which practices what it believes?

III: These Things Did Not Exist in the Original Religion

This is also another justification that they use. For instance, when you criticize the disunity of the Moslems, they are at a loss for an answer. Hence, once again they change their position and say: "These things did not exist in the original religion" or "This was not the essence of the original religion."

I say: What concern do you have with the essence of religion? There is a world of difference between your beliefs and the essence of religion. The religion of every group of people is that which they profess and practice. Religion is not like clothing, of which one can have two sets, one to put on and one to pack up and put away. Their answer itself is the best indication of their ignorance about religion. They do not want religion for life, and do not seek any benefits from it for their lives. Hence, they ignore the impurities of religion and its detriments.

It is quite astonishing: A religion has become full of misguided beliefs, its followers are disunited, and are subject to much degradation and humiliation. They pay no attention to their condition and are only happy that the essence of religion was pure. This is like a family who lives in a ruined palace and puts up with snakes and scorpions in the midst of rubble and garbage but is content to say, "This palace was not always like it is now."

Most astonishing about the Shi'ites is that for more than a thousand years this group has separated itself from other Moslems. It has followed a different course in regards to the "imamate" (or caliphate) and has waged war against other Moslems and spilled blood. Now, there are domes erected in every corner. Pilgrimage prayers hang everywhere. And the Shi'ites await the Invisible Imam night and day. They consider salvation in the next world possible only through the mediation of the imams. They consider all of these to be "religious mandates" and have written a hundred thousand books about them. Still, when they are unable to respond to you, in order to avoid defeat, they say: "These things were not part of the original religion." One does not know how to respond to them; one does not know what to call such ignorance.

One should ask: If these did not exist in the original religion, from where did you get them? Why did you spill so much blood? Why did you write so many books?

Your story is like the chintz seller who kept two yardsticks, one exact, which he kept under his cushion, and a shorter one, which he used to measure out fabrics. He used the shorter one to measure the fabric he sold. And if occasionally a buyer realized what had occurred, the man would pull out the correct yardstick, saying, This yardstick is not short.

Once, in a meeting, the discussion turned to the Invisible Imam. A cleric said, "This is a mandate of the religion. Anyone who denies it will be considered an apostate. Anyone who dies without knowing the imam of his age will die as if in the Age of Ignorance." Then the subject

84

changed, and this time the cleric said: "I do not know why these Westerners do not convert to Islam." In protest, one of those present said: "Many of the Westerners want to convert to Islam, but cannot decide whether they should become Sunnis or Shi'ites, follow the sheikhs or the religious jurists, and then, what to do with Sufism. These are all obstacles in their way." The cleric responded hurriedly: "They should not accept any of these. They should accept the original Islam." The person who had spoken in protest said: "Then, it becomes clear that the original Islam is different from these sects, and I have no idea where it is practiced. Besides, why don't you follow it yourself? In this meeting you said that the idea of the Imam of the Age is one of the mandates of the religion, and anyone who refuses to accept it will die an apostate. And then you quote us the *hadith*s. Hence, how can you say that the Westerners should accept the original Islam? Suppose a Westerner converts to Islam but does not accept the Invisible Imam. Will you consider him a Moslem?" The poor cleric did not have an answer and began to make a series of nonsensical statements.

On another occasion, I told one of them: If religion is supposed to be pure only originally, but then falls into any condition and becomes polluted, then what objections could you have to Zoroastrianism, Judaism, or Christianity? Were those religions not pure originally? What could the difference be between Islam and these others? Why is it that they are polluted and should be eliminated but Islam should remain in place despite hundreds of impurities, without anyone objecting to them?

IV: Let Us Return Religion to Its Origins

Sometimes they even go a step further saying: "Let us return religion to its origins" or "Reform the religion." This is also an idea which appeared during the time of Seyyed Jamal al-Din Asadabadi and became popular. This is another justification they use.

It must be said: First of all, this is merely a justification. No cleric has ever given up his sect and tried to understand and teach the original religion. The Wahabis have taken some steps in this direction, but for this reason, they are also considered to have abandoned religion.[10]

Secondly, returning religion to its origins is not a task of which just anyone is capable. They must be asked: Who was the cause of the religion deviating from its original course, to which now you want to return it? Had you chosen this "secondary religion" or "the secondary principles of religion" willingly, that you could willingly leave it and follow the original? If you knew and are capable of knowing the original religion, why did you not accept it from the very beginning? Is it not true that you have considered and accepted certain misguided beliefs as religion in accordance with your own intellects? And then, is it not true that you only realized you have been misguided once we had told you? In any case, how are you going to find the original religion? Have you now changed your perceptions?

So boldly do they want to return the religion to its origins--as if such were as easy as drinking water; as if there are two things standing before them, the original religion and its deviant form, and since they see that the deviant form of the religion which they have been following has not turned out to be the right one, now they want to abandon it, and this time embrace the original; as if they have purchased some item from the market which has turned out to be an "imitation" and now they want to return it to the shopkeeper and exchange it for the authentic one.

It would be no more of an exaggeration for someone to say that he wanted to move a mountain than it is for them to say that they want to "return the religion to its origins."

As we said, this idea started during the time of Seyyed Jamal al-Din and has become a source of an extremely chaotic situation in the religion. On the one hand, it has become a justification for the followers of the sects, who use it to insist on their ignorant ways. Sometimes it has become an escape for them when they have no answer to a criticism, rather than submitting to the truth and accepting that their sect is without any foundation, they respond: "This is not the original religion. We must return religion to its origins. If we return religion to its origins, all of these problems will be eliminated."

On the other hand, certain charlatans have used this as a means to deceive people. And every one of them has gathered a group of those who have little awareness of the corruption of the Moslems. The term "reformist" has become a title, which many capricious clerics have taken on.

In this short period of time, many people of this kind have appeared here and there, and the "path to reform" which they have identified takes several turns: One is that when someone makes a criticism, they respond that this is not a part of the original religion. As long as something has not been criticized, it is a part of the religion. But as soon as it is criticized, it is no longer a part of the religion.

Another is whenever someone expresses a good idea, they say that it exists in Islam, too, and by finding a Koranic verse or a *hadith*, they try to force an interpretation to conform to that idea. They can find anything in the Koran, provided someone has expressed it once.

Still another is that they try to conform the new sciences to the Koran and *hadiths* and make it appear that the Prophet of Islam (as well as the Shi'ite imams) knew all the sciences and had talked about them.

This is the way these "reformists" think religion should be reformed.

You can see well that religion has become a plaything in their hands, one which they alter and patch up from time to time. Ask one of them, "What is the origin of the religion that you are talking about? Tell us what it is." You will receive no answer, because they have no inkling of what is involved in this matter. They have no understanding of anything, whether outside or inside the realm of religion, before it is criticized or pointed out to them.

One of these reformists, who lives in Iraq, has written a book claiming that the Prophet and the twelve imams knew modern astronomy, that whatever Galileo, Kepler, Newton and others have labored to discover were known by them, and that they had been explained a thousand years ago. All this he embellishes with countless quotations of Koranic verses and *hadiths*, which has helped his book become very popular.

This "Mr. Reformist" did not realize that every prophet knows of sciences only what is known during his own time, and that divine power or inspiration exists only in the realm of religion.

He did not realize that for one to say the Prophet of Islam knew everything would create hundreds of problems regarding the Koran and its verses.

It is interesting that the Koran describes in the story of Zo al-Qarnayn that the earth is flat.[11] (This was what people understood at the time.) But this Mr. Reformist has disregarded this and only refers to verses that explain that the earth is round and that it revolves around the sun. We do not know what to make of this.

Another one of these reformists was in Tehran. This one, too, would find a place for whatever he heard in Islam. Since newspapers wrote articles concerning the importance of physical exercise, he too on the pulpit began praising exercise, considering prayers [*namaz*] a form of exercise. When the Ferdowsi conference was held and so much commotion about poets and poetry was made, he, too, went along with the idea and began praising Sa'di, Hafez, Khayyam and Mowlavi on the pulpit, quoting verses from the Koran about them.[12] Since for many years in Egypt and elsewhere there had been discussions about the Moslems' belief in worshiping the dead, that it is contrary to the principles of Islam, and then, since we had written about this subject in *Peyman*, he, too, published a book, entitled *Yektaparasti* [Monotheism]. When we wrote about the Invisible Imam, he, too, was inspired and began to deny the Invisible Imam to many of his followers. These are examples of the accomplishments of that reformist.

More astonishingly, none of these reformists gives up his sect or wishes to offend anyone. For instance, the same man from Iraq, who gives himself the title of "al-Mosleh al-Kabir" [the Great Reformist] in his writings, is still a Shi'ite and has not uttered a word so far that would offend the Shi'ites. The man from Tehran, too, continued to be a Shi'ite, and always called himself a Shi'ite. On the one hand, he writes a book entitled *Monotheism*, pretending that he understands the basis of Islam, and placates a group of people. And on the other hand, he would not let go of the Shi'ite sect, which is founded on polytheism. His followers went to Qom, Mashhad, and Karbala in groups to worship domes. In fact, he went on a pilgrimage himself. He would deny the existence of the Invisible Imam before one group of people, but before another group, he would not confess to his own denial saying, "I never said such a thing. I am a Shi'ite."

As we said, they expect to benefit from the term "reform" (or returning the religion to its origins) in two ways:

First, to preserve the sects and to use it as a shield. This is precisely like the story of the chintz seller and his two yardsticks. And from this you can see how ignorant and desperate they are.

Second, some charlatans use these ideas to please some people and gather them around. It must be said that they are like shopkeepers who think of these ideas as new merchandise, with which to operate a thriving business. For years, they have made a living from the secondary precepts and trappings of religion. Now, they are making a living from religion itself.

Their story is like that milkman who watered down his milk, all the while swearing to the contrary. As time passed, and all his customers found out about him, he spread the rumor that he had repented, that from then on he would sell undiluted milk and that he would use the money to make a pilgrimage to Karbala. But again, he mixed water with the milk, and continued his fraudulent practice. When people objected, he would say: "This is pure milk. You are just being suspicious for no reason."

V: As Long As the Koran Exists, Islam Will Also Exist

This is the final justification. Once all of their statements have been refuted, they say: "The book of Islam is the Koran, and as long as it exists, Islam will exist." Or they say: "We must find the original religion in the Koran."

They must be asked: The Koran is the book of which Islam? If you are talking about the original Islam, that has nothing to do with you. There is a world of difference between what you profess and that Islam. If you are talking about these different, and confusing, sects that are your Islam of today, the Koran is not the book of any of them.

In any case, all of these misguided and ignorant beliefs and practices have appeared despite the existence of the Koran. If the Koran could have prevented these beliefs and practices, it would have done so already. What use is the Koran to you, even though every one of your various sects uses the Koran to support its arguments and each sect calls the Koran its own.

The answer to those who say, "Let us find the original Islam in the Koran" is, Why have you not done so already? Why have you abandoned the principles and followed the secondary precepts, in spite of the Koran?

This is one of the ignorant ways of the Moslems, who live with their misguided beliefs and corrupt practices and do not know it, always having the purity of the original Islam and the original Moslems before them. They do the same in regards to the Koran as well. They boast about that book, never remembering how far removed they are from it, nor realizing the problems that these disunited sects have created which prevent its effectiveness.

We see people come to us and ask: Does the Koran not state, "Do not consider God as having a partner"?[13] I respond: There is such a verse in the Koran. They continue: "Then, how can you write that Moslems are dualists?" One is at a loss what to answer and how to make them understand how ignorant they are. Today, the masses of Moslems have sunken into "dualism," and the foundation of the sect of the Shi'ites, who ask these questions, is on worshiping the dead and not understanding God. Nevertheless, they imagine that they are the followers of the Koran and recite in support of their argument, "Do not consider God as having a partner."

My answer is: It is true that such a verse exists in the Koran. But then, in your sect, you claim: "Making a pilgrimage to Hoseyn in Karbala is like visiting God in Empyrean"; "We are created by God, and the people are created by us"; and "It is because of his being that the earth is in place, and it is in gratitude for his being that people receive sustenance." On the one hand is that Koranic verse, and on the other, those domes in Mashhad, Qom, Abd al-Azim, Baghdad, Samaria, Karbala, Najaf, Baqi', and elsewhere, to which you set out from hundreds of miles away in order to stand before with bowed heads and ask for absolution of your sins and solutions to your problems.

They respond: "Do these beliefs constitute dualism?"

I say: If these do not constitute dualism, then what does?

It must be known that since the rise of Mohammad ebn Abd al-Wahab from Najd and the wars and other actions of the Wahabis, some sort of movement has appeared among Moslems. Everywhere, some group or other has become a supporter of the ideas of Mohammad ebn Abd al-Wahab, and everywhere groups have appeared, calling themselves "followers of the Koran," who, according to their own claims, want to read the Koran, understand it, and evaluate their beliefs accordingly. Such groups have also appeared in Iranian cities.

On the surface, this is appealing. But, beneath the surface, it is not good, as it has yielded nothing but unpleasant results. There are several reasons for this, which I will mention briefly:

(1) These groups do with the Koran what the founders of the sects have done. The founders of the sects have explained the Koranic verses as they saw fit and have fabricated interpretations for every verse that they have not found in conformity with their own ideas. The same is true of these recent groups. For instance, when a Shi'ite becomes a Follower of the Koran, rather than evaluating his beliefs in accordance with the Koran, he evaluates the Koran in accordance with his beliefs. For example, it has been clearly stated in the Koran in two places: "I do not know the unknown." The leader of the Followers of the Koran told me: "From myself."[14]

(2) The Koran cannot respond to many of the misguided beliefs and practices of this age, including Sufism, Kharabatism, determinism, and materialism. And those whose minds are filled with such misguided beliefs will gain nothing from reading the Koran and devoting themselves to it. In fact, they will become skeptical and confused.

(3) Many of the valuable instructions of the Koran, such as cooperation and unity among Moslems, fighting the infidels, obeying those who have authority vested in them, and paying *zakat* and similar religious taxes are no longer valid. That is why their reading verses on these subjects and discussing them will have no affect but to cause them to become anachronistic and removed from the necessities of the times.

(4) Because of their love for the Koran, whenever they hear anything valuable or learn of a science, they try to conform it to the verses of the Koran and presume that this is a praiseworthy practice, which is nothing more than a display of ignorance and lack of understanding.

(5) This itself has become an excuse for them to presume that they have attained salvation, refusing to listen to any statement or idea, even if it is supported by evidence, and they do not accept any guid-

ance. Instead, they use this excuse to boast of their superiority to everyone else.

On the whole, instead of reaping benefits from it, harm comes to them. And rather than becoming better, they become worse. This is something that we have tested well. Indeed, the Wahabis have achieved good results through their devotion to the Koran and are the best group among Moslems. This is because, on the one hand, Mohammad ebn Abd al-Wahab was a scholar and understood the meaning of the Koran better than others, and, on the other hand, the nomadic Arabs were simple people whose minds were not as polluted as those of others.

In short, the Koran has become an excuse in the hands of Moslems. This book, which was once a source of salvation for nations, is now a pretext for them to insist on their misguided beliefs and practices and resist salvation.

There is much confusion about the Koran among the Moslems. I will tell you a story in order to clarify what I am saying:

Some time ago, one of the clerics came to me and said: "It would be better if you would call the people to the Koran." I said: You can do that. If it is so simple for someone to rise up on his own and accept the request of this or that person, then, you take the step and call the people to the Koran. Why do you order me to do so? Why should one person issue instructions and another carry them out?

I then asked: Is the Koran popular among the Followers of the Koran today? He was at a loss to answer. I continued: It goes without saying that it is not. Today, few of the Koranic instructions are followed. For instance, the Koran states: "Fight the infidels who are near you." It instructs Moslems to be constantly at war with the non-Moslems around them. Yet, how can the Moslems be at war with non-Moslems today when they do not even desire their own independence and freedom but live joyfully and happily under the rule of foreigners. The Koran states: "Obey God. Obey His messenger and those who have authority vested in them." It considers obedience to the calif obligatory for everyone. But there is no calif of Islam in the world today, and we have forgotten how the Moslems treated the calif of Islam at the time when there was one. We have not forgotten that in wars, Moslems from India and Morocco picked up their rifles and fought against the army of the calif (the Ottoman sultan). We have not forgotten that in the past World War, the Arabs disobeyed the calif and formed an alliance with his enemies, the great European governments, and fought against him. Such is the importance the Moslems place on "those with authority vested in them." The Koran criticizes poetry, but Moslems, especially the educated ones, consider poetry a praiseworthy practice. The Koran forbids the drinking of wine, yet Moslems drink wine as if it were water.

One does not need to speak at length. We have seen that in most Islamic countries, the Koran and its instructions have been rebelled against and replaced with "constitutional laws" brought from Europe. It goes without saying then, that the Koran is not practiced by the Followers of the Koran. I ask: Why has this happened; why does the Koran have no affect on its followers? Answer me that!

He said: "Beliefs have become weakened; people have become bad."

I said: First, I ask why the people have become weak in their beliefs. Everything in the world has a cause. What is the cause in this case? Secondly, I say that people are always bad, and religion must change them. When the Koran was revealed, people were worse than they are today. The Arabs worshiped idols, killed their daughters, and plundered each other's property and homes. But, the Koran helped them overcome their misguided ways. Out of the ignorant idol worshipers of Arabia, it created true self-sacrificing men, such as Ali, Abu Bakr, Omar, Ammar, Abazar, Abdollah Rawaheh, and Khaled Walid. This was the effect of the Koran at that time. But today, it does not have the slightest effect. The clerics read the Koran from beginning to end without taking the slightest heed. Why is this so?

You ask why I do not call the people to the Koran. I ask: Would they come if I were to call them? There are so many clerics and others as well as the fellow members of your sect, who have written and who write so many books about Islam and the Koran. Have they been effective? Have any of the Christians or others come to believe in the Koran? Suppose that they do, will they be better people than followers of the Koran? First, you must clarify the reasons for the Moslems' failure to be attentive to the Koran and its instructions so that we know what should be done.

I said this and waited silently for a response. Once he realized that he had to give an answer, he said: "People do not follow the Koran in practice."

I said: Again, you are offering a pedestrian answer. Why do they not follow it in practice? There are a hundred million Moslems who strongly believe in the Koran and consider it their holy book. Why is it that they do not follow its instructions? Is there no reason behind it? I am asking you for the reason.

On the other hand, what do they follow? Do they draw their swords and kill the non-Moslems? Do they obey "those with authority vested in them," who do not exist? Do they destroy the tax offices and the banks and engage in collecting *khoms* and *zakat* religious taxes? Do they disregard the new sciences, which are not compatible with the Koranic dictums? Others aside, tell me, do you yourself follow the instructions of the Koran to the letter?

Since he kept silent and would not speak, I did not continue the conversation, because they refuse to understand and agree. They do not have the capacity and insight necessary to benefit from what we say. As I mentioned, they have made of the Koran a tool and they speak in confusion. But since I know that the readers would like to know the reason for the weakness in the beliefs of the Moslems and their failure to pay attention to the Koran and its instructions, I will respond to the question I posed to that cleric and which he was unable to answer.

We must know that at the time when the founder of Islam rose from among the Arabs, their greatest misguided belief was idol worshipping, which is why the Koran dealt with this subject and provided many sharp responses, such as: "Do you worship what you have sculptured?" and "Would you worship anything other than God, which can neither benefit nor harm you?" A large part of the Koran is devoted to this subject. Hence, the simple Arab people were saved from their misguided beliefs and practices and, with pure hearts and strong faith, they rose up to work and self sacrifice. At that time there was no book among the Moslems except the Koran, and no instructions except those in the Koran were common. Moslems read the Koran with simple, pure hearts and were inspired by its very valuable instructions.

However, later on, certain confusions occurred in the Islamic world and very deep-rooted, poisonous misguided beliefs appeared, one after another. Before all else, the Shi'ites rose and created another organization to compete with Islam.[15] They used the Koran as a tool to advance their sect, explained the verses as they saw fit, and interpreted whatever they wanted. Along with them appeared the Batenis, who followed an even worse course. This group said: "There is an apparent side to the Koran and a hidden side, and no one knows the hidden side but us." Thus, all at once, they devalued and made ineffectual that sacred book and made it a tool in the hands of false teachers and charlatans. Later, Greek philosophy, which was incompatible with religion from the root, became popular among Moslems. Anyone who accepted it considered religion insignificant and unimportant and turned away from it. Also, Sufism, which came from Rome, and which also was incompatible with Islam and the Koran in every respect, was spread among the Moslems. Then, among the Moslems in Iran, Kharabatism appeared. And this inculcated the most poisonous false teachings in the minds of the people, making them absolutely turn away from religion.

In this way, misguided beliefs were established and defeated the Koran, reducing its effectiveness. For this reason, Islam became weak and many of its instructions became obsolete.

It must be said that although Moslems considered the Koran to be their book, they did not have strong faith in its instructions and their minds were full of teachings contrary to the Koran. That is why they could not properly follow it and make use of its instructions.

This was how it was in the past. In our time, other things have been added to it. Now, the flood of materialism has risen, which is the greatest and most deeply rooted of misguided beliefs in the world, a misguided belief which has shaken the very roots of all the religions. On the other hand, as a result of the advancement of the sciences concerning the workings of the universe (the sky, the earth, the stars, etc.), certain contradictions have become apparent between the Koran and other religious books, on the one hand, and those sciences, on the other. Although one cannot criticize those books because of these contradictions, their importance is diminished. On the other hand, in the present age, the political foundations of Islam have fallen apart, and as we said, many of the Koranic instructions have become obsolete. These have been added to the past causes and have made the Koran altogether ineffectual.

Those who say, "As long as the Koran exists, so will Islam" are absolutely oblivious of these issues.

In short this is one of the justifications, all of which are unimportant and unfounded, as we have shown one by one, that Moslems present in response to our assertions. The most irrational and unfounded of their claims is wanting to return the religion to its origins, of which we will later also speak.

CHAPTER 3

God Is Weary of This Islam

As we said, today, there is no Islam left. What remains consists of various sects of Sunni, Shi'ite, Karimkhanism, Aliyollahism, Sufism, and the like, which are called Islam. Not only is this establishment not Islam, it is not even a religion. It is irreligiosity itself.

As we have said elsewhere, religion is not something useless. We expect benefits from religion. Religion must familiarize the people with the truths of the world and life. It must prevent them from disunity and set everyone on one main course. What we value and consider necessary for the people of the world are these benefits. But this establishment neither teaches the truth to people nor sets them on one main course. Instead of truths, it fills the hearts of its followers with misguided and ignorant beliefs and creates disunity among them. Let me repeat: Not only is this not religion, it is, in fact, irreligiosity. Religion is for the purpose of preventing people from sinking into such ignorance, and, as a result, becoming disunited. It is for the purpose of preventing the people from becoming so base and ignorant.

Religion is for the purpose of helping the people to advance, and religious people must be superior to irreligious people. But this establishment is exactly the opposite. We all know that today, Moslems (or better, Sunnis, Shi'ites, Sheykhists, Karimkhanis, Aliyollahis, and Sufis) are inferior to and more backward than others. As we said, in any of the Islamic countries, people are divided into two groups: The first consists of those who have turned away from religion and are interested in the freedom, advancement, and development of the country as well as the spread of sciences. The other group consists of those who

95

maintain religion (or better, their sect) and know nothing of honor, pride, and interest in the development of the country. This is the result of this establishment called Islam.

Let those who support this establishment tell us what benefit they gained from it.

If they say that these sects "teach certain truths to the people," they lie. What truths do Shi'ism, Sheykhism, Karimkhanism, Aliyollahism or Sufism teach the people? Is it not a fact that each one of them fills the minds of their followers with the basest of ignorant beliefs? The most simple of these is Sunnism, which is less corrupt than the others. We mentioned six examples of their misguided beliefs (which the others share) in the beginning of this book.

If they say that they "draw the people toward monotheism and purity of heart," they lie. Today, the masses of Moslems are idol worshipers and there are few cities in which one or more domes have not been built. Moslems mention the name of God, but as we said in the beginning of this book, they do not consider Him anything more than a whimsical, autocratic ruler, not to mention the kind of impudence that the Shi'ites, Batenis and Sufis have displayed toward God.

If they say that they "teach the laws of freedom and pride," still they lie. We witness the contrary to be true. Today, Moslems (those who display devotion to religion) are the most abject and inferior of nations. And, as we said, they openly display hostility towards freedom, independence and bravery.

If they say that they "improve life and enlighten Moslems in this regard," again they lie. We see that Moslems know nothing of commerce, nor do they understand the meaning of agriculture, nor do they desire the development of the land and an abundance of foodstuff. In this regard, too, they are inferior to others.

The best example of the detriments deriving from these sects and the evil that they create in their followers is the condition of the clerics, who are the leaders of the religion. One would learn a great deal from studying their condition, and calling to mind the extent of their ignorance. Is the purpose of religion to nurture such people? Is it to nurture such people that God appoints prophets?

In short, nothing is derived from this establishment but detriments. Undoubtedly, it is one of the major causes of the misfortune of the East.

This itself shows the ignorance of the Moslems, who always have the original Islam before their eyes and recall the victories of its early days, but are altogether unaware of their own conditions, never remembering the corruption that exists today. Let me repeat: This itself is a manifestation of their ignorant and misguided beliefs.

This is the result of failing to understand the meaning of religion. They do not understand that religion is a way of life and the religion of every people is that which they believe in and follow. For example, the religion of Iranians today is Shi'ism, with all its corruption. And it is very ignorant for Iranians to speak about the original Islam and try to tie themselves to it. There is quite a bit of difference between that Islam and the one they follow.

In order to show this ignorance (or better, lack of awareness and intelligence), and understand the extent of its harmfulness, I will recount an anecdote.

Since for years we have spoken about the disunity that exists among the Iranians and have tried to find a solution to it, one group has stood before us and engaged in hostile and disruptive actions. One of those people wrote articles in the Tabriz newspapers and boasted to us of "Islamic brotherhood." This article reminded me that forty years ago, in Tabriz, there was a barefooted, mad ruffian by the name of Ghaffar Vakil, who used to run around from one end of the bazaar to the other and, despite his pitiable condition and poverty, always talked about money and property and spoke of thousands, even tens of thousands, of *tomans*.

I am reminded that in Tabriz, in Azarbaijan, Moslems consist of three groups: Sunnis, Shi'ites and Aliyollahis (Guran).[16] The Shi'ites, as well, consist of three groups: The Sheykhists, the followers of Shar', and the Karimkhanis, in addition to the Sufis, who are another group, and the Baha'is, who rose from among the Shi'ites.

I am reminded that these groups spilled much of each other's blood. And until the beginning of the Constitutional movement, they lived apart, and that the relative peace and integration that exists today in the name of Iranianism is the result of the Constitutional movement.

I remember that in Tabriz, in 1330 HQ, on the day of Ashura, the Seqqat ol-Eslam, the leader of the Sheykhis, was hanged. The followers of Shar' were overjoyed, and it was said that some of them dyed their hands with henna in celebration.

I remember that in Tabriz, in that same year, 1330 HQ, when the agents of Nicholas arrested the leaders of the liberationists and hanged them one by one, the clerics and others sent telegrams to him expressing their joy and gratitude.

I remember that in Azarbaijan, whenever the Kurds had an opportunity, they would attack Shi'ite villages, kill and plunder. One of those instances occurred in 1320 HS [1941/42], when they attacked the villages around Urmia and cut off the breasts of women (or better, their Islamic sisters).

I remember all of these and do not know whether I should

laugh at the ignorance of that writer and thousands like him or weep for the misfortune and the misguided beliefs and practices of these people.

I will not elaborate on this subject any more than this. This establishment is by no means related to the original Islam (as the Moslems imagine). This establishment is far removed from Islam. When they say that they "will return it to its origins," as we said, this is an ignorant and ill-thought-out statement. To return this establishment to that Islam would require someone to deal with all the misguided beliefs of the Moslems, including Shi'ism, Batenism, determinism, Kharabatism, Greek philosophy, Sufism, Aliyollahism, Karimkhanism, and, finally, materialism, and to fight and reject each one of them. On the other hand, he would have to explain the meaning of the Koran as the early Moslems understood it and show the original foundations of the religion. This is the way to return religion to its origins, which is ten times more difficult than founding Islam itself, because in founding Islam, an effort was made to fight only one misguided belief (the simple idol worshipping of the Arabs). In the present effort, however, dozens of more deeply-rooted and stronger misguided beliefs must be fought. How could anyone, of those misguided ones, accomplish such a task?

Then, suppose that they could do so. Would Moslems accept it? Is it not true that the followers of every sect consider their sect to be the true Islam, and refuse to accept anything that does not conform to their sect? Could there, therefore, be any solution but to eliminate those sects?

In any case, this establishment is detrimental through and through and will not accept improvement. That is why I say, God is weary of this establishment. That is why I say, this establishment must be eliminated.

Should this establishment remain, it will always be a shackle for the nation; it will prevent their progressing (as it has done so far). Now that the movement of the sciences has occurred in the world and the people of the world are ready for advancement, if this establishment is to remain, it will bring misfortune to the Easterners and keep them backwards forever.

Even today you see them disregard all honor and dignity, becoming subservient to foreigners in order to preserve their sects. As we said, today, Moslems are content with their mosques being open, with their Friday Islamic holidays being observed, with their being free to go to Mecca and other places of pilgrimage, with having their Koran recited on the radio every evening and every morning, and with, every once in a while, having some Orientalist write and publish a book praising Islam and its founder. They will be content to be subservient to any foreign government, with only these few conditions.

You see that constitutionalism, or the government of the masses, is the best method of government. Today, most advanced nations benefit from it and have become powerful because of it. But a Moslem (an intelligent and informed Moslem) is only happy to conform constitutionalism with a Koranic verse, "Ask for consultation in affairs," boasting and saying, "Constitutionalism is in the Koran, too."

This is itself an example of their misguided ways and ignorance. On the one hand, they surmise that constitutionalism is merely consultation and display their lack of awareness of its meaning. On the other hand, they misrepresent the Koran by quoting it out of context and do not avoid any sort of audacity. Islam has given the calif (or the one with authority vested in him) the right to govern, and everyone must obey him. These people want to cover the truth and say that in Islam, too, government is given to the people.

This is their way in everything. They sacrifice all dignity and benefits for their sects. Today, all the people of the world are seeking to benefit from the new sciences. But Moslems are content with finding verses in the Koran to conform to the sciences and pretending that those sciences also exist in the Koran. Any time an important idea is presented by someone, Moslems say that it is also found in the Koran or in the *hadith*s.

Religion must guide the people and protect them. Here, the contrary is true. They have to preserve religion by patching it up and fabricating lies, changing its color with each new day. One of their most disgusting practices is that when you explain certain negative aspects of some sect and criticize them, they persist as long as they can; and then, when they cannot respond to the criticism, they deny it completely. This is one of the great faults of their sects, which have no stable foundation; anyone can accept certain things and reject others, as he sees fit.

Their case is like that of the foolish family living in a ramshackle building, with weak foundations and demolished doors and windows, which has become a nest for snakes, scorpions, and tarantulas, refusing to come out. And in response to your criticism, you see that overnight they have gone and taken doors and windows from some new palace and haphazardly installed them on their old, ugly building, boasting to you, "You see, our building has doors and windows, too." Or you see that they have filled the cracks in the walls with mud and say: "There is nothing wrong with these walls."

Ten years ago, when we had just begun our efforts, speaking of the rational faculties, we said: "Religion must be susceptible to rational faculties." Many of the clerics started to make a ruckus and said: "'God's religion cannot be measured with the rational faculties'; religion cannot be conformed to the rational faculties. Our rational faculties are imperfect, and there must be an infallible person to guide us." They have frequently come to me to speak, or rather, to debate. But, now that they have nothing to respond, some of them return and say: "Of course, religion must conform to the rational faculties. Our imams have also said this." Sometimes they even quote a *hadith*: "When God created the rational faculties, he addressed them and said, 'Come forward.' They came. He said, 'Go back.' They did. He then said, 'I swear on my honor and glory that it would be with you that I shall punish and with you that I shall reward.' " They say all of these and do not remember that this establishment called Islam in name only (or better, a few scattered sects) which exists today is incompatible in many ways with the rational faculties, and this is precisely like the story of removing the beautiful doors and the windows of the new palace that we mentioned above.

There may be those who think that these people are so persistent because they are worshippers of God and religious and are devoted to religion and God's name, hence, they are working to preserve that establishment called Islam. But this supposition is not correct. We have seen and tested that when we speak to them of a much higher and stronger religion, which glorifies the name of God, they do not accept it. Rather, as we said, they would not stop at any kind of hostility and disruption and engage in every barbarian and base practice.

The truth is that their devotion to what they know and their insistence on their ignorant and misguided ways indicate one of the base characteristics existing in the nature of man. When the soul is sick and the rational faculties weak, this base characteristic becomes powerful and effective. This is the secret behind the devotion and insistence that we see in Moslems.

On the other hand, today, hundreds of thousands or rather millions of people make a living off this establishment. Clerics, seminary students, professional religious mourners, prayer readers, seyyeds, Sufi elders, wandering dervishes, and prayer writers exist in large numbers in every city. In every city, including Najaf, Karbala, Samaria, Baghdad, Mashhad, Qom, Medina, and Mecca, several thousand people have gathered around the domes, freeloading in the name of custodians, servants, prayer readers, and *mojaver*s [persons choosing to live close to a holy shrine]. They live happily in the name of religion and consider themselves superior to others. Some have even gained fame and prominence.

As we have said, the Shi'ite *mojtahed*s have arranged a ruling establishment for themselves and rule without a throne and crown. They collect taxes from the people as "*mal-e emam*." The leaders of the

Batenists (Esma'ilis) pretend to be "the manifestation of God" and govern the lives and property of their followers. A similar establishment exists for the leaders of the Karimkhanis in Kerman.

Today this establishment is useful for two purposes: First, it is useful for freeloading. That is, millions of people have made a business out of it. Second, it is useful for the policies of greedy governments, which have made a tool of it to dominate the Eastern nations.

In addition, in this religion (especially in the Shi'ite sect, in Sufism and the like), the way is open to everyone to be capricious and selfish. Everyone can find what he wants and follow whatever path he wants in the name of religion. A greedy person can accumulate wealth any way he can and ease his conscience merely by giving some of it to the clerics. A lazy person can live idly off the fruits of the labor of others and call himself a pious man or a dervish. A government employee can shamelessly engage in all sorts of theft and corruption, and be proud that he supports religion. A degenerate man can be a tool in the hands of foreigners and call it religious.

This is how a religion which has lost its essence and the foundation of which has fallen apart, becomes a tool in the hands of the capricious, the selfish, and the evil doers. There is much to say in this regard, which time and space preclude here.[17]

After all these, this establishment called Islam, or Christianity or other religions, is greatly harmful to the world today. That is, as a result of being tainted with myths and their incompatibility with sciences and also because their time has passed, they cause the people to turn away from religion.

This is the great malady from which the world suffers today. As we have said, from the time that the movement of sciences occurred, people have turned away from religion, group by group. They flee not only Christianity, Islam or Judaism, but any religion. In their opinion, religion is without foundation and will be eliminated by the sciences. And many books have been written on this subject. However, religion is one of the ways to progress. We have clearly explained elsewhere that from the time human beings have appeared on earth, they have continually progressed and improved.[18] But the point is that human progress must always be in one of two ways: first, through the sciences, and second, through religion. Otherwise, nothing will be gained. Religion is one of the two ways for progress, and the people of the world need it dearly.

This detriment and similar ones caused by that establishment cannot be ignored. They cause the people to be misguided. They are the stones blocking the way to progress, which must be removed, and the world must be cleansed of them.

These few worthless and baseless establishments must never stop world progress. God's laws must never change. This is what we mean when we say: God is weary of this Islam (and also of other establishments like it).

CHAPTER 4

All Religions Have
The Same Foundation

There is much to say about religion. Religion is an important establishment and has many secrets.

The story of religion is that from the time human beings appeared on earth and were progressing, once in every age, someone rose to deal with the existing misguided beliefs and practices, tried to eliminate them, explained certain truths about life, instructed people on how to live together, shook the rational faculties, and advanced humanity a few steps.

This is the story of religion. And one of its secrets that must be known is that all those who rose wanted the same thing, and the foundation of all religions is the same. This is proof that those who rose did not do so capriciously and on their own, but they all had the same source.

Religion has several purposes, which we will list here briefly.

(1) The world has a Creator and Owner. And no one else has a hand in the affairs of this world. This is one of the points where humans err, and there have been misguided beliefs in this regard from the very beginning. In searching for God, humans have created certain things out of their own imagination and have been enslaved by the very idols they themselves have created. Prophets have pursued and explained several things in this regard:

First, there is one system throughout the world and it has only one Creator and Possessor.

Second, that Creator and Possessor is beyond this superficial, material world.

Third, no one else but He has or could have a hand in the affairs of the world, and no one else but He must be worshipped.

(2) This world is an orderly and organized system and its operation is based on certain laws. This shows that the world is not without a purpose, that there is a purpose in it.

(3) The human being is the Creator's chosen creature. Even though human beings are of the same material as animals, they are not equal with them. In human beings there exists an essence called the soul, which is itself a separate system.

(4) Good and evil both exist in the world and also in the composition of every human being, and humans must always desire good and fight against evil.

(5) Beyond all the misguided and deviant beliefs and practices and the conflicts and battles that people rage against each other when they live together are a series of very important truths and an open pathway for living together in joy and tranquility. On the other hand, a power has been placed in the composition of human beings called *kherad* [rational faculties] for understanding those truths and finding that main path. Human beings have been created to live happily and benefit from tranquility and joy and have no need of wars and conflicts.

(6) The soul is not destroyed along with the body, and after this life, there can be and must be another life, a better and worthier life than this.

These are what every religion must (more or less) want and pursue. These must be the foundations of every religion. For this reason, in most places, when religion is mentioned, these ideas are desired. When we say, "Religion is not a thing which becomes new or old," these are the ideas that we have in mind. This is a truth that the masses of the people, especially the Moslems, do not know, but which, by all means, are unquestionable.

Nevertheless, every religion must follow a path and establish a foundation to advance these ideas, in accordance with the dictates of the time. In this connection, there are several issues which must be considered:

First, every religion must deal with the misguided and ignorant beliefs and practices of the time and fight them in order to cleanse the hearts and make room for the truths. Obviously, misguided and ignorant beliefs and practices differ with every age.

Religion is like the practice of medicine. A physician who comes to the bedside of a patient has two concerns. One is to restore health to the patient who has lost it; another is to drive away the illness that has overtaken his body. Health is always one thing. It consists of eating well, sleeping well, and being well. But there are many kinds of illness, and they can change each time.

For instance, in ancient times, because of their ignorance, people did not understand that the world is one system, and thought that many hands were involved in its operation. That is why they created many gods from their own imagination, built idols for each, worshipped them, and enslaved themselves to them. But today, such ignorance has been eliminated and now many more deeply-rooted ignorant ideas have appeared. For example, one group has appeared, calling themselves Kharabatis saying: This world is nothing. It is futile, and we must not be preoccupied with it. We must not pay attention to the past nor think of the future. We must value the present moment and engage in pleasure seeking and drunkenness. They have made these ignorant ideas into a philosophy and have inculcated them into the minds of the people. Another group, called Sufis, has appeared and made these fabrications: We are from God and we shall return to God. What has distanced us from God is this material system. We must forget about this world and think about the next. We must suffer in order to reach God. They call these nonsensical ideas "*erfan*" [mysticism] and have spread them with much embellishment everywhere. Yet another group, called Shi'ites, has appeared. Its members consider certain dead people who have left nothing behind but a name to have a hand in God's affairs and have forced people to keep these names alive, revitalize their stories, and go on pilgrimage to their tombs. They have called these very irrational, misguided beliefs religion, and insist upon them. Finally, there is a group called Scientists and and New Thinkers, which has committed many errors, including lowering human beings to the level of animals, considering them incapable of any good. They explain life in terms of a battle and the world as a battle field. They have misguided the masses of the people through these errors, especially in Europe and America, and have caused many problems in people's lives.

Today, religion must rise up to engage in a series of extensive, expansive efforts to battle such misguided beliefs, to cleanse the hearts of these beliefs, and to create a basis to establish itself in order to prevent the return of such ideas. In truth, such misguided beliefs have disrupted the religious path that once existed and have destroyed its foundation. That is why another path must be created and a new foundation established.

Second, the world is advancing and human beings are gradually becoming more susceptible to and more prepared to accept good. Many good ideas that could not have existed in the past can now exist. And, many evil ideas that could not have been prevented in the past can be prevented now. For this reason, every religion must take new steps in its own time for the advancement of the people.

For example, at the dawn of Islam, government was dictatorial and autocratic and there was no readiness for the government of the people (or democracy), which is the best type of government. For this reason, Islam was only able to decrease the autocratic nature of that kind of government and couple it with justice and good will. But today, as a result of lofty ideas, the grounds for democracy have been prepared and most countries have accepted it. In any case, religion must accept this and add other good ideas to it.

At the dawn of Islam, the grounds were not prepared to prevent the practice of sacrificing, which was a remnant of the days of idol worshipping. And Islam only changed its method. But today, this practice must be prevented altogether and eliminated. How could the cutting off of a sheep's head bring one closer to God? And how could it prevent accidents?

Third, sciences and knowledge increase as time goes on. For this reason, a religion which is established after another must be superior to it, explain things more clearly, and contain higher and more numerous truths.

For example, at the dawn of Islam, the present sciences did not exist and the Arab people possessed simple knowledge. For this reason, Islam chose a simple language and followed the knowledge of the time in terms of the sky, the earth, and so on. However, it is obvious that in the present age, nothing can be accomplished with that language, and the kind of pursuit of the knowledge of its time that Islam followed can do nothing but cause people to turn away from it.

These are the reasons why every religion must choose another path. This is the path that we sometimes call religion, and this is what we mean when we say, "Islam, Christianity, and Zoroastrianism are out of date," or we say, "They are anachronistic."

The masses of people, particularly Moslems, are not aware of what we have said. In their minds, when a prophet or a founder of a religion appears, an angel comes to him from the sky and continually brings him messages from God. He must in turn give those messages to the people. Obviously, this kind of thinking (or better, superstition) is very immature and pedestrian and differs greatly from what we have said.

In any case, there are two reasons for any religion to take the place of another:

One, when a religion loses its essence and becomes irreligion itself.

Two, when the time or age requires a new path.

106

It is for these two reasons that at any age, when need be and God wills it, a divine movement appears in the world and a new path begins. This is the law of God and is necessary for the advancement of the world.

The Moslems' claim that Islam was the last religion is a baseless statement and is incompatible with God's law and progress. Besides, there is a very clear answer to it. We must ask: Which Islam are you talking about? If you are talking about the original Islam, it no longer exists, that it can be the last religion. If you are talking about today's Islam, it is nothing but irreligion.

To say that God made this contraband, insignificant establishment the final religion is a grand lie ascribed to God. To say that God wants Shi'ism, Sufism, Aliyollahism and the like to last forever is ascribing a grand lie to God .

I know that you will quote me the Koranic verse, "Wa khatam al-Nabiyyin" [and the Seal of the Prophets]. That is why I say that undoubtedly these two terms do not and cannot mean what Moslems have understood them to mean, for several reasons:

(1) First, as we said, that meaning is incompatible with God's law. Besides, the present condition of Islam is proof that that meaning is incorrect. Even if we do not know its true meaning, we should not give it an incorrect meaning.

(2) A method in the Koran is that it repeats its important teachings not once, but several times. If this was what that noble man meant, since it is an important issue, he would not have sufficed with saying it once (and then, in an ambiguous language).

(3) There are in the Koran statements contrary to that interpretation. For instance: "And we do not send messengers except as harbingers of good news and those who give warning," or, "He inspires any one of His creatures that He wants in order for Him to warn the people of the Day of Judgment." The fact that he does not say, "We did not send" or "We did not inspire" indicates that such was not intended by those two terms.

CHAPTER 5

Islam and *Pakdini*

Concerning Islam, we have said all that we should say. And since for many years we have been engaged in certain endeavors in the name of *Pakdini*, here we would like to explain its relationship to Islam.

As we have said, the foundation of all religions and their aspirations are the same; only their paths differ, as the times require, or for other reasons. Therefore, the foundations of *Pakdini* and Islam are the same. The efforts that we have made in the name of *Pakdini* are, in fact, to advance the intentions of Islam and revitalize its foundations.

Islam had created a path, but that path was for certain purposes and now, we want to advance those purposes in a much better way.

That is why we say, if Moslems are truly religious and truly understand Islam, they should be very happy with our efforts and cooperate with us. The fact that they are unhappy and rather than cooperating try to disrupt our efforts shows that they are irreligious and do not understand Islam.

There is another important point here, which is, when one religion rises out of another, it must continue the course of the previous one. That is, it must return the previous religion to its origins and explain its strong foundation to the people. Then, it must begin its own path and accomplish what it wants.

Islam itself did a similar thing. When that religion appeared among the Arabs, there existed in Arabia from ancient times a group called " Hanafa'," whose members were theists and worshiped God. *Tahannof* was considered a religion among the Arabs. In fact, the founder of Islam initially called the people to follow that religion.

Once having done so, he founded Islam on the basis of that religion.

The same has been done in connection with *Pakdini*. *Pakdini* is the continuation of Islam and its foundations are the same as those of that religion. *Pakdini* has appeared in a different age, and in this respect is different from Islam. However, it is founded on the same six objectives of Islam and other religions. The differences between Islam and *Pakdini* are the same as the differences between Islam and *Tahannof*.

This is hard for Moslems to accept, as they do not understand these ideas because of their polluted minds. They imagine that we have replaced Islam, whereas we have revitalized it and are advancing its objectives in a better way.

The history of our endeavors will clarify this point, and I will briefly mention it here.

Our endeavors began in 1312 HS [1933/34]. In that year, we began our work writing the monthly publication *Peyman*. Europeanism had reached the height of its popularity in Iran and other Eastern countries; it had even reached a point of madness.

What was Europeanism? It is possible that many of our readers do not remember it, and we must remind them of it.

In Eastern countries, including Egypt, Syria, Iraq, Iran and India, certain movements had appeared and people had been stirred and had opened their eyes, looking at the Europeans, with their many sciences, astonishing skills, dazzling advancements, unmatched tools, and great glory and power. They were enchanted by all this and imagined that Europeans had found another world. Their lives were all pleasure and comfort and their words and deeds all goodness and purity. For this reason, they were trying to catch up with the Europeans as soon as possible and follow them in everything. This was the meaning of progress and civilization to them. Their prominent people often said: "We must become Europeans inside and out." A person who would go to Europe and return would bring back exaggerated praise as a souvenir, and he could capitalize on this one trip, boasting about it for many years. He would tell stories about Europe proudly in every meeting.

Rational faculties began to fail to distinguish the good from the bad and there was no basis for measurement, except whether something existed in Europe or not. Everyone had to document whatever he said on the basis of some Monsieur or Madame, otherwise, his word was not accepted.

This was Europeanism, one of the most detrimental affects of which was the spread of irreligiosity. As we have said, materialism had long become popular in Europe and had uprooted religion. Now, in the East, the uproar--yes, the uproar--had shaken the foundations of religion. Many people felt proud to be irreligious and expressed disdain for religion. In their opinion, science had uprooted religions and had shown that they were all without foundation. Many said openly: "In the twentieth century, no one would submit to religion." Darwin and his philosophy were on the tongues of everyone, and a large group of people, without knowing what Darwin had said and what criticisms he had of religion, openly displayed irreligiosity in the name of his philosophy. Statements such as, "Life is a battle," "The weak are prey to the strong," and "Everyone must concern himself only with his own pleasures," were commonly heard.

At such a time, when the widespread uproar of Europeanism and irreligiosity, support for Khayyam and Hafez, and love of poetry and literature had begun and madness of all kinds had commingled, we began our efforts. Since we had to tread the path step by step, as a first step, we dealt with and battled Europeanism. For more than one year, we explained in our writings that Europeanism itself had lost the way to life and was confronted with many problems and that it was very immature for the Easterners to follow. After disputes with many of the educated, with God's help, we silenced and eliminated that uproar.

This was the first step. As a second step, we rose in support of religions and showed that sciences do not make the world needless of religion. We showed that in the area of understanding the world and life and attaining tranquility and happiness, there are a series of very important truths which religions have pursued and shown to the people. We showed that what the materialists have surmised about religion, considering it full of unfounded fabrications, is merely the result of being uninformed and is itself an unfounded supposition. In this connection, too, we wrote for more than a year. And it was at this time that we began to speak of *kherad* (or rather, the power which judges between right and wrong and distinguishes between good and evil) and wrote strong answers to the materialists and others, who expressed their lack of awareness of such a power in human beings. Because in our writings more than anything else we seek judgment from *kherad* (as we must), we began to write many very important discourses on this subject.

Then, as our third step, we dealt with the religion of Islam, which was the last of the past religions and is itself a religion that has been current in and around Iran. On the one hand, we wrote discourses about its truthfulness and strength, and, on the other, we showed the foundation of that religion, or better stated, we returned it to its essence [*gowhar*].

What is the essence of Islam? The essence of Islam is belief in

110

God and His oneness, considering no one as the operator of the world, pursuit of the good and the pure, striving along the path of life, enmity towards the misguided and the irreligious, belief in a world of reward and punishment, and the like. These are the objectives of Islam. These are the foundations of that religion.

We explained these issues and showed that the sects that have branched out from Islam are nothing but blind alleys. We showed that the main path itself has been destroyed and that these blind alleys, which are misleading, have replaced it.

Those who say today, "Let us return Islam to its origins," and have made of this a justification do not know that we have already done so. Not only do they not know the meaning of religion, but they are also ignorant of the meaning of "returning Islam to its true essence."

Once this step was also taken, we had to engage in another part of our task. We had to establish "*Pakdini*" on the foundations of Islam. We had to advance the same objectives of Islam and other religions on a better and higher path, a path more in keeping with this age.

In order to do so, on the one hand, many religious truths, more than those which existed in Islam, had to be presented and much stronger truths or evidence provided. Islam had risen among the Arab people and had employed a very simple language, without having felt a need for proof in many instances. In this age, which is the age of sciences, another language must be used, and every statement must be supported with evidence equal to that of the sciences.

The advancements of the time must be noted and other great steps taken to improve the world.

In the wake of the extensive progress made over the past two hundred years in the area of sciences and the manufacture of tools, religion would have a very grave obligation; it would have to engage in establishing very strong foundations in the face of the sciences.

These are issues that we have written down here briefly, and not clearly, and we have neither the time nor the space to explain them with examples. Those who would like to understand these statements well and know what they are about must read our books.

On the other hand, many of the various misguided beliefs and practices which exist have to be confronted and fought one by one. As we said, when Islam appeared, the great misguided belief and practice of the Arabs was idolatry. For this reason, the Koran engaged in condemning it and tried to eliminate it. But today, there are several other much greater misguided beliefs and practices, including Shi'ism, Batenism, Kharabatism, Sufism, Aliyollahism, Baha'ism, and Greek philosophy, each of which alone is no less, if not more, evil and harmful than the worship of Lat and Hobal.

Most of these misguided beliefs have tied themselves to Islam and turn to the Koran for support. We must deal with all of these, write about each, and show the foundation of each one of them separately.

On the other hand, the greatest of the misguided beliefs of this age is materialism, which we must battle against the hardest. Materialism is the greatest and the most deeply rooted of misguided beliefs the world has ever known. This misguided belief is not a pedestrian matter; it is considered a philosophy which is supported by all the sciences (openly) and is founded by all the great scientists of the world.

On the other hand, this misguided belief has rooted itself in all fields of thought and has found its way into every segment of life. Materialists consider the system of existence to be merely this tangible world, and do not believe in God, the soul, or the hereafter. They group human beings together with animals and do not consider them capable of improvement. They do not accept *kherad* [rational faculties], which distinguishes between right and wrong and good and evil. They consider life as a battle and permit everyone to be concerned with his own interests, without having any consideration for others. They consider the weak to be the prey of the strong, and regard all laws and rules to be irrelevant and useless. One can say that this is a misguided belief, which indeed has been created to fight religion. That is why it stands against it in every respect, displays its hostility towards it, fights it from every corner, and tries to eliminate it.

We must deal with this issue too, provide responses, and each time start from another corner and express other views.

In short, we must strive along this path for many years in order to revive religion, and this is the endeavor which we are still pursuing.

This is a brief history of our endeavor. As we said, we are following the path of Islam and advancing its objectives. The apparent differences are in the methodology (or rather, in the path of religion). In foundation, there are no differences, and there must not be. Let me repeat: We have done the same with Islam that Islam did with "Hana-fiyyat" (or *Tahannof*). Those Moslems who oppose us are altogether devoid of Islam and have sunk so deeply into their misguided ways that they know nothing of Islamic truths, or they are those who are uninformed in this regard and do not understand what we want of religion.

They do not know that religion is not selfishness. Rather, its purpose is the salvation of the people of the world. That is why a religion that cannot bring people to salvation and stop their misguided beliefs and practices no longer exists as a religion and is of no value. On the other hand, when another path is open to salvation, it becomes valuable, and there is no room for complaining and enmity.

In those days, when we spoke about Islam and its truths and we

112

explained the essence of that religion, making people's eyes open to it, it was assumed that our efforts would be exclusively to revitalize the original Islam (in the path that it followed). This was an assumption of our own supporters as well as strangers, because up until then, it was not clear that "every religion has a foundation and a path," and that life is advancing and religion must advance along with it. There was very little understanding of these issues. We have always written: "Religion is not something that can become old or new. It is the same old religion, the path of which must be taken anew." But the meaning of these statements was not understood at the time. Today, after many years, it is understood, and what had to be done has been accomplished.

It is quite astonishing that Moslems, or rather, Shi'ites, Sufis, Aliollahis, Sheykhists, and Karimkhanists, under the pretext of supporting Islam, display their hostility towards us and make such a ruckus because we have named our efforts "Pakdini" or we have changed certain other things. It is quite astonishing that they who have destroyed the foundations of religion altogether and have eliminated the objectives of religion do not find anything to criticize in their own actions, instead criticizing us, who have revitalized the foundations of religion and have established the strongest of foundations for it. Yes, it is quite astonishing that that group which has displayed the worst hostility towards Islam and has replaced it with a series of very base, misguided beliefs ties itself to that religion and confronts us with its big mouth.

Here, let me conclude by saying once again: *Pakdini* is a replacement for Islam; it is what follows it. In essence and foundation, there is no difference. The differences lie in the path and some of its bases. And this must be so. This has been the will of God and this is His law.

NOTES

1. Kasravi commonly refers to Mohammad, the Prophet of Islam, as " that noble Arab." (tr)

2. Esma'ilism: a Shi'ite sect that followed Esma'il instead of Musa as the successor to their father, Ja'far ebn Sadeq, the sixth imam of the Shi'ites. Aliollahism: a sect believing in the divinity of Ali, the son-in-law of the Prophet Mohammad. Sheykhism: a Twelver Shi'ite sect following Sheykh Ahmad Ehsa'i, belonging to the Akhbari school and opposing *ejtehad* (independent reasoning in religious jurisprudence). Karimshanism: sect of followers of Mohammad Karim Khan Kermani, successor to Sheykh Ahmad Ehsa'i. (tr)

3. Batenis refers to a sect of Sevener Shi'ites believing in "hidden truth." Kharabatis, literally "those who dwell in taverns." The allusion is to the frequent references in classical Persian poetry to praise of wine drinking and taverns. (tr)

4. Reference is to World War I. (tr)

5. *Kherad*, as Kasravi's text shows, is the power to distinguish between good and evil, right and wrong, and so on. *Aql* is quoted by Kasravi here as a synonym for *kherad*. (tr)

6. The idols of Lat and Hobal were worshipped in pre-Islamic Arabia. (tr)

7. The Pakdini movement: *Pak*, literally "pure" or "total" (according to Kasravi's lexical explanations provided in "Vazhehnameh-ye Zaban-e Pak") and *din*, meaning "religion"; hence, Pakdini may be translated as "pure religion." "Pakdini" refers to a system of beliefs advocated by Kasravi in his writings, and which found some followers in Iran. (tr)

8. On this matter, see *Varjavand Bonyad*. (Kasravi)

Varjavand Bonyad [Sacred Foundation] is a book which Kasravi, in an advertisement at the end of *Bekhanand va Davari Konand*, calls "the most valuable of our books" and urges readers to read. (tr)

9. See *Davari* on this point. (Kasravi)

Davari is the shortened title of *Bekhanand va Davari Konand* [Let Them Read and Judge], which has also appeared under the title *Shi'igari* [Shi'ism], and which follows the text of *On Islam* in the present volume. (tr)

10. Wahabis. Followers of Mohammad ebn Abd ol-Wahab. Wahabism is a Moslem movement which appeared in Saudi Arabia in the 18th century and considers all other Islamic sects to be infidels, dualists and idol worshippers. (tr)

11. That story states: "Zo al-Qarnayn reached where the sun rises" and "It reached where the sun sets," and this cannot occur unless the earth is flat. If the earth is round, the sun cannot sink anywhere and cannot come up from anywhere, and no one could reach where it sets or where it rises. Today, if someone travels around the globe, he will never reach where the sun sets or rises. (Kasravi)

12. Accounts of this were published in *Kanun* newspaper.

13. Kasravi quotes original Arabic phrases in his text and provides Persian translations in footnotes. The English translations of such phrases throughout the remainder of the present text are based on Kasravi's Persian translations and are indicated by quotation marks. (tr)

14. What he meant was that when the Prophet said, "I do not know the unknown," he meant that he did not know it by himself, but that he knew it from God. (Kasravi)

15. On this subject, read *Davari*. (Kasravi)

Bekhanand va Davari Konand [*Shi'ism* in the present volume.] (tr)

16. According to *Farhang-e Mo'in*, a Kurdish tribe in Kermanshahan. The reference here may be to another tribe called "Guranzaza," who are not Kurds and follow the Aliollahi sect. (tr)

17. See *Davari* in this connection. (Kasravi)

18. On this subject, we have written in the second chapter of *Varjavand Bonyad*, but an even better source is *Khoda Ba Mast* [God Is With Us]. (Kasravi)

Let Them Read and Judge

SHI'ISM

Oh God, we shall combat aberrations; we shall fight greed and oppression; we shall eliminate the houses of idols; and Your support and guidance will make us victorious.

(First Azar worship)

FOREWORD

In The Pure Name Of The Creator

As many readers know, four months ago, we published a book on the Shi'ite sect. As we had anticipated, that book created an uproar. Rather than responding to our criticism and questions or, realizing that they have no answers, trying to seek the truth and accepting our statements, the ill-wishers rose in uproar. The government found a pretext to ban the book and, presuming that a "crime" had been committed, tried to make a case out of this matter to be judged in the penal court.

We did not become saddened by this event, because the uproar brought our efforts to the attention of a large number of people who were previously unaware of them. They sought out and found our books and began to read them intelligently. Our enemies helped us with their ill-intentioned deeds. As a matter of fact, we would like all of our statements to be judged. This is precisely what we want. The only way to distinguish truth from falsehood and the rational from the irrational is through judgment.

But the question must be asked: Who is qualified to judge this matter? What law can be employed to examine it? Are three or five "arbitrators," employees of the Justice Department, competent to pass such a judgment? Do Iranian laws contain anything that would indicate the truth or falsity of our statements?

There is no question that Justice Department arbitrators are incompetent to adjudicate in such a matter, and nothing can be found in Iranian laws on the basis of which such a judgment can be made.

As far as we know, such a judgment is possible in two ways:

Firstly, once the government becomes aware of the publication of such a book, it should organize a meeting of the clerics and ask them to respond. A well-intentioned and concerned government would do so, because this book concerns the problems of Iran and deals with vital issues. The book concerns the Iranian people, who have, unconsciously and unwittingly, been caught up in a series of very harmful misguided beliefs and practices, and while these beliefs and practices exist, the condition of the nation will not improve. The book addresses vital and worthwhile issues, providing very clear evidence.

More than anyone else, the government should be interested in such matters. It should value them and not hesitate to support us. In order to obtain beneficial results, it must step forward and ask the clerics to respond. It should then organize an assembly of scholars and well-intentioned people and ask them to judge the matter. In doing so, it would be engaged in a great historical task, making an immortal name for itself in history. But alas, such a government did not exist, and this was not done.

Secondly, the enlightened and people of good intentions of the world, from Iran and elsewhere, who are not small in number in this country, should read our assertions and judge for themselves.

First, they should read and realize what all the uproar is about, what we have said, what barbarian responses we have received, and what we wanted that resulted in our being prosecuted.

Second, they must understand for what reason this nation has fallen into misfortune and destitution, for what reason this country has turned to ruins, for what reason large groups of people are hostile towards the country and its progress and always wish its misfortune.

Third, they must know what we are aiming for, why we are tolerating so much suffering and abuse, and for what reason we experience so many insults and such uncivilized behavior from ill-wishers.

They should understand all this and then judge in accordance with the dictates of their rational faculties and their sense of fairness, without hesitating to help, as much as their courage and honor will allow.

Judgment in this regard must be carried out in one or the other of these two ways. Since the former did not occur, we have been forced to request the latter. We have found it more useful to put our views in writing in a more clear and concise language, to publish a small number of copies and send them to those on whose wisdom and good intentions one can set one's hopes. This is the story behind the writing and publication of this book.

Another point that must be remembered here is that, since this book concerns a set of worthwhile inquiries and then seeks the help of the reader, everyone must read it carefully, evaluate the statements with regard to the evidence and allow his rational faculties to pass judgment. Only then must he move from one issue to the next.

We have often observed in those who read our books that when they come across statements they have not heard before, they are initially offended and cannot readily accept them. And since every statement is accompanied by strong, irrefutable evidence, they consequently become undecided. These readers must not stop after one reading of the book; rather, they must read it two or three times. Undoubtedly, what they were unable to accept after the first reading they will be able to accept after the second or third reading.

In any case, we have not said anything which is unfounded, and we do not want anyone to accept any statement we make without understanding or believing it.

As we have requested, we would like every reader to be the judge of the truth, not to accept any statement we make without proof, and not to overlook any statement that is supported by evidence. He must imagine that he is a judge in a great court of law and behave in a way deserving of such a position.

After reading the book, those who are able to implement their judgment in the form of writing their conclusions should send an article to a newspaper or publish a book on the subject. This will be very beneficial and will achieve very good results.

Ahmad Kasravi

CHAPTER 1

How Shi'ism Began

Shi'ism has a long history; in fact, it is a history in itself. But we will make brief mention of it here.

Shi'ism, in the sense used here, began during the Omayyad period. Mo'aviyeh, under the pretext of responding to the killing of Osman, declared war on Imam Ali ebn Abitaleb, and after the latter's death, through force and deception, gained the caliphate and made it hereditary to his own family. This action did not please many of the Moslems, and many coveting the caliphate wanted to take it away from the Omayyads.

However, while Mo'aviyeh was alive, no one could challenge him. After his death, Hoseyn ebn Ali initiated a campaign, which did not succeed because of the lack of perseverance on the part of his supporters. As is well known, he was killed. Later on, when Yazid, the son of Mo'aviyeh, died, his son, also named Mo'aviyeh, ruled for only forty days when, amidst the confusion, Obeydollah ebn Zobeyr in Mecca and Mohammad ebn Hanifeh in Medina rose up with claims to the caliphate. Also, Mokhtar, who was secretly trying to become the calif, engaged in an uprising in Kufeh. However, none of these efforts was successful; they were eliminated one after another.

Then, two great families engaged in fighting the Omayyads, the

Abbasids (descendants of Abbas, the paternal uncle of the founder of Islam) and the Alavids (descendants of Ali). The Abbasids concentrated on preparing the groundwork. Since they considered the Omayyads to be the source of the displeasure of the Iranians and were aware of the Iranians' readiness to rebel, the Abbasids sent representatives to Iran, where they engaged in secret efforts and gathered some followers. On the other hand, the Alavids simply engaged in battles and were killed (as were Zeyd ebn Ali; his son, Yahya; Mohammad Nafs Zakiyyeh; his brother Ebrahim; Hoseyn, the author of *Fakh*; and others). Hence, the Abbasids succeeded and, with the help of Abu Moslem, overthrew and replaced the Omayyads.

In short, beginning with the second half of the first Islamic century, many severe conflicts arose over the caliphate and many wars were waged. Those who desired to become calif would not stop at any attempt to achieve their objective.

To that end, they shed each other's blood, destroyed families, and employed lies and deceit.

In these struggles, the followers of the Alavids were called "Shi'ite," which means "followers." "Shi'ism" began from that point.

Initially, Shi'ism was a simple political effort and most Shi'ites were praiseworthy, good men who were sincere and honest in their efforts to achieve their goal. Without a doubt, the Alavids were better suited and more deserving to be califs. Among them there were a greater number of honest and pious people, particularly compared to the Omayyads, most of whom were dishonest men.

The important point, however, is that Shi'ism did not remain in its initial simple form. In various periods, it took on various taints. From the very early times, one group of extremists claimed that during the time of Abu Bakr, Omar and Osman, Ali was more deserving to be a calif and that his three predecessors had unjustly held the position. With this statement, they expressed their displeasure in Abu Bakr, Omar and Osman.

This was the first tainting of Shi'ism. In truth, after the death of the founder of Islam, his companions, who were considered the leaders of the Moslems, first conferred the office of calif on Abu Bakr, then on Omar, then on Osman. Ali did not display any displeasure, and rightly so. At the time when Islam was on its way to great advancements, coveting the office of calif and creating schism among Moslems was considered a break with Islam. Obviously, Ali ebn Abitaleb would not have committed such an act. During his own office as calif, that imam wrote to Mo'aviyeh:

"The same group that gave their allegiance to Abu Bakr, Omar and Osman also swore allegiance to me, without one refusal. Choosing a calif is a prerogative of the *mohajers* [fellow travelers] and the *ansar* [companions] of the Prophet. Whomever they choose as their leader would please God."[1]

Ali's intention with this letter is to scold Mo'aviyeh, who opposes the calif, and to remind him of his error, or rather, his break with Islam.

How could the author of such a letter have expressed discontent and opposition during the period of the caliphates of Abu Bakr and others? Had he done so, would he be any different from Mo'aviyeh?

On the contrary, history clearly shows that Ali lived kindly and happily with those three. He even gave his twelve-year-old daughter, Omm-e Kolsum, in marriage to Omar. Also, when Osman became mortally wounded, he openly displayed his displeasure and sent his son, Hasan, to Osman's home to nurse him.

But the Shi'ite extremists, after fifty or sixty years of wishful thinking and ignorance, would try to create enmity between him and Abu Bakr, Omar and Osman and would not stop at any insult regarding the three califs. As we said, this was the first tainting of Shi'ism. These Shi'ite extremists, one must note, did not include all the Shi'ites, only a small group of them. In fact, during the same period, they were called "*rafezi*" [heretics] as a result of an event which in itself indicates their evil and perverted behavior.

The story was that late during the reign of the Omayyads, Zeyd ebn Ali ebn Hoseyn came to Kufeh from Medina. When he decided to return, the Shi'ites prevented him, and fifteen thousand people swore allegiance to him, hoping that he would rebel and take over the caliphate. Zeyd was deceived by them and began to work on the scheme. However, when the time came for him to prepare for the war, a large group of Shi'ites (the same extremists) came to him and asked: "What is your opinion concerning Abu Bakr and Omar?" Zeyd expressed his satisfaction with them and praised them. The Shi'ites made an excuse, left Zeyd and scattered. Zeyd said: "You abandoned me in my hour of need." From then on, that group was called *rafezeh* (or abandoners). Because of their lack of honor, Zeyd did not succeed and was killed.

As we said, the Abbasids were gathering followers in Iran and were preparing the grounds to ultimately take over the caliphate, with the help of Abu Moslem. Obviously, they also were hostile towards the Alavids. Once the Omayyads were eliminated, a conflict arose between the Alavids and the Abbasids. It was during this time that Mohammad Nafs Zakiyyeh, his brother Ebrahim, Yahya ebn Zeyd, Hoseyn Saheb Fakh, and others were killed. Since these people would rise up in arms, they were eliminated quickly.

At that time, one of those who made claims to the caliphate was

Ja'far ebn Mohammad ebn Ali ebn al-Hoseyn (the nephew of Zeyd). This man, who had some followers, followed a new path, stating: A calif must be chosen by God. The person who is chosen by God is a calif, whether he is capable of taking over the affairs or incapable and merely sits at home. Those who want to attain salvation must submit to this person chosen by God, obey him and pay *khoms* and *mal-e imam* [religious taxes].

Hence, he sat in a corner, claiming to be a calif (without any headaches). His followers submitted to his claims and accepted his views. But, afraid to call himself a "calif," he hid behind the name of "imam." Up to this point, the words "calif" and "imam" were used synonymously; the calif was also called "imam."[2] However, during this period, as the terms were used by this group, a slight distinction between the meanings of the two terms appeared. This group interpreted imam to mean "chosen by God."

This was a very astonishing story, because there would no longer be a need for war and struggle for the office of calif. A person could merely sit at home, claim to be a calif, and gather a small or large group around himself. On the other hand, the office of the caliphate or the imamate would lose its value and become insignificant.

This was the second taint appearing in Shi'ism, and a political movement started to become a sect. In addition, the meaning of the caliphate changed and, as we said, the calif (or, according to them, the imam) was a religious leader and not a political one.

The followers of this imam, who were the extremists (or the *rafezis*), found the opportunity to take another large, extremist step and said: "Imam Ali ebn Abitaleb was chosen by God to succeed the Prophet, and the Prophet himself made him his successor. Abu Bakr and Omar pushed him aside and coerced him into submitting to Abu Bakr as calif." In this manner, they found a pretext to curse and insult Abu Bakr, Omar, Osman and many of the companions of the Prophet. They impudently engaged in the fabrication of such lies as: "When Omar went to forcefully bring Ali to swear allegiance to Abu Bakr, the Prophet's daughter would not open the door. Omar forced the door open, pinning her between the door and the wall, as a result of which she lost a baby called ' Mohsen '; as a result of this same incident, she later died." They told many stories of this kind, which had no historical basis.

Because they had begun their efforts with exaggeration and extremism, they gradually surpassed even this level and began to make other statements: "Anyone who dies without having recognized the imam of his age dies as an infidel."[3] "God created us from superior water and clay and created our Shi'ites from the leftover water and clay."[4] "God revealed to the lands how to love and follow us. Those that accepted became fruitful and those that refused became salt deserts. He revealed the same to the mountains and those that accepted became high and those that did not became low. He revealed the same to the waters, and those that accepted became fresh water and those that did not became salt water." "Your deeds are shown to us every day. If you have done good deeds, we rejoice, and if you have done evil, we are saddened." "No one knows the meaning of the Koran but us; everyone must ask us." Such statements can be considered nothing more than boasting and exaggeration, and their utterers were undoubtedly irreligious and ungodly. We do not know who has said all of these statements and whether they are truth or lies and fabrications.

In this manner, a rift was created in Islam and a group of people separated themselves from the Moslems. This group displayed strong animosity towards other groups, not hesitating to curse and insult Islamic leaders, including Abu Bakr and Omar. In their opinion, others were all irreligious and only this group of Shi'ites was religious; others would all go to hell, and only this group would go to heaven. They called themselves the "saved sect" and considered all others to be misguided. However, because of their animosity and insistence, upon the instruction of their leaders, they would hide their beliefs and sentiments and practiced "*taqiyyeh*" [dissimulation].

Ja'far ebn Mohammad, whom we recognize as the founder of this sect, chose his son Esma'il as his successor; but Esma'il died before his father (and his death became the source of a story, which we will write about later on). Hence, his other son Musa al-Kazem succeeded him.

During the time of this imam, the Abbasid calif became suspicious and brought him from Medina to Baghdad, where he was kept in jail for twenty-seven years, until his death.

After him, his son Ali al-Reza succeeded him. He is the same person chosen by Ma'mun as heir apparent and summoned to Khorasan. This appointment raises the question: How could a person who considers himself to be chosen by God as calif and considers the Abbasid calif to be "oppressive and a usurper" accept being his heir apparent?

After his death, his son Mohammad al-Taqi, who had married Ma'mun's daughter, became the imam.

Succeeding him was his son Ali al-Naqi, who was succeeded by Hasan al-Askari, who is the eleventh imam of the Shi'ites, according to their calculation. However, after his death, something astonishing occurred in Shi'ite history, and once again Shi'ism took on another color.

The story was that the eleventh imam had no known offspring. For this reason, after his death, a schism arose among his followers. One group said: "The imamate has ended." Another group accepted his brother Ja'far (who is called Ja'far the Liar by Shi'ites) as their imam. Still another group said: "The late imam is survived by a five-year-old son who is hidden in a cellar and who is the living imam." The leader of this group, who had made the claim, was a person by the name of Osman ebn Sa'id, who called himself the "Bab" (or the gate to the imam). He said: "The imam has appointed me as the medium between him and the people. Whatever you have to say, tell me and whatever money you want to donate, give to me." Sometimes, too, he brought messages (or, as he called them, "decrees") to the people from the Invisible Imam.

Let us repeat that it was a very strange story. The child that they spoke of was not seen by anyone; no one knew of his existence. One cannot accept that someone would have an offspring without anyone knowing of it. And then, why would the imam hide himself? Why would he not come out of the cellar? If an imam is the leader, he must be among the people to guide them. For what reason would he hide?

But in Shi'ism, asking for proof or letting wisdom be the guide had not existed from the beginning and could not be expected to exist in this instance either. At that time, given their fanaticism and their distance from other Moslems (the Sunnis), it would be impossible for the Shi'ites to change their course and they would have to accept and submit to anything that occurred.

Nevertheless, many found the actions of Osman ebn Sa'id and the lofty position that he had established for himself to rule the Shi'ites hard to tolerate, particularly those who were intelligent and knew where it had all begun. For this reason, there were many struggles among more than ten persons, whose names appear in books and who also claimed to be intermediaries to the imam, calling themselves "gates," like Osman ebn Sa'id had done. Osman and his successors called them liars and brought "decrees" from the imam concerning his displeasure with such persons.

After Osman, his son Mohammad claimed to be a gate. He, too, brought "decrees" from the "sacred quarters" of the Invisible Imam, collecting money from the people and, according to them, sending it to the imam in animal hides made for ghee. He was followed by a person by the name of Hoseyn ebn Ruh. Then Mohammad ebn Ali Saymari, who was an Iranian, became the "gate."[5]

This was the situation, more or less, for seventy years. However, upon his death, Saymari did not appoint a successor to himself and

127

brought a "decree" from the imam that there would be no other gates and that the imam would be invisible altogether. It is not known what his secret reasoning was for such an action.

From then on, the Shi'ites were left without an imam and leader. However, there existed such "*hadiths*" [reported sayings] from the imams as: "In incidents, turn to those who have learned our sayings. They are my '*hojjat*' [proof] to you and I am God's '*hojjat*' to them."[6] With this justification, the clerics and religious jurists called themselves the successors of the imam and began to lead the Shi'ites.

According to them, the four successors were the "*navvab-e khasseh*" [special deputies], and clerics were all "*navvab-e ammeh*" [general deputies].

The fact is that today the clerics have established such a position for themselves. They consider the people to be their inferiors, collect *khoms* and *mal-e imam*, and even claim the right to leadership (or government) and regard the government as a "usurper" and "unjust," yet this extensive organization is merely rooted in and founded on those two *hadiths*.

On the other hand, during the time of Osman ebn Sa'id and his successors, they took advantage of the story of "Mahdi-ism" and recognized their invisible imam as "Mahdi." Hence, Shi'ism assumed another coloring. However, since "Mahdi-ism" has a history of its own, let us first explain it, before returning to our present discussion.

The idea of someone appearing in the future and, through a series of extraordinary acts, bringing goodness to the world exists in many religions: The Jews expect the Messiah; the Zoroastrians await King Bahram; the Christians hope for the return of Christ from heaven; and Moslems await Mahdi.

As Darmesteter (the Jewish, French orientalist) has said in this regard,[7] this idea has existed from ancient times among Iranians and Jews.

Iranians who believed in Ahriman and ascribed all evil in the world to him thought that a day would come when a person from the race of Zoroaster by the name of "Soshyant" would appear, who would kill Ahriman and cleanse the world of all evil. As for the Jews, because they had lost their freedom in their homeland and had become slaves in Assyria and Chaldea, one of their prophets had prophesied that a king (messiah) would rise in the world who would restore freedom to the Jews. The Jews have always awaited the Messiah, as they do now.

These ideas have existed among the Jews and Iranians and, with the passage of time, would become rooted in the hearts of the people and increasingly important in their minds. Then, at the dawn of Islam, as Darmesteter, who provides evidence about which we have spoken in

128

detail elsewhere,[8] says, this idea found its way among the Moslems, with the help of Iranians, and became widespread within a brief period of time. Those who desired to hold the office of calif took advantage of this idea, each calling himself Mahdi, promising goodness in the world, and, in order to advance their purpose, not hesitating to lie, each fabricating a *hadith* or *hadith*s from the Prophet or Imam Ali ebn Abitaleb.

Mohammad ebn Hanifeh, whom we said claimed the office of calif in Medina, was the first person to be called Mahdi by his followers. When he died, they said that he had not died but was alive in Razavi Mountain and would return one day.

Zeyd ebn Ali, who rose up in Kufeh, was also called Mahdi by his followers. He, too, promised the people good days for Islam through him.

The Alavids, who assembled in Medina, swore allegiance to Mohammad Nafs Zakiyyeh, whom they recognized as Mahdi, and who became known everywhere by this name.

The Abbasids, whom we said sent representatives to Khorasan, thereby preparing the grounds for themselves, also took advantage of Mahdi-ism and pretended that their rise was the same as the coming of Mahdi.

In this manner, the name Madhi existed from the first century of Islam. And it appears that the Ja'fari Shi'ites also took advantage of it. However, since they were a weak group, they lived under the cover of "dissimulation," promising themselves that "Mahdi shall be ours; he shall evenge us against our enemies and shall bring us to victory and power."

The following verse has been ascribed to Ja'far in books: All people await a government, and ours shall appear at the end of time.

Later, when the story of the Invisible Imam developed and they were forced to await his return, they made a Mahdi out of him, but this time, they took proper advantage of the legend. Whereas others had made up one *hadith*, they fabricated a hundred, and strongly established the foundations of their idea. But they added a new tint to Mahdi-ism and made strange statements: "Before Mahdi, a *dajjal* [impostor] shall appear; on the day of Mahdi's advent, the sun shall rise from the West; the supporters of the imam, who consist of 313 persons, shall rise up from various Shi'ite towns (Shi'ite towns at the time)--from Taleqan, Qom, Sabzevar, Kashan, etc.; he shall instantaneously appear in Mecca by way of *teyy al-arz* [instantaneous transmigration from one point to another]; the Imam shall draw his sword, saying ' Oh, avengers of Hoseyn, ' and shall avenge the blood of Hoseyn by killing all offspring of the Omayyads and Abbasids; he shall kill so many that a sea of blood shall surround the Kaaba; people shall say ' He knows no limits to bloodshed '; in response, the Imam shall mount the pulpit and, with tearful eyes, hold a torn, bloodstained shoe (belonging to Ali Akbar) and shall say: 'Were I to kill everyone in the world, it would not suffice as retribution for this shoe.'"

Such statements are so numerous that, if I were to write them down, as have Majlesi and others, I would have to write a separate book.

This is the history of the creation of the Shi'ite sect (the Shi'ite sect that exists today). In this manner it appeared, from the second century A.H., and has had followers in Baghdad and other cities of Iraq as well as some Iranian cities. It was founded on exaggerations and suppositions, and as time passed, it was embellished.

The imams had the knowledge of the past and future, understood the language of four-legged animals and birds, knew the invisible, and controlled the events of the world. Tranquility on earth and in the heavens depends on the existence of an imam, and the sustinance of people exists in gratitude for his being.[9]

Also, their enmity towards the three califs and other Islamic leaders, which is another basis for this sect, knew no bounds and they insisted upon it increasingly, day by day. They consider all praise in the Koran to concern their imams and all reprimands to concern the three califs.

In the meantime, two things have aided the advancement of this sect, first, the good name of Imam Ali ebn Abitaleb and, second, the heart-rending story of Karbala.

Imam Ali ebn Abitaleb was a great man, possessing many praiseworthy qualities. Shi'ites took advantage of his good name and pretended to be his followers. They presented that great man as the founder of Shi'ism and claimed that from the days of that imam, the differences between Shi'ites and Sunnis stemmed from the differences between him and Abu Bakr and Omar over the office of calif, and that all this conflict and hostility was engaged in for his sake. In addition, they engaged in exaggerations regarding that imam, ascribing to him a status beyond his own: "The Prophet has said, 'If you love Ali, no harm shall come to you from any sin.'"[10] "God said: Love of Ali is my fortress; anyone who enters that fortress shall be saved from my wrath."[11] There are so many such statements that were they written down, they would fill a large book.

And now, as to the heart-rending story of Karbala. From the day this event occurred, it caused anger and despair for most Moslems. Many rose up to avenge the blood spilled, and much blood was spilled. However, the Ja'fari Shi'ites took political advantage of it, kept it alive by holding mourning ceremonies, and made strange statements about it: "Anyone who weeps, makes others weep, or pretends to be weeping will certainly go to heaven."

They built domes over the graves of Imam Ali Abitaleb, Hoseyn ebn Ali and others, making them places of pilgrimage, and created pilgrimage prayers for each: "Anyone who makes a pilgrimage to Hoseyn in Karbala is like a person who has made a pilgrimage to God in heaven."

Such exaggerations, even if they existed during the time of Ja'far ebn Mohammad and his successors and were uttered by them, have undoubtedly been embellished and have grown and multiplied day by day.

Besides these, the idleness that in Shi'ism was considered an important Islamic mandate and would free a Shi'ite from holy war, Friday prayers and the like--he could even ignore the performance of prayers, fasting and avoiding evil and still be be forgiven all his sins merely by making a pilgrimage to the tomb of Hoseyn and weeping for him; the promises given concerning the mediation of the imams on Resurrection Day, when all Shi'ites would go to heaven; the superiority that Shi'ites believe they have possessed in their nature from the day of creation, considering themselves to be of superior, purer stuff; the organization of the imam's deputyship; and the leadership and governing role that the Shi'ite clerics established for themselves, each was an added incentive to attract simple people to Shi'ism and make them steadfast in this sect.

Another thing that we must mention here is that Batenism stemmed from Shi'ism, and the Batenis had gone a few steps beyond Shi'ites in their enmity towards Moslems and in destroying unity and cooperation. In later years, Shi'ism took many things from Batenism. Furthermore, the efforts of the Batenis to gain the office of calif, the forces that they gathered, and the governments that they established in Egypt, Yemen, Iran and other places were influential in spreading Shi'ism, not to mention the boldness and fearlessness of the Shi'ites themselves. However, since we have not spoken of Batenism in this book, we will not speak of its intermingling with Shi'ism. Such would require a different book altogether.

However, the spread of Shi'ism in Iran has a long history, which we shall briefly mention here.

It should be noted that from the day that the Arabs conquered Iran, the masses of Iranians refused to accept their victory and engaged in certain liberation efforts. Particularly during the time of the Ommayads, when pressure on them was more intense, Iranians increased their enmity towards Arabs. And when the Alavids fought the Ommayads, Iranians supported the Alavids "not only for the love of Ali, but for the hatred of Mo'aviyeh." For this reason, Iran was susceptible to Shi'ism, and some of the Alavids who escaped and came here established governments in Mazandaran and Gilan.

Then, whether because of their beliefs or for political reasons, the Buyids, who established a monarchy and advanced up to Baghdad, supported Shi'ism and helped spread this sect in Iraq and Iran.

During the Seljuks, because the kings of that dynasty were Sunnis, the spread of Shi'ism declined. Then, during the Mongols, because the family of Genghis did not believe in one religion, once again the spread of Shi'ism increased, and one of their great kings (Soltan Mohammad Khodabandeh) converted to Shi'ism, minting coins in the name of the Twelve Imams.

After the overthrow of the Mongols, the Sarbedars, who rose up in Khorasan; the Mar'ashis, who appeared in Mazandaran; and the Qarehquyunluys, who governed a large part of Iran, were Shi'ites and helped the advancement of Shi'ism in Iran. Seyyed Mohammad Mosha'sha' in Khuzestan, who claimed to be Mahdi, mixed Shi'ism and Batenism and began new ways to misguide the people.

After all of this, it was Shah Esma'il's turn. When he came to power, he began to kill Sunnis, and, by the sword, spread Shi'ism throughout Iran and made cursing Abu Bakr, Omar and other companions of the Prophet a common practice among Iranians.

From this time on, Shi'ism became the official religion of Iran, and the policies of the sect became enmeshed with those of the country. And the behavior of Esma'il and the killing of Sunnis were avenged. Soltan Salim, the Ottoman king, also engaged in killing Shi'ites in his country, destroying forty thousand people, including adults and children, men and women. Later, he acquired a "decree" from Sunni clerics, engaged in a war against Shah Esma'il, and defeated him in Chaldoran, and the latter was forced to flee.

From this point on, a serious rift was created between Iran and the Ottoman Empire, and the Ottoman kings invaded Iran at every opportunity. Then, during the time of Shah Tahmasb (Esma'il's son) and Soltan Soleyman (Salim's son), wars continued and much blood was spilt.

Esma'il the Second (son of Tahmasb) tried to rid Iran of Shi'ism and to stop the cursing and abuse. However, time was not on his side, and he died.

After him, during the time of Soltan Mohammad, Shah Abbas and Shah Safi, once again many wars occurred. This time, the Ottomans had acquired a decree from their clerics, engaged in slaughter and plundering as well, took women and girls as slaves and sold them at the markets in Istanbul, Sofia and Belgrade.

At the end of the Safavid period, the Afghans rebelled because of the conflicts between Shi'ites and Sunnis and, after a number of wars, conquered Esfahan. Because of the ensuing disorder in Iran, the Ottomans once again found the opportunity to send armies to Azarbaijan, Kurdistan and Hamadan, where they achieved victory and spilt much blood.

Later, when Nader came to power, this brave king attacked the Ottomans, on the one hand, driving them out of Iran and many times dispersed their large armies. On the other hand, he tried to stop enmity and hostility and wanted to cleanse Shi'ism of curses and abuses and purge it of exaggerated beliefs and make it into a "religious jurisprudential" school, making Shi'ites (or rather Ja'faris) sit side by side with the Malekis, Hanafis, Hanbalis and Shafe'is, and to create love and friendship among them. To this end, he engaged in many efforts, many times bringing Shi'ite and Sunni clerics together to sit side by side and engage in discussions. He frequently sent envoys to the Ottomans proposing reconciliation upon the conditions stated above. In Dasht-e Moghan, when he agreed to become king, he made Iranians pledge to do the same. However, all these efforts were in vain, and that courageous king was killed and thus eliminated. Shi'ism remained as it was and reached the situation that exists today. We all know its history during the Constitutional Movement. This is a brief history of the spread of Shi'ism in Iran.

CHAPTER 2

Criticisms That Can Be
Made Of Shi'ism

As we have seen, Shi'ism was initially a political effort which later became a sect. We would now like to discuss this sect and briefly mention many criticisms that can be made of it:

I: As we said, Shi'ism is founded on the idea that a calif must be chosen by God and not by the people. We ask: What is the reason behind such a claim? The holy book of Islam is the Koran. Where in the Koran is there such a claim? How could this be true without any mention made of it in the Koran?

The actions of the Islamic leaders clearly prove that such a statement is unfounded: After the death of that righteous Arab, they assembled, held discussions and chose as califs first, Abu Bakr; after his death, Omar; after his death, Osman; and after he was killed, Ali.

It is hard to believe that those who had sincerely converted to Islam at a time when Islam was weak, and had suffered and fought for its advancement, would abandon all their convictions once that righteous Arab died and appoint a calif on a whim.

The Shi'ites say: "Everyone turned away from religion, except for three persons."[12] But is this statement not hard to believe? What occurred which suddenly caused everyone to turn away from religion? Suppose Abu Bakr and Omar had wanted to rule and did turn away from religion with that desire. What would be the others' gain? This is a practice of the Shi'ites, who would not hesitate to lie in order to advance their opinions.

We have already spoken of the letter by Imam Ali ebn Abitaleb

134

to Mo'aviyeh in which he states: "The people have sworn allegiance to me as they had done to Abu Bakr and Osman." This is the proof that he offers for his position as calif and does not write: "God has chosen me" or "The Prophet had foretold it." In that letter, he openly states: "Choosing a calif is the right of the fellow travelers [*mohajeran*] and the companions [*ansar*] of the Prophet; whomever they choose as their imam will please God." I do not know what similarity exists between what the Imam said and what the Shi'ites say.

The clerics reason: "A calif must not have committed any sins and he must be the bravest, wisest, and most superior among the people. No one but God can choose such a person." I respond: What is your reason for saying so? If this were true, the founder of Islam should have said it; rather than you fabricating it as you see fit.

One proof that they offer in this regard is the story of Ghadir-e Khom and another the story of the Prophet asking for paper and pen at the moment of his death. Since I have an anecdote in this regard, about which there was a discussion, I will repeat it here.

In Dey 1321 [December/January 1943], I traveled to Qazvin with Mr. Va'ezpur to visit our supporters. In a meeting at Mr. Nasri's home, Mr. Pakravan said: "Some of the religious scholars and others who heard you were coming to visit told me that they had some points to argue with you. I responded that Mr. Kasravi does not argue, but if questions are asked, he will answer. They then asked me to bring these questions and get answers to them: If you support the Sunnis, what do you have to say in regards to the story of Ghadir-e Khom? On that day, the Prophet chose Ali as the calif and said: 'To whomever I am the lord [*mowla*], so also is Ali his lord.' Also, what would you answer in regards to the Prophet's asking for paper and pen and Omar's preventing it? On his death bed, the Prophet wanted to choose Imam Ali ebn Abitaleb as calif so that there would be no room for conflict among others. That is why he said: 'Bring me pen and paper to write down something for you so you will never be misguided.' When Omar realized what was taking place, he prevented it and said: 'This man is suffering from delirium, God's book will be sufficient for us.' He accused the Prophet of being delirious. I know well that you do not consider such stories as part of religion, and in truth religion does not consist of such statements. However, because such statements are imprinted on people's minds and whenever the discussion comes to religion, they immediately call to mind these statements and ask questions, until we have responded to them, they will not stop. For this reason, I deliver these questions to you for your response."

This was what Pakravan had said. Since there were others in the gathering besides our supporters, I responded: It is true that such statements are not a part of religion. One thousand three hundred years ago, some conflicts took place in regards to the office of the calif, and whatever happened has ended. What would we gain from those arguments today?

Not only do these statements have nothing to do with religion, but they are indicative of irreligiosity. In truth, the purpose of religion is to prevent the people from becoming so irrational [*bikherad*] and ignorant as to abandon their lives, argue about conflicts that occurred thirteen hundred years ago, and fabricate conflicts among the dead. Those who consider these stories as a part of religion do not understand the meaning of religion.

Religion reflects the understanding of the meaning of the world, life and living, in accordance with the dictates of the rational faculties [*kherad*]. Today, for Iranians, religion should be a guide to making the land that God has given them prosper, to benefitting from that land, and to living together comfortably without having families suffer poverty and hunger, without having villages remain in ruins and land left unutilized. Religion today should be a guide to the wealthy in Iran to use their capital to invest in building streams, creating springs, and ensuring the prosperity of villages, so as to eliminate ruins, as well as to save thousands, even hundreds of thousands, of hungry, destitute families from misfortune. Such is religion. Such actions please God. How could arguing about the conflicts between Ali and Abu Bakr please God and be deserving of reward? I am saying all of this so that the gentlemen will understand and comprehend the proper meaning of religion.

On the other hand, it is also true that such ideas are imprinted on the minds of Iranians and will not be eliminated until we speak about them. And that is why I will respond to their questions.

As for the story of "Ghadir-e Khom," it is very astonishing that the clerics do not understand this sentence. Do they not study religious jurisprudential books in which *vala'* [friendship] is a section [*bab*] of religious jurisprudence? This is a familial will and testament. The Prophet had a *vala'* relationship with certain people and that is why he said: "Ali will be my successor in regards to those for whom I had *vala'*." How could they interpret *mowla* to mean calif?

Besides, if the Prophet wished to appoint a "calif," he should have said from the start that the selection and appointment of a calif must be made only by God and not the people. Once he had clarified the issue thus, he should have stated clearly: "Now, my first calif is Ali, who is chosen by God." How could he have made a statement on such an important issue in passing, in an ambiguous, brief sentence, and then move on to other matters?

Furthermore, did the companions of the Prophet, who had lived with him for many years and fought for him with their very lives, not understand him? Or were they less fond of the Prophet and his instructions than the Shi'ites in Qazvin? How could one believe that the Prophet appointed Ali as the calif, but his companions ignored his wish and rallied around Abu Bakr? Why, then, did they not do the same in regards to the other instructions of the Prophet?

In regards to the story of the Prophet's death and Omar's hindrance, I do not know how true the story is, even whether or not it occurred. I have not conducted any research in this regard. Nevertheless, if it is true, Omar behaved quite properly. This is proof that Omar behaved properly. This is proof that Omar understood the meaning of Islam better than others. It is proof that that man had a very strong belief in God and Islam. The objection made that he accused the Prophet of having "delusions" is not correct. He said, "This man suffers from meningitis." The Arabic word *bajara* means meningitis [*sarsam*], not delusion [*bazyan*]. Delusion indicates deficient rational faculties [*kberad*], while meningitis is an illness. Omar said that this man suffers from meningitis as a statement which would not offend the Prophet, because any Prophet who becomes ill, who becomes emaciated, and whose color turns yellow might also display delirious speech. Meningitis is the result of illness and would not offend anyone. If the Prophets were exempt from such symptoms, they should be exempt from diseases and never become ill. It would be no surprise for a prophet who becomes ill to also suffer from delirium.

On the other hand, you say: The Prophet was illiterate and could not read or write. Then, why would he ask for a paper and pen to write? Besides, why did he not utter a word concerning his successor during his twenty-three years as a Prophet and wait to do so on his death bed? How could he have neglected such an important issue? Furthermore, do you not differentiate between the guiding and prophetic statements of a prophet and his other statements? Was whatever the Prophet said at any given time a revelation? You can see that the Prophet himself differentiated between his statements and considered a revelation to be a part of the Koran. In this connection, too, if he had a revelation, it must appear in the Koran, rather than as a statement made on his death bed.

All this aside, how could we know that the Prophet wished to write something about his successor? And then, how could we know that he wanted to appoint Ali as his successor? What evidence is there for such a claim?

Finally, I repeat: Why would the Shi'ites of Qazvin be more fond of Islam and the instructions of the Prophet of Islam than the

137

companions of the Prophet? Why would those men who would give their lives on the path of the Prophet and his religion and who had suffered so many harms not place as much value on the instructions of the Prophet as those of the gluttonous clerics of Iran? Why did Omar, as you state, insult the Prophet without anyone protesting?

The next day, when Mr. Pakravan informed them of the answers, they responded as follows: "It is true that the Prophet was illiterate, but he wanted them to bring pen and paper so that he could dictate and someone else could write it down."

Discussions were held once again on another evening, and Mr. Pakravan mentioned this response. I said: The Prophet of Islam was not Baha'ollah, who did not know Arabic and was unable to use that language. The Prophet could easily say whatever he wished. If he wanted others to write it down, he would have said "bring me a pen and ink pot to dictate to you" rather than "to write for you." These mean two different things.

Astonishingly enough, someone in that meeting began to speak, saying: "Since the Prophet knew that if he were to reveal the appointment of the commander of the faithful as calif during his life, certain people would not accept it and it would cause differences of opinion and disunity, he waited until the last hours of his life . . ."

One of those present interrupted him and completed his statement with: "To create a conflict and escape."

Everyone laughed and there was no need for a response.

This is as far as the story goes. More astonishing is that some clerics had read this story, which we published in "Parcham," the monthly newspaper, and rather than coming to their senses and realizing how misguided and ignorant they were, they put their last arrow in the bow and said: "Then why did the Commander of the Faithful always complain of his right being usurped?" My response is: As far as we know, Ali ebn Abitaleb did not do so. It is possible that he considered himself to be more competent than Abu Bakr and Omar and had a secret complaint in this regard (even the Shaqshaqeh sermon, if it is actually that imam's, would not reveal more than this). But it would be impossible for him to consider those two califs to be "usurpers," to be hostile towards them and oppose them. Even so, if evidence becomes available that he considered himself to be chosen by God as calif, as the Shi'ites state, and tried to do something about it, we would consider him to be as misguided as others and would not honor him. We love him not because his name was Ali nor because he was the son-in-law of the Prophet, but because he was a thoroughly honorable man who would not submit to his personal wishes.

It is grossly impudent on the part of the Shi'ites, who, in order to advance their politics, attribute such actions to that pure imam. It is because of their gross impudence that they tell such lies.

II: If we suppose that in Islam a calif must be chosen by God, then that representative of God must show himself to the people, state his evidence, make every effort to become a calif, and take over the affairs, guide the Moslem masses and protect the Islamic countries from enemies. Sitting at home, secretly calling oneself calif, gathering a small group around oneself and telling them not to tell anyone, but to practice "assimilation" is something I do not know what to term. In any case, such actions could not and cannot accomplish anything but to create disunity among the Moslems and diminish their power.

They may respond: The fault rests with the people, who did not accept God's calif. My answer is: The calif of God must strive to be accepted by the people. He must behave towards the misguided as did the Prophet, who brought them to the right path. When a calif of God hides himself and even occasionally denies being one, how could the people be blamed for not accepting him?

It is astonishing that of the eleven imams who existed, none but Ali ebn Abitaleb became a calif, and none but Hoseyn ebn Ali made an effort to gain the office. Among the rest, Hasan ebn Ali was the person who gained the office of calif, but did not retain it. Ali ebn Hoseyn was such a recluse, so concerned with seeking comfort and so reluctant to take on this task, that in the year 63 AH [circa 683], when the people of Medina rebelled against Yazid, he withdrew, left town, and wrote a letter to Yazid saying that he did not support the people. Later, when Yazid died and many tried to gain the office of calif, not only did he not make any attempts, but when Mokhtar, who had incited an uprising in Kufeh, sent him an envoy asking his permission to call the people to support him as calif, he refused to accept it. Hence, Mokhtar had to call the people to support Mohammad Hanafiyyeh. We know nothing of Mohammad al-Baqer, except that he lived in seclusion. I have mentioned Ja'far al-Sadeq, who wanted the office of calif but did not make any efforts towards this end and hid his desire altogether, because he feared for his life. Like his father, his son Musa al-Kazem strongly hid his desire to become a calif, but was arrested and spent twenty-seven years in prison for it. His son Ali al-Reza was appointed as heir apparent by Ma'mun, and yet he did not become a calif. Others did nothing but sit at home and live a life of pleasure. Is this the meaning of being chosen for the office of calif?

III: Is there any proof for statements such as "God created us from a higher water and clay," "God created the world because of our existence," "Your deeds are brought to our attention every day," and the like, which abound in Shi'ite books? Should the persons who made such statements not offer proof? Did making such unfounded claims not serve to open the way to charlatans and opportunists to boast? For instance, can it not be said that such statements provided the incentive for Baha'ollah, who claimed to be God?

On the other hand, why were those imams different from the people? Is it not true that each came into this world unwillingly and left this world just like anyone else, ate, slept, became ill, and proved to be vulnerable, like anyone else, without being superior to them? Then, what is the meaning of all this exaggeration?

While the founder of Islam, despite his position and appointment, called himself an individual like any other, what so distinguishes his survivors that they can make such claims?

Besides being lies, such statements are impudent before God. We do not know for sure whether such statements were made by one of them or attributed to one of their followers. In any case, we cannot consider such claims anything but irreligiosity and ungodliness.

One of the benefits we seek from religion is that the people properly understand the meaning of the world and life. That is, God has created everyone equal, and superiority over others can only be in terms of good deeds. We also hope that no one will boast so undeservedly and that people will not believe in such exaggerations. Such boasting, or accepting it, is nothing but irreligiosity.

IV: The Shi'ites, with their beliefs concerning their imams, place their imams on the same level as prophets, and even consider them as more exalted at times, because, to the Shi'ites, an imam was chosen by God, knew all things, understood all languages, and had knowledge of the unknown. Everyone had to obey him. Heaven and earth could be at peace because of his being. And no one but the imams knew the meaning of the Koran and religion. With such praise for the imams, the Shi'ites place them above the prophets. We ask: What is the proof behind such beliefs? And why have such imams not been mentioned in the Koran?

It is astonishing that while the Prophet of Islam openly stated, "I have no knowledge of the unknown,"[13] they claim that their imams did, and they tell stories about their imams' knowledge of the unknown.

It is astonishing that the Prophet of Islam expressed his inability to perform miracles.[14] Yet, they report miracles performed by the imams, and many stories are written about them.

Most astonishing is that in recent years, since European knowledge has been recognized in the East, some clerics have stated that their imams knew all of it, and that all these sciences are mentioned in the reported traditions. Some of them take sentences out of context from one reported tradition or another, drop the beginning and the end, and ascribe meanings to them, about which they boast before scientists. I do not know what to term this action of theirs.

In the same reported traditions, they quote their imams with thousands of statements concerning the sky, earth, clouds, rain, stars, earthquakes and the like. When you look carefully at them, you will find that they are more worthless than old wives tales: "When Adam fell from Paradise to earth, Gabriel brought him some wheat from heaven to plant, so that he would not suffer from hunger. The part of the wheat that was planted by Adam grew as wheat, and the part planted by Eve as barley." "The people of Sham [Damascus] asked about the tides. He answered that an angel called Ruman has been given the task of watching over the seas. When he puts his foot in the sea, it rises, and when he takes his foot out, it recedes." "I asked, What does the earth stand on; he said, On a fish. I asked, What does the fish stand on; he said, On water. I asked, What does the water stand on; he said, On a rock. I asked, What does the rock stand on; he said, On the horns of the bull."[15] Do these represent the knowledge of the past and the present? Is it not disgraceful for some people to pride themselves on such statements, and to boast of them before scientists? Is it not disgraceful for them to say that their imams possessed all that knowledge?

We see clearly that the imams did not possess any of the attributes ascribed to them. Imam Ali ebn Abitaleb aside, the remainder were people just like any others. For instance, Ja'far ebn Mohammad chose his son Esma'il as his successor; but Esma'il died before his father. What evidence could be more convincing that he did not know about the future?

In fact, a story in this regard is quoted in their books: When Esma'il died, his father said: "God changed his mind about Esma'il as His choice."[16]

However, this very story requires some discussion. This statement means that God, Who had chosen Esma'il as the successor to his father, regretted His decision and took him out of the world sooner. Is the attribution of such a statement to God not impudent? Does this not point out the speaker's ignorance of God?

Readers know what we have said about prophets (or messengers, as they call them) and how we have made clarifications in this regard. At a time when the sciences have severely shaken the world and the followers of materialism, who consist of the masses of scientists, not only do not believe in prophets but have no belief in God either, we clarified the fact that prophethood does not contradict science but is itself one of the secrets of the universe.

Also, readers know what positions we have ascribed to the

founder of Islam and how we praise him.

But to say that a group of imams with divine power who were chosen by God succeeded him is completely without foundation and is unacceptable.

When we praise the founder of Islam as a prophet and boast about him before the world, we are not trying impose our beliefs on anyone. Rather, we present evidence. At a time when the people of the world were misguided, that righteous man rose and fought idolatry and other ignorant beliefs, shook the minds of the people, and opened a great path for life. For such actions, we consider him to be a prophet of God and boast about him before the world.

But, in regards to those imams, the questions must first be asked: After that Prophet, what need was there for them? In other words, had the Prophet so utterly failed to complete his task that they needed to complete it? Secondly, what did they accomplish that is worthy for us to boast to the world? What aberration did they remove? What movement did they create? What distinguishing or superior characteristic did they display?

Yes, Mohammad ebn Ali and Ja'far ebn Mohammad, the father and the son, were somewhat knowledgeable regarding "religious jurisprudence," but so were Malek, Abu Hanifeh, Shafe'i and Ahmad ebn Hanbal.

V: The Shi'ites consider those imams to be the administrators of the world. "The Fourteen Infallible Ones" are fully in charge of God's organization and help Him run the world.

Such statements are quoted from those imams in books. And although we may not know which ones were made by them and which ones were added by others, on the whole, the imams were clearly the sources of such statements. After all, the masses of Shi'ites believe such statements, turn to them in times of hardship, and expect them to solve their problems. The imams aside, the Shi'ites imagine their relatives--including "his holiness, Abbas," "his excellency, Ali Akbar," "Zeynab," "Omm-e Kolsum" and "Sakineh"--to be in charge of the affairs of the world, and assistants to God. In fact, the Shi'ites believe that every dome can provide a solution to their problems and every religious water trough can grant "wishes."

The purpose of all of these domes which have been built, both big and small, is nothing but for them to stand before, to ask for solutions to their problems, to hold those pieces of metal in their hands and request their needs from them.

Statements such as the following are common among Shi'ites: "Resort to the imams," "Plead with Imam Hoseyn," and "This is the way to salvation."

142

There are now several thousand panhandlers in Tehran who roam around the alleys, stand before house doors, and continually say, "May His Holiness Abbas cure your pain," "May Imam Hoseyn not let you become miserable," "May the Sick Imam not let you fall into a sick bed," and "May the Imam in Exile pay your debts." And the people reward them with bread and money for such statements.

Last year in Tehran, a man who limped with a broken leg had wrapped a green shawl around his head and was begging. All of his prayers concerned Imamzadeh Davud: "May Imamzadeh Davud grant your wish. May Imamzadeh Davud pay your debts." Several kilometers from Tehran, there is a dome called Imamzadeh Davud, in a filthy village where the people of Tehran visit every summer, slaughter sheep and ask for their "wishes." Recently, when there were elections for parliamentary representatives, a charlatan had printed and distributed a statement that if he were elected representative, he would use his salary to pave the road to Imamzadeh Davud.

Now, one must ask: Are people who have such beliefs not misguided? What could be more misguided than to consider the dead who have no position to be God's colleagues? One must ask: What proof is there of your imams being assistants to God? What do you think God is that you think Him to be in need of assistants?

Now, if we ask the clerics these questions, first they will respond: Yes, they were imams, God created them from "light." Then, when we object and ask for proof, they will be at a loss and will respond this time: "These are the beliefs of the common people." This is their method to first argue about their misguided beliefs and engage in debates, and once they are at a loss, suddenly they change their argument and blame the "common people."

But we know that these beliefs stem from the books. And, as I have said, there are "reported traditions" about them.[17]

In any case, the guides of the "common people" are the clerics who have taught and are teaching them such irreligious beliefs. Even today, if a person is ill and mentions the word physician before a cleric, he will immediately say, "What is a physician? Ask the pure imams for your recovery."

VI: Another criticism concerns the Shi'ites considering themselves to be the chosen, made of superior water and clay. The Shi'ite leaders imagine themselves to be of a higher nature, and claim that the rest of the Shi'ites were created from the water and clay left over from making them.[18]

A person who becomes a Shi'ite and accepts "the guardianship of Ali" [velayat-e Ali] has a pure nature, and a person who does not has an impure nature. Shi'ites are a chosen group who will all go to heaven in the next world.

These statements are so false that some of the Shi'ites them-selves have criticized them. We see in their books that Safvan Jamal, who was a Shi'ite, has criticized the founder of Shi'ism and said: "You say that our Shi'ites shall go to Paradise even though among the Shi'ites there are groups of sinners who engage in every evil deed." He reinter-prets the statement and responds that a Shi'ite will not pass away from this world unless he becomes ill or suffers from an ill-tempered woman and cruel neighbor and that all of these are punishment for his sins. In the absence of these, his death will be difficult, if he is to leave this world without any sin. Safvan again criticizes and says: "Then what about the injustice towards the people and the money embezzled from them?" He responds: Since we will be in charge of the people's reckon-ing on the Day of Resurrection, we will accept *khoms* [religious taxes] to bring them out of debt.[19]

In some books this issue is represented in another light: On Resurrection Day, when the report cards of the people are examined one by one, the sins of the Shi'ites will be blamed on the Sunnis, and the Shi'ites will be rewarded for the good deeds of the Sunnis, so that the former will be sent to Paradise and the latter to Hell.

On the one hand, such statements are deceptive and misguide the people. On the other hand, they reveal impudence towards God, as if God runs the world the way they do their own kitchens, which is in truth a very great sin. According to the Koran, "the most cruel of people is he who lies about God."[20]

The statement that God has created one group of higher water and clay is a clear lie, no matter how you look at it. The statement that God has especially chosen one group, ignores their evil deeds, and grants them excessive reward is a totally detrimental statement. Such statements will destroy the roots of Islam and render the efforts of that righteous Arab man futile.

VII: The shrines that exist in Mashhad, Qom, Abdol'azim, Baghdad, Sumaria, Karbala, Najaf and other cities, and to which the Shi'ites go on pilgrimage, are another story. If you have seen them, each is a magnificent house of idols. Shi'ites go on pilgrimage to them from hundreds of miles away and stand before them with bowed heads and moist eyes. A seyyed or a cleric shouts, "May I enter, oh God; may I enter, oh Messenger of God." Then they enter, circumambulate the iron or silver box, kiss it, drop their heads, and pray. Is this not idolatry?

It offends them when we call these shrines houses of idols. But what else should they be called, for they truly are so? Whatever is wor-shipped, other than God, and is considered to be in charge of the world is an idol.

144

The argument concerning theism and idolatry concerns whether there is anyone but God in charge of this world. Theism states that there is not. Idolatry says there is. Then, theism (or better stated, religion) says: God operates this world in accordance with a set of laws and there is an unalterable way of doing things. A person who is ill must seek treatment. A person who is poor must engage in work or a trade to acquire wealth. A person who wants to please God must do good deeds, and the same goes with other things. This is the subject of discussion and not worshiping wooden and metal statues or silver and golden domes. Even if the people were to consider a living person in charge of God's affairs and were to ask him, for instance, for the recovery of a patient or a solution to problems, such would be considered idolatry.

Astonishingly, they quote the "reported sayings" of their leaders: Anyone who goes on pilgrimage will be forgiven all his sins; paradise is mandatory for him; for every step he takes, a palace of gold, silver and crystal will be built for him and hundreds of nymphs [*huri*] shall be registered in his name. They have been involved in politics so much that they do not hesitate to make any exaggeration.

No one has asked, Of what use is going to visit a shrine so that God will grant a reward? After all, a reward is given for a beneficial act. How could a futile act be deserving of a reward from God? Is telling such lies not a sign of atheism? Is saying "He who makes a pilgrimage to Hoseyn in Karbala makes a pilgrimage to God in Heaven" not impudence and rudeness towards God?[21]

More strangely, they even expect miracles from those shrines and fabricate stories about them: He gave sight to a blind person, or health to some ill person, or killed some enemy and turned an evil-wisher into stone.

[Or they make up verses such as:] "A king who with the blow of two fingers/ Miraculously killed Ebn Qeys."

In spite of his lofty position and the advancements he made on the path of God, when the Jews and Christians pressured him to perform miracles, the founder of Islam responded to them: I am not capable of doing so. The Koran is full of such responses. But his idle progeny are said to have performed miracles, and continue to do so, even after death. Woe be unto us for such ignorance!

If we look at history, killings have often occurred around those domes and no action was taken (as is to be expected). During the time of Shah Abbas, in 988 AH, when Abdolmo'menkhan Ozbak conquered Mashhad through war and bloodshed, masses of people, including clerics, seyyeds and others, took refuge in the "sacred shrine" and thought that they would be safe from being killed. But the Uzbeks entered with their drawn swords and began slaughtering them, leaving no one alive. It is stated in *Alamara*: "A reliable source was heard to say of Mir Mohammad Hoseyn, known as the *mir* [custodian] of the head of the shrine, who was a seyyed from holy Mashhad, highly ranked in good deeds, piety and worship, who performed prayers, worshipped and read the Koran at the head of the blessed sepulcher and rarely left that noble position, that one horrible day, he was sitting at the head of the sepulchre, as was his custom, engaged in reading the Koran, when one of the ungodly Uzbeks grabbed him by the waist and dragged him out. Fearing for his life, struggling and worried, the custodian grabbed the blessed sepulchre tightly. Another Uzbek cut off his arm with a sword. His hand was left on the lattice work. He was dragged out and torn to shreds."

Many such stories have happened in Mashhad. In 1324 AH, during the Constitutional movement, a group of theological students and others rioted because of a shortage of bread. They assembled in the courtyard of the shrine. A person by the name of Haji Mohammad Hasan, who had a contract for the bread and meat in the city, sent soldiers, who killed forty of them in the courtyard.

In 1330 AH, when Seyyed Mohammad Yazdi took sanctuary with a group of people in the courtyard of the shrine, demanding the return of Mohammad Ali Mirza, in order to disperse them, the Russians fired artillery at the shrine, and the soldiers entered the courtyard, killed some people, and arrested Seyyed Mohammad. The places where shots hit the dome were visible for several years.

The last incident of slaughter happened during the reign of Reza Shah, when a large group assembled in that place, refusing government orders to wear Western-style hats and to allow the women to unveil. The government sent the army, and it is reported that several thousand people were killed.

In Karbala, large-scale slaughter and plunder have taken place many times and the coffer has been broken and removed many times.

In 858 HQ, Mowla Ali, son of Seyyed Mohammad Mosha'sha', took over the place and plundered, slaughtered and captured many people and carried them off.

In 1216 HQ, when the Wahabis attacked Iraq to plunder and slaughter, on the day of Ashura, they invaded the city, slaughtered around the shrines, entered homes and raped women and girls, cut off the heads of infants, broke open the coffers, dug up the graves, and within a few hours killed nearly seven thousand religious jurists, seyyeds and others, plundered the shrines and left victoriously.

Once again, in 1260 HQ, Najib Pasha, the governor of Baghdad, sent an army to that city, conquered the city with cannons and guns,

146

and in three hours killed nine thousand people. It is reported in *Naseklu ol-Tavarikh*: "They made streams of the blood of the people in the shrines of the Sire of the Martyrs and His Holiness Abbas, changed these two blessed shrines into stables for horses and camels, plundered the treasury and every piece of property that they could find in that city, and broke to pieces the tablets in the sacred garden." It is reported in one book: More than three hundred slaughtered bodies were taken out through the cellar beneath the courtyard of the shrine of Abbas.

In the year 858 HQ, again, Mowla Ali, son of Seyyed Mohammad Mosha'sha', conquered Najaf and destroyed the shrine. His soldiers used the wood from the sepulchre to cook food.

One should ask, Then why were no miracles performed by those domes in the course of such bloodshed? Is it not shameful that, despite such historical accounts, with each event, you fabricate and spread another lie regarding miracles?

Strangely enough, the Wahabis in their invasion of Iraq first set out for Najaf, but since that city had a strong fortress, they could not conquer it. They left that city and set out for Karbala, where they engaged in slaughter and plunder. From that event in Najaf, the Shi'ites found an excuse to fabricate another "miracle": "One of the pious" saw in his dream the Commander of the Faithful, whose palms had turned black. He asked, Why did this happen? The response was, "Who do you think turned away those cannons?"

Witness the extent of ignorance! Rather than realizing that Najaf was saved because it had a fortress and Karbala was sacked because it did not, thereby realizing the fact that in this world nothing is possible unless it is done according to natural laws, and that no benefit will come from those graves and domes, they displayed their ignorance and fabricated and spread such an infamous lie.

Now, the problem is that if we discuss such pilgrimages with the clerics and others, first they will resist, then they will answer. And once they are at a loss, they will retreat and say: "We do not consider the imams to be God. They are regarded highly before God and we turn to them (making them mediators)."

My response is: This is nothing but idolatry. The idol worshipers of Qoreysh made the same excuse to the founder of Islam, saying, "We worship them in order to become closer to God."[22] Or they would say, "These are our mediators."[23] We must answer: "Idol worshipers are all the same, and they always have the same excuse."

When they hear this, they retreat once more and say: "After all they are our prominent people. Do you not visit the graves of your prominent people?" In this manner, they color their sect differently several times in one meeting.

147

My response is: Yes, they are your prominent people. They were the founders of your sect. But where in the world are gold and silver domes built for a prominent person, such establishments arranged and traveled to for visits from hundreds of miles away, and such actions engaged in? Besides, do we not know your books and prayer texts for the shrines, and do we not know what sorts of exaggerated praise you make about the good-for-nothing dead? Do we not know that you consider those dead people to be the assistants of God and the operators of the world?

VIII: The story of weeping and crying for those killed in Karbala is another matter to be greatly criticized. Of what use is crying after the fact? Are repeating a story, holding mourning ceremonies, weeping and making others weep rational actions?

It has been said, "Anyone who weeps or makes others weep or pretend to be weeping will certainly go to heaven." The question must be raised, Why? Why would God grant them such a great reward just for weeping and making others weep? Besides, where do you find such a statement? What channel of communication has there been between you and God? Oh, irrational people, do you think God is Alexander of Macedonia who so loved Hephestion that upon his death he forced the people to mourn him for several months?

Hoseyn ebn Ali attempted unsuccessfully to gain the caliphate. However, he displayed very praiseworthy bravery. He did not behave abjectly. He preferred that he himself, his children and his followers be killed rather than submit to Yazid and Ebn Ziyad. He insisted bravely, and he and his followers were killed.

This action of his was praiseworthy, but no matter what happened, all that is in the past. What is the use of crying for thirteen hundred years? What can you call these irrational exhibitions during the months of Moharram and Safar?

These stories of pilgrimage and weeping along with the reported traditions about them must be criticized in another way as well. Such actions destroy religion from the root. When making one pilgrimage ensures that all sins will be forgiven and weeping one time ensures that one will go to heaven, why should one resist any kind of pleasure? Why should some greedy haji not engage in hoarding? Why should some oppressor not engage in bloodshed? Why should greedy people not engage in the accumulation of wealth? Why should men not chase after other men's wives? The leaders of the Shi'ites have not taken anything into consideration in their political efforts. They have said and done whatever they wished. But can we ignore their totally harmful actions?

IX: There are many statements in Shi'ite books regarding the next world. They do not stop with this world, but engage in exaggerated fabrications about the next world as well: On the Day of Resurrection, God will sit in justice with prophets lining both sides. Ali will hold "Lawa'ol-Hamd," the flag which stretches from east to west and is one thousand years long. The imams will support and mediate for the Shi'ites. They will give their sins to the Sunnis and will give the good deeds of the Sunnis to the Shi'ites. They will send the former to Hell and the latter to Paradise. The "pool of Kowsar" is under the control of Ali, who will give water to no one but the Shi'ites. In the burning heat, the hearts of the Sunnis will roast, and they will not find any water.

They have fabricated enough of these political exaggerations to fill a large book. We are discussing mediation. This is one of foundations of the Shi'ite sect. Hoseyn ebn Ali was killed merely to support the Shi'ites on the Day of Resurrection and forgive them their sins. On the Day of "Creation," an agreement was made between him and God: Hoseyn was to give up his life, property and children, and God would accept his "mediation" on behalf of the Shi'ites on the Day of Resurrection. The belief of Christians concerning Christ and his crucifixion as a "compensation" for the sins of mankind is similar to the belief of the Shi'ites about Hoseyn and his being killed. Undoubtedly, they have taken this idea from the Christians.

In any case, this is one criticism that can be made of that sect. They imagine God to be like one of the autocratic kings of history. For this reason, they have provided Him with "those held in reverence" as His supporters. The clerics have frequently been heard to say: "Kings have ministers, should God not have them?" Such statements reveal the ignorance and ungodliness of this group.

One should ask, Oh, ignorant people, how could you compare God with the autocratic kings? One should say, Mediation need not exist except in the face of ignorance or oppression. In the organization of a king who dominates the lives and property of the people, and often, out of anger, destroys people's lives, one who might consider an innocent person guilty and order his death, a need might be felt to fall at the king's feet and subdue his anger through flattery, in order to save an innocent person. Such an organization would require a mediator. In a completely just and truthful organization, what need is there for mediators? I ask you, can there be a mediator in a court of justice or other legal office?

X: Cursing and using abusive language concerning the companions of the Prophet, which they call "*tabarra*," is another foundation of the Shi'ite sect, which is a shameful, heinous practice. Expressing hostility towards the dead for no reason, fabricating lies and curses and using abusive language indicates nothing but the unenlightened minds of a group.

As we said, this improper practice began before the time of Ja'far ebn Mohammad, but became official and was escalated during the time of this imam. I am astonished that Zeyd ebn Ali supported Saddiq and Faruq against the *Rafezis* [heathens] and gave that sincere and brave answer, but his nephew put fuel on the fire of the *Rafezis* as he did and made them more impudent in their heinous behavior.

Shi'ite books are full of curses and abusive language. Khajeh Nasir, that irreligious glutton, who was sometimes a Bateni and sometimes a Shi'ite, has written a book of "curses." Many of the clerics have written books about the "infidelity of the two sheykhs."

The Shi'ites believe that if Omar and Abu Bakr had not been obstacles to Ali's becoming calif, so that the office would remain in his family and benefit Ja'far ebn Mohammad and others, no evil would have occurred in the world. Therefore, those two are to be blamed for all sins. Some even go so far as to imagine that even all the sins before that time must be blamed on them. On the Day of Resurrection, when Cain is interrogated for killing his brother Abel, he will provide evidence that Omar and Abu Bakr were the cause of his fratricide. Cain's sin is also blamed on these two. These are statements that clerics have written, said and inculcated in the minds of the common people. It is not without reason that Moslems considered *Rafezis*" to be non-Moslems and spilled their blood. It is not without reason that the imams instructed their followers to practice "dissimulation."

As we said, one of the accomplishments of Shah Esma'il was to spread Shi'ism in Iran. This king, who despised the Sunnis, also spread the heinous practice of cursing and using abusive language. Since his time, a group of dervishes called "Tabara'i" appeared, who would walk before the horses of some vizier or prince, calling out the names of the leaders of Islam one by one and cursing them. Esma'il Mirza, the grandson of that king, realized the ugliness of this practice and tried to prevent it. But Shi'ism had already been deeply rooted in Iran, and the idea of "Tabara" had been inculcated in the minds of the clerics, dervishes and their followers, and the efforts of Esma'il Mirza were all for naught.

Later, during the reign of Nader Shah, similar efforts were made on a larger and more appropriate scale. That honorable king considered peace in Iran impossible without the abolition of that heinous practice. For this reason, on the one hand, he held negotiations with and offered proposals to the Ottomans, while on the other hand, he tried to abolish this heinous practice in Iran, frequently holding joint sessions between Sunni and Shi'ite clerics. However, these efforts as well failed, and that honorable king was killed, taking his hopes with him to his grave.

During the Zand and Qajar dynasties, the clerics had an open field, and this heinous practice flourished. Until the Constitutional Movement, every year in the month of Rabi' I, clerics, seyyeds and seminarians took the lead in a series of evil, heinous acts. The survivors of the Tabara'i dervishes, mentioned above, roamed the alleys and bazaars in Tabriz and other cities under the name of "cursers," using their abusive language to solicit money. One of the beneficial results of the Constitutional movement was the abolition of such heinous practices in Iranian cities.

As we said, these heinous acts led directly to bloodshed involving millions of people and the destruction of thousands of families, and resulted in hundreds of thousands of Iranian girls and women being captured by the Uzbeks, Turkomans, and Ottomans and kept as slaves or sold on the markets in Bukhara, Khiva, Istanbul, Sofia and Belgrade. During the reign of Nader Shah, several thousand of these women were in captivity, and that shah tried, more than anything else, to free them.

As has been said that the stories written in Shi'ite books concerning the conflict between Ali ebn Abitaleb, Abu Bakr and Omar are all lies and fabrications. May God expose politics for what it is!

Abu Bakr was elected by the companions of the Prophet to become calif, and after him, Omar. These two were among the most distinguished companions of the Prophet. After Omar, Osman was chosen. But this man committed certain evil deeds, and in the end, a group of Moslems rebelled against him and, as history records, killed him, deservedly.

The reason for the companions of the Prophet not choosing Ali first to become calif has been given in books. At that time, Ali was young, despite his praiseworthy character, and Abu Bakr was more competent to become calif, particularly because of the blood spilled by Ali for Islam, which had brought him many enemies. In any case, no ill will was involved in his not being chosen, and no conflict occurred because of it.

The story that is told so enthusiastically about Omar going to Ali's home and pressing the daughter of the Prophet between the house door and the wall is an out and out lie. It is said that the daughter of the Prophet had a "miscarriage" of a child called "Mohsen." Should one not ask, Oh ignorant people, what need of a name did a child who had not yet been born have? Who could know that the child was to be a boy, to have called him "Mohsen"?

In short, Abu Bakr and Omar were praiseworthy men. As we note the praiseworthiness of Ali, we must also note the praiseworthiness of these two and honor them. This Shi'ite practice is the best evidence of how tainted Shi'ism is.

XI: The practice of "dissimulation" is another point for criticism. If Shi'ism was political, it should have been out in the open, for everyone to know. Even though it may have been necessary to keep it a secret for a while initially, it should not have remained a secret forever. And if it was a religion and a guide, it should have been out in the open for people to know about it and benefit from it.

It is most unfortunate that a group, on the one hand, forces people into exaggerated and unfounded beliefs and instigates them to use abusive language against the leaders of Islam, and, on the other hand, instructs them to hide their religion and not reveal it to anyone. It is most unfortunate that they act one way and believe another. More strangely, the leaders of Shi'ism have instructed Shi'ites to practice "dissimulation" as a permanent obligation, to ensure that people do not discontinue that practice until such time as the Invisible Imam appears.[24] This shows that they had no hopes for the advancement of Shi'ism or for a day when a king would rise up and spread it by force of his sword, and they would not want such advancement.

"Dissimulation," or hiding one's beliefs, besides being deceptive and no different from lying, has always been coupled with other deceptive practices and lies. There are some stories in this regard worth mentioning. In order to explain the hideousness of this behavior and the evil that can be coupled with it, I will mention the following anecdote.

Qesas al-Olama' is a book which has undergone many printings. It was written by Mirza Mohammad Tonokaboni in praise of his teacher, Seyyed Ebrahim Qazvini (the author of *Zavabet*), who was one of the grand sources of emulation in Karbala during the time of Mohammad Shah. In that book, we read:

His excellency converted the governor of Karbala, who was a Sunni, to Shi'ism. The story was that the Pasha of Baghdad conquered Karbala by imposing a siege and carrying out a slaughter in that city, placing a man by the name of Rashid Beyk, who was of the common sect, as the governor of Karbala. The teacher treated the governor kindly, and any time the governor visited the teacher, his excellency would himself take a fan to fan the governor, and would see him off or welcome him in person. Indeed, the love and companionship between the two was so great that the governor often visited his reverence, and in the evening, after the people had gone to sleep, he would visit the teacher and stay with him until the middle of the night. Eventually, the religious sects were discussed and since the governor was a believer in the common sect, the teacher spoke about the truth of the sect in terms that the governor could understand. Every night he would speak on one aspect or another of the corruption of the Sunni sect and the truth of the Shi'ite sect. Finally, when he found the governor inclined toward Shi'ism, he proved to the governor that, as is indicated by the statements of the majority of the Sunnis as well as the divine verses and reported sayings of the Prophet, Ali was superior to all the companions. Now judge for yourself. Suppose you were to compare one of my students with me and make me sit at home idly without any authority, do you think you would be doing a proper thing or performing an improper and heinous act? The governor said: Of course, common sense indicates that it would be a heinous act. His excellency said: Abu Bakr's taking over the office of calif for the common believers is not in accordance with the text [of the Koran], but rather, based on the allegiance and unanimous vote of the people. Therefore the companions made Ali, who was more virtuous, more knowledgeable, more devout, more pious, more brave, more magnanimous, more of a worshipper, and more of a pioneer in Islam, and who was closer to the Prophet of God, sit in a corner in a position of weakness at home and put Abu Bakr, who was like his student, in his stead, thereby committing an improper, heinous act. Hence, after hearing this reasoning and other such proof, the governor converted to Shi'ism. However, the teacher said: He became a Shi'ite in every respect, but I did not teach him the cursing of the califs. Because of his strong adherence to dissimulation, the master did not reveal this subject to him. In short, this story spread until the Pasha was informed of the events, and the Pasha dismissed the governor and appointed another in his place. The second governor and the teacher did not establish a friendship or relationship. That governor did not socialize with the teacher because of the action of the former governor, and the teacher would not even visit him. It so happened that one day, one of the Shi'ites quarreled with someone in the bazaar. The Shi'ite cursed the second calif. One of the officials of the governor, who had heard it, arrested him and took him before the governor. The governor ordered him to be imprisoned and sent to Baghdad for the Pasha to punish. The relatives of the Shi'ite were informed of the incident and went to the teacher, explaining to him what had occurred. His excellency said: Inform him today that if the governor himself summons him and asks him why he had cursed, he should answer that we consider the calif to be obedient and would never curse him. What was meant here was Omar ebn Sa'd, the killer of Imam Hoseyn, blessings be upon him. Hence, the relatives of that person related this matter to him in prison. In the morning, after the morning prayers, when the sun rose, the teacher pulled his garb over his head and set out for one of the alleys near the camp, not allowing anyone to accompany him. When he reached the governor's home, where there was an opening towards the alley, the door of which was open, the governor himself was sitting there watching the passersby in the alley. The teacher put the garb down on his shoulders and was about to pass by, pretending that he was going somewhere else. The governor initiated the greeting and asked him to join him for coffee and a water pipe. His excellency accepted and sat down. After having partaken of what was served, the governor said: Yesterday, one of your people, who had cursed the second calif, was brought here. We jailed him in order to send him to the Pasha to be punished. The teacher said: This could not have happened, because we consider the second calif to be a good man, a companion of the Prophet and the father of his spouse, and we consider cursing him to be prohibited, and all the Shi'ites emulate us. This claim is a slanderous accusation. The governor said: Some have borne witness that they have heard the phrase from him. The teacher said: If it is true that that common person was heard saying it, of course, he meant Omar ebn Sa'd, who was the killer of the offspring of the Prophet, the killer of the favorite son of Heydar, and the oppressor of Zahra. You can summon that person now and ask him this question orally. The governor summoned the prisoner. When he came, the governor asked him to explain what he had meant. The man answered that he had cursed Omar ebn Sa'd, the killer of the offspring of the seal of the Prophet, the Sire of the Young People of Paradise. We do not curse the second calif. The religious scholars prohibit cursing him and we emulate them. The governor said: Thank God this matter has been clarified to me and the blood of an innocent Moslem has not been spilled. The teacher said: I have told you the truth. Hence, the governor ordered the man to be released. In this incident, the teacher was an example of the noble verse: He who saves a life has saved the life of all the people.

XII: Another very strong criticism that can be made of Shi'ism concerns the disrespect shown by its members for the Koran, and their demeaning of it. The Shi'ite leaders have been very disrespectful towards the Koran on several occasions.

1. The Koran was a book for reading, understanding and finding salvation. These people say that no one can know the meaning of it except the imams. In this manner, they have made the Koran ineffective, and even devalued. The Shi'ite scholars consider the Koran to be of "doubtful evidence" and prefer "reported sayings" to it.

2. They learned interpretation (or as they call it *ta'vil*) from the Batenis and totally misinterpret most of the Koranic verses.

As though the Koran were a book of poetry, they interpret all verses about good news and reward as related to their imams and all verses about fear and punishment related to Abu Bakr, Omar and oth-

154

ers. Rather than following the Koran and achieving salvation, they have made the Koran a tool for advancing their own misguided beliefs and practices.

3. Some of them are even more impudent and have fabricated words or sentences as they saw fit, adding them to the Koran.[25] In addition, two separate suras, one called "Surat al-Nurin" and another called "Surat al-Velayah," have been fabricated and added to the Koran, the claim being made that they were omitted by Abu Bakr, Omar and Osman.

More astonishingly, they have said: "The correct Koran is kept by the Imam of the Age, who will bring it when he comes out of occultation." It is not known where they found a copy of it.

Whatever the case may be, such a Koran has existed and exists among the Shi'ites. In fact, a copy fell into the hands of protestant ministers who have spoken in detail about it. The English journal of the Moslem world[26] has published these two separate suras and we have published one of them here.[27]

XIII: There is much to say about the Invisible Imam and much criticism can be made.

1. How could a child be born and no one know about it? How could five years pass without his being identified? Did Hasan al-Askari not live among the people in Samaria? Did no one come and go to his home? Can one believe it because Osman ebn Sa'id said it?

Besides, what was the secret of his being hidden? Would he have been harmed had he not been hidden? They say: He was afraid of his enemies. My answer is: Then, why where his ancestors not afraid? How could a group who can practice "dissimulation" and hide their beliefs from others be afraid of anything?

2. If an imam is a leader, he must be among the people and guide them. What could an Invisible Imam mean? They answer: "An Invisible Imam is like the sun behind the clouds." I say: It is a very false analogy. The sun stays behind the clouds for a very short time and then comes out. Besides, the light and heat of the sun are manifested from behind the cloud. From your imam, there is nothing but a name.

3. Living for a thousand years is beyond belief. They say: "It is not farfetched in terms of God's power." I say: This response is an example of your ignorance concerning the meaning of religion. If you knew the meaning of religion, you would know that God has established laws for everything and would never change them. You would know that God has determined that no one lives or can live more than one hundred twenty or one hundred forty years.

They say: The Koran states that "Noah lived for nine hundred fifty years among his people"; what is your answer to that? I respond:

That in itself is objectionable. Such statements in the Koran are among the "doubtful statements" [*motashabehat*] which must be set aside and not discussed.

4. Why would God need to keep someone alive for a thousand years and make him wander in the deserts until one day he would bring him out and by his hand turn the world into a good one? Could God not bring him into the world at any time He wanted and put him to work? The fact that people store something up for the future is out of necessity and weakness (for example, since there are no eggplants in the winter and the people cannot have them, they store them up from summer). What can we imagine that God would need or what weakness might He have?

5. Mahdi-ism is nothing but a myth. That someone would rise and, through a series of extraordinary actions, make the world good is nothing more than a figment of someone's imagination. I repeat: God operates this world in accordance with certain laws, and those laws will never change.

Yes, God appoints certain guides, and through them shows the way to the people. But there is never any need for extraordinary acts. Whenever He wants, God appoints a person from among the people, removes the obstacles from his vision, and makes him see the truth. The person who is chosen or appointed engages in an effort to fight misguided beliefs and practices, shakes people's minds by telling truth, through effort and insistence, gains the support of the wise and those of pure heart, and fights and eliminates the ignorant and the impure. This is God's law. This is what has been so far and shall be from here on. Mahdi-ism, as it stands, can never be.

They say: Such beliefs exist in other religions as well. The Jews expect the Messiah, Christians hope for the descent of Christ from Heaven, and Zoroastrians await King Bahram. I respond: What good proof you have found! Does the recognition of a myth among one group or another indicate that it is true?

They say: The Prophet predicted the coming of Mahdi. I respond: The Prophet openly said, "I have no knowledge of the unknown." How could he have predicted the future? Why was such an astonishing story not mentioned in the Koran?

6. As we said, the Shi'ites took the idea of Mahdi-ism, but did not allow it to remain simple. Rather, they embellished it themselves: Before Mahdi an imposter [*dajjal*] shall appear. The sun shall rise from the west. A call will be heard from the sky. The supporters of the Imam will hurry towards him by "traveling the earth instantly [*tey al-arz*]." These are all exaggerations and outside the laws of God.

They have said that he shall avenge the blood of Hoseyn and kill the Omayyads and Abbasids. These all indicate nothing but political profiteering and that they thereby hoped to prevent their followers from despairing and dispersing.

Now that there are no Omayyads or Abbasids, it is unclear who Mahdi will kill. And what can one say in regards to these predictions that have proven to be clear lies?

7. Following these exaggerations in the Shi'ite books, there is another more astonishing exaggeration: When Mahdi accomplishes his task and his time ends, he will be killed by a bearded old woman. After him, the imams will return to the world one by one and rule the world prosperously. The supporters and enemies of each will also be resurrected, and every imam will kill his enemies, avenge himself, and live in comfort with his supporters.

See to what extent they exaggerate! See how they ridicule the system of creation, how impudent they are towards God!

The imam's have not had their fill of the world, and the fire of revenge has not subsided in their hearts. They will return to rule as they please and by avenging themselves against their enemies, put out the fire in their hearts. Shame on you, oh liars! Should one not ask, Why do you say such things? What proof do you have, after all?

Because of this myth of Mahdi, hundreds of disturbances have taken place so far. An example was the Babism conspiracy. A seyyed from Shiraz desired to become Mahdi and call on the people. Since the people were in expectation, a group of people gathered around him. That man, who had little education, engaged in fabricating nonsensical Arabic, and after conflicts and bloodshed, in which he himself was killed, the result, now, is that a group of people called Baha'is or Azalis, who have taken a step further in ignorance than the Shi'ites, have appeared and live most hideously. This is one of the bitter fruits of that political tree.

CHAPTER 3

Detriments Of This Sect

Besides failing to conform to rational faculties [*kherad*], because of which much criticism can be made of it, Shi'ism is detrimental to life itself. In this chapter, we will point out a few of the detriments.

I: This sect has misguided its followers, turning them away from religion. The Shi'ites call themselves the "saved sect" and consider salvation to be exclusive to their sect. But the truth is to the contrary. Indeed, they are altogether outside the realm of religion.

What is religion? People do not understand the meaning of religion, and regard it as being without value. But we ascribe to religion an exalted meaning.

Religion is one thing: "Understanding the meaning of the world and life, and living in accordance with the dictates of the rational faculties" [*kherad*]. Hence, two kinds of results are gained thereby: first, "understanding God, realizing His wishes, and knowing His laws"; second, "recognizing the realities of life, using them, and making the world prosper and benefit from comfort and happiness."

These two results comprise the benefits that are gained from religion. But Shi'ism is the reverse of all this. We have shown what constitutes understanding God and His laws. The leaders of this religion have not understood the religion of God and have demeaned Him. We have shown what impudent acts they have committed against God, what lies they have ascribed to Him, and how they have ridiculed Him. Sometimes they have imagined God to be a Mongol king to whom a mediator must be sent. Sometimes they have considered him Alexander the Macedonian, who demands a thousand years of mourning for a few

158

people who were killed. Sometimes they have considered themselves to be His supporters. Sometimes they have considered creation to be the result of their own existence. Every time, they have used God as a tool to advance their own affairs.

See to how far their impudence extends: "Making a pilgrimage to Hoseyn in Karbala is like making a pilgrimage to God in Heaven." "Because of the existence of the imam, the earth and sky remain in place, and it is because of his being that people receive nourishment."

"Anyone who weeps, makes others weep, or pretends to weep will go to Paradise." The question must be asked, Why? What sort of activity is weeping for those who were killed, and what good does it do that God should grant such a reward for it? Is it right for God to grant such excessive rewards?

"Anyone who makes a pilgrimage will be forgiven all sins." The question must be asked: "Then what is the use of religion? Why speak about good and evil and permitted and prohibited acts? When weeping or making a pilgrimage will absolve any sin and Paradise will become a reward for it, why should anyone abstain from sinning? Why should anyone bother with what is good or evil, permitted or prohibited?"

The story of the death of Esma'il is unforgettable: "God changed His mind about Esma'il." In order to cover up their own transgression, they ascribe regret to God. What could be more impudent than this?

As we said, the story of the Invisible Imam and whatever they have said about his thousand years of life, about his appearance and the return of the imams, are all contrary to the laws of God.

Now, let us turn to understanding the realities of life and working towards the prosperity of the world, which is another benefit of religion. Shi'ism is a total stranger to all of this. In this religion, neither is there talk of the goodness of life nor any desire for the prosperity of the world. Their teachings are as follows: The world was created in gratitude for the existence of the "Fourteen Infallible Ones"; everyone must know them, consider them as God's supporters, not fail to mention their names, not hesitate to curse and insult their enemies, mourn the ones of whom were killed, make pilgrimages to their shrines whenever possible and hope that they will mediate on their behalf in the next world. These are the teachings of Shi'ism.

These are the instructions of that sect, and we are in Iran, living among the Shi'ites, and witnessing the results of these instructions with our own eyes. A Shi'ite who is steadfast in his beliefs has no wish but to hold religious mourning sessions and make pilgrimages. Other affairs hold no value for him.

I have written this elsewhere, but in 1336 HQ, during the World

War, there was inflation, and one could easily say that the war had caused the destruction of one-third of the people. At that time, I was in Tabriz and clearly saw that most of the rich people did not help the poor. They would not even notice their relatives and neighbors who were dying. They would ignore the dead, who were left unburied because they had no shrouds. Many of those who had wheat and groceries would hide them and sell them at inflated prices, thus accumulating money. What they had in common was religious mourning ceremonies. Later, in spring, when the road to Iraq, which had been closed for years, reopened, they became overjoyed and mobilized large caravans of people to make pilgrimages.

Worse than this happened two years ago. In 1320 HS [1941], when Russia and England sent troops to Iran and Reza Shah was removed, the restrictions that he had imposed on traveling to Iraq were lifted. The Shi'ites forgot everything else and, at a time when foreign armies had come to the country and Iran had become closer to the battle field (rather it had become a battle field) and there was much fear, jubilantly, the people set out for Tehran, and twenty-one thousand people bought pounds at a rate of 140 rials and departed for Karbala and Najaf.

This year, another experiment is underway. For years, wheat and barley were inexpensive in Iran and farmers suffered hardship and losses. Last year, because of the war and the shortage of grains, the prices increased tremendously. Even this year they are still high, despite the abundance. Now, the farmers sell their grain at twenty times the price of the previous years. Rather than realizing the value of this opportunity and increasing production, improving their farms, creating orchards, cleaning out the water springs and increasing the water output, buying clothes for their wives and children, and taking children suffering from trachoma to a doctor, they have forgotten all of these and only remember pilgrimages. From every village, a group of people organizes a caravan and, taking their cleric along, they set out happily with cheers and incantations.

Also, the bazaar merchants, who have accumulated much wealth in these two years as a result of the increase in prices, as well as merchants who have increased their wealth by hoarding and price hiking, entertain the sole wish of making a pilgrimage to Karbala and Najaf (or Mecca). Many of them evade paying taxes to the government through ruses and bribery and yet set out on a pilgrimage.

Now, the streets of Tehran are full of villagers from Khorasan, Mazandaran and other places, who have come here to go to Karbala, wandering in groups in the streets in their tattered, soiled clothing. It has gone so far that the government of Iraq, which makes a huge profit every year from the visits of these groups, has refused to grant visas. Hence, many of these people set out without passports and are caught at the border. There are also people who forge passports, and now a number of them are being interrogated by the Police Department.

Such are the ideals of the Shi'ites. What they lack is a desire to improve agriculture or commerce, to engage in other efforts, and to take an interest in the nation and the country. That is why we say, Shi'ism is the reverse of religion in every respect.

One of the valuable truths that religion teaches is that in this world nothing out of the laws of the universe can occur. It cannot be that someone exists in this world who can be seen by no one. It cannot be that one can live for a thousand years. It is impossible for the sun to rise from where it sets. The dead cannot return to the world. But we have seen that Shi'ism is full of such beliefs which are contrary to the laws of the universe.

Another valuable truth is that there is a proper way to accomplish every task. A sick person must be taken to the doctor for medical treatment. To get rich, one must work hard. And to acquire honor among the people, one must do good deeds. But Shi'ism teaches the opposite of all these. Any "wish" that a Shi'ite has is supposed to be granted from the shrines, from the shrines of Imamzadeh Davud, Shah Abdol'azim, and Ma'sumeh of Qom, not to mention the shrines of higher and mightier imams.

II: A great misconception of Shi'ites is that, as they imagine, God has created the world in gratitude for the existence of the "Fourteen Infallible Ones." This itself is a baseless exaggeration. God has not created the world in gratitude for the existence of anyone. God is beyond granting favors to His creation. He is greater than choosing "certain favorite ones," like a capricious king. Whoever made such a statement is an irreligious liar and is shamed before God.

The founder of Islam was an ordinary person, like others. God chose him and appointed him as a guide. He became superior for this and for no other reason. If that righteous man, who was appointed by God, was an ordinary person, how could his offspring, who were nobodies, be any different?

In any case, this belief, despite having no foundation, has been the basis of the Shi'ite sect and has been harmful in two ways: First, the Shi'ites have been "personality worshippers." Second, they value only the times of their imams and stories related to them and have become strangers to their own time.

In regards to personality worshipping, a Shi'ite's heart must be full of love for the imams and value nothing else. If you scrutinize this idea, you will see that they do not even value the Prophet as much.

161

The Prophet was appointed at the age of forty. Even then, Gabriel had to come and go and bring him instructions. But the imams were imams from childhood and, without any need of Gabriel, knew everything. In helping God operate the world, too, the ability and effort displayed by the imams and "His Holiness Abbas" is not displayed even by the Prophet.

A Shi'ite believes that the twelve imams were the flowers of the Garden of Creation and that others have and will have no value or worth compared to them. No matter whether a person does good deeds, tries to stay on the path of God or makes self-sacrifices, he will never achieve the status of Salman, Abazar and Meqdad, let alone that of the imams. They have done all the good deeds, and there is no room for anyone else.

Good and bad are all the same. A Shi'ite does not recognize a cruel person other than Yazid, Ebn Ziyad and Shemr. Neither Genghis Khan, who spilled so much blood; Tamerlane, who engaged in so much slaughter; nor Samad Khan, who committed so many atrocities, can be compared to Yazid, Shemr or Ebn Ziyad. Yazid and Ebn Ziyad occupy the position of injustice, and there is no room for anyone else. After the passage of thirteen hundred years, they still "curse" Yazid, but they do not mention Genghis Khan and Tamerlane, who engaged in so much bloodshed.

A Shi'ite must take every opportunity to praise his imams or reproach their enemies. This is an obligation for him as a Shi'ite. For instance, because Abu Bakr became a calif, went on the pulpit and said, "I have become your leader, even though I am no better than you are," the Shi'ite must not miss an opportunity to add [in Arabic] "Ali is one of you" to Abu Bakr's statement in order to make it known that despite all his enmity toward Ali, Abu Bakr confessed that Ali was superior to him, and that it was because of Ali's status that Abu Bakr said, "I am no better than you are."

There is a sentence in the books concerning God having told the Prophet of Islam: "*Lowlak lama khalaqta al-aflak*" [If not for you, I would not have created the galaxies]. This sentence is incorrect and was obviously made by an Iranian who knew some Arabic. In Arabic, one must say: "*Lowla ant...*". "*Lowlak...*" [If not for you...] is incorrect and has only been used to rhyme with "*aflak*" [galaxies]. The Shi'ites have not let such an untrue and incorrect sentence be, but have added to it: "And, if not for Ali, I would not have created you either."

As we said, in this connection, they have also tampered with the verses of the Koran, and whenever they have found an opportunity, they have added to them.

No matter what movement or event occurs in the world, the

Shi'ites must search for a reported saying to show that the imams had predicted it. This is an obligation for Shi'ites.

In recent years, during which time European knowledge has become widespread in Iran, the only use that Shi'ite clerics have made of these sciences has been to search for certain reported sayings to boast to the world that all this was predicted by one imam or another. Hobbatoddin (the minister of education of Iraq) writes that astronomy is nothing new. Its findings have all been revealed in the verses of the Koran and mentioned in the reported sayings.

According to Khalesizadeh, the imams knew of the "force of gravity" and have explained it in their discussions, and it is very unfair that the Europeans have recorded it in the name of the Englishman, Newton.

In the course of these ten years that we have attempted to write about life, in the early years, many of the seminarians and others would come and say, "These ideas are also found in the reported sayings. Why do you not mention that, so that the people will accept them more readily?" Then, when they were disappointed in us, they would set to the task, and whenever we wrote something, they would search the books and find a statement among the reported sayings that would more or less be like what we had said and would boast of it to us. For instance, in the area of rational faculties [*kberad*], we had disputes with the sects, with Sufism, with the *kharabatigari*, and with the new psychologists, and we would offer clear proof to support each one of our statements. They would boast of a reported saying to us: "When God created *kberad* [rational faculties], He told it to step forward, which it did. Then, He said to step back, which it did. He said, It is with you that I shall punish and with you that I shall reward."

This is itself a question of whether religion is for the sake of the people or the people for the sake of religion. The truth is, religion is for the sake of the people. Religion is for teaching the realities of life to the people and guiding them on the right path. God sees fit to appoint someone every now and then, and through him to show the people a main path for their lives. This is the purpose of religion. But the Shi'ites think the opposite. They believe that people are for the sake of religion. In other words, God created the "Fourteen Infallible Ones" and has honored them. He has created this world and the people to recognize the Honored Ones, to recognize their place next to God, to please God, to always repeat their names and greet them, to build silver and golden domes over their graves and visit these domes from far away, to never forget but keep alive their life histories, to remain an enemy of their enemies forever and not hesitate to curse and insult them. Obviously, as a reward for these actions, they will go to heaven in the next world and drink water from the *kowsar*, and every sin they have committed will be forgiven upon the mediation of those Honored Ones. This is the perception of the Shi'ites.

In ancient times, when they wanted to express appreciation for a hero, they would form a parade. They would form a great caravan with groups of people surrounding the champions, who would be positioned in the middle, and they would march through the city with music and songs, all praising the champions.

The Shi'ites imagine that creation is such a parade to honor the position of the "Fourteen Infallible Ones." Groups of people have come before The Fourteen, with their relatives and cohorts, and will be followed by other groups who will come and go.

With this belief, the Shi'ites consider the time of The Fourteen (the early centuries of Islam) to be the best of times, and in their opinion, the time that passes afterwards is worse and less valuable.

Given this belief, they do not value their own time and the events of the present; rather they are always bound by the times of The Fourteen and the events of that period.

For example, now that a very great war is under way among the European governments, and every nation should be moved by these events and engage in efforts to shape its future, the Shi'ites pay no attention to it, and often refuse to even listen to the news of it. But if you speak about the Safayn battle or tell the story of Mokhtar, they will listen enthusiastically and happily.

The greedy governments of Europe dominate the Easterners and have taken over all the Eastern countries. The Shi'ites pay no attention to this. Yet, after thirteen hundred years, they have not forgotten the story of Fadak, and whenever the occasion arises, they discuss it and do not hesitate to insult Abu Bakr, Omar and others.

In 1320 HQ, when there was a battle against the Russian army in Tabriz and the Russians were victorious, arresting Seqat ol-Eslam with eight other people for loving their country and people and hanging them on the day of Ashura, simultaneous with the hanging of those eight people, the followers of Ja'far ebn Mohammad engaged in self-flagellation with chains in the bazaars and crying out, "Save us from the tyranny of Yazid."

In Shahrivar 1320 HS [August/September 1941], when the Russian and British armies crossed the Iranian border and entered the country, I had to travel to Shiraz and Bushehr. When I sat down on the bus, there was also a group of "pilgrims" returning from Mashhad. I cannot put into words the degree of ignorance I witnessed among them. Despite the damage that the country had suffered, they did not pay the slightest attention and spoke only of their trip and true or false stories about their imams, continuously chanting "incantations." Only once did the discussion turn to the subject of the country. One of them responded: "They will leave. The Russians said in Mashhad, 'This is the country of Imam Reza; we will not stay.'"

From Shiraz to Bushehr, I had to put up with another group, about whose ignorance pages would be required, if I were to write. An elementary school principal instructed others: "Recite 'Qol hovallah'[28] six times and blow in six directions, and you will need not fear bombs or anything else." On the road, they did nothing but "incantations," once in a while displaying their evil character and shouting out, "... on all three unjust califs."

No need to mention that such people, without paying any attention to the realities of life and alienated from their own time, will have no fate but helplessness and misfortune. It is a punishment for their ignorance and misguided ways that they are always subjugated by foreigners. To tell the truth, with all these problems, the Shi'ites are anachronistic. They are, rather, the dead people of thirteen hundred years ago who have mingled with the living. That is why they do not understand the ways of life.

If we were to liken them to anyone, they would be like a man with impaired vision, who cannot see anything in front of his feet, but can see a village several miles away and watches what happens there. Obviously, such a man with strange vision would be unable to live, because without being able to see what is around him while he is watching the village several miles away, suddenly he will slip and fall down or into a well. The misfortunes that the Easterners suffer today and the reason they have become subservient to Westerners are direct results of such ignorance.

We know that some will object and say: During the Safavid era, how did the Iranians, who were all Shi'ites, engage in great wars and preserve the country? How did they achieve those victories?

I respond: Firstly, during the Safavids, the Shi'ites were not solely preoccupied with religious mournings and pilgrimages, but were involved in the affairs of the country as well. The proof is that they sacrificed their lives to protect the country.

Secondly, the time of the Safavids was different from our own. At that time, the masses of people had no authority and the kings were able to lead them as they wished and to force them to do anything. At that time, too, it was the courage and sense of honor of Shah Esma'il, Shah Tahmasb and Shah Abbas that made Iranian Shi'ites into warriors. Furthermore, as we have written in detail elsewhere, Shah Esma'il and his successors did not use Iranians, but Turkish tribesmen, who were zealous desert warriors and had not learned anything from Shi'ism but fighting the Sunnis.

Thirdly, during the Safavids, the Iranians were confronted with the Ottomans and Uzbeks, who were not far superior to them. But today they are confronting the Europeans, who have become far superior to them.

Fourthly, during the Safavids, the world was different from what it is now. Today, life is not limited to war and sword fights, and every nation must take an interest in all the affairs of its life and employ all its intellect and attention to improving life, otherwise, it will be left behind and eliminated. Safavid times were different from the present in every respect.

III: One of the detriments of Shi'ism that I must mention separately is the impudent attitude of the followers of this sect towards lying. Lying, which is among the worst of sins, is not avoided by them to advance their sect, and they do not consider it a sin. It has been so from the beginning and it is so now. For instance, concerning the Invisible Imam, in addition to other lies, they say: "There are two cities called Jabalqa and Jabalsa, one in the East and another in the West. The Invisible Imam is in those two cities." Now that all parts of the earth are known, ask the clerics: Where are Jabalqa and Jabalsa; to which country do they belong?

As for the Invisible Imam, we know what his story is. Many have said that they have seen him, and each has a story to tell. One of the clerics (Haji Mirza Hoseyn Nuri) has compiled them into a book, a book full of lies.

They frequently ascribed "miracles" to the domes of the imams in Karbala, Najaf and Mashhad. Before the Constitutional era, once every few years, news would arrive from Karbala or Najaf that on some given night, everything became illuminated, some blind man was given sight, or a lame man was cured. Such news would be reported by telegram, and the cities in Iran would be decorated with lights in celebration. We must be thankful for the Constitutional movement in Iran and the Ottoman Empire, which put a stop to such fabrications of "miracles."

Rarely does an Iranian or anyone else return from Karbala without bringing back a few lies. When I was a child, I frequently heard: There is a bird in Karbala that clearly says, "Hoseyn was killed." Such an obvious lie was told and is still being told.

It has been frequently observed in Mashhad that two or three people will roll a rock into the courtyard of the shrine and then claim: "The rock has come on pilgrimage." They have played this game many times, but none of the clerics has ever objected, because they believe: "It will strengthen the beliefs of the public."

In 1307 HS [1928/29], for a month I saw this game played over and over again. Once I asked: "Did this rock come by itself?" They responded: "Yes, it came on pilgrimage. Many rocks do." I said, "From which door? Did it roll along the ground or fly through the air?" Here, they did not know what to answer. One of them said: "We did not see all of that . We saw it here, having come on pilgrimage." They answered in this manner because there was a gendarme standing behind me, otherwise they would have behaved differently.

It is their practice to fabricate "miracles," and if someone were not to accept them and begin to ask questions, they would consider him weak in his beliefs or call him a Babi and try to harm him. To their way of thinking, whatever is said about the imams must be accepted. This is precisely a Shi'ite obligation.

In 1330 HQ, when the Russians shelled the dome in Mashhad, and the marks left by cannon balls, which I saw myself, were seen for a long time, they used to say in many cities: "The cannon ball turned back and hit them." This lie is still told; one still hears it.

They have frequently told the lie that on the day of Ashura or the eve of someone's killing, a man copulated with a woman and they were stuck together and could not be separated. They imagine this to be an attempt to promote their sect, to fabricate and spread such lies. I remember once they spread another lie during Moharram in Baku. I was very young and heard the story in Tabriz: "A man by the name of Haji Reza had copulated with a Russian woman on the day of Ashura and both were stuck together." Shi'ites congratulated each other and repeated the story with more embellishments. Shokuhi-Maragheh'i put this story into verse and published it. This year, too, the story was spread during Ramazan in Tehran: "An Indian or an American soldier copulated with a prostitute in Shahr-e No on the eve of the twenty-first of Ramazan, and in the morning when they awoke, they were stuck together and had to be taken to the hospital."

They spread this lie so many times that it was published in the newspapers. A large group of people assembled in front of the hospital and no matter how much they were told that it was a lie and that nothing like that had happened, they would not believe it. Worse still were those who returned from the hospital. If someone asked, they would say, "Yes, it happened. I saw it myself." They would tell such an utter lie without shame.

Because the Shi'ites believe that the imams are in charge of God's operations, any exaggerated statement or thought about them is possible. The imams are capable of any act (or as the clerics say, it is possible to occur). That is why even if it has not happened, it is not considered a lie. It is possible for an imam to give sight to a blind person. That is why it would not be considered a lie for such a miracle to be fabricated and spread. Rather, "since it publicizes the virtues of the imams and strengthens the beliefs of the public, it is considered a good deed."

In *Alam Ara-ye Abbasi*, concerning Shah Tahmasb I, it is reported: "Mowlana Mohtashem-Kashani composed an ode praising his excellency . . . and sent it from Kashan . . . His excellency said, 'I am not pleased to have poets eulogize me. They should write about His Holiness Ali and the Infallible Imams, peace be upon them, and expect their primary reward from their sacred spirits, and then from us, because, taken in light of the saying that 'the greatest praise is the greatest lie,' the farfetched and profound ideas, meanings, and metaphors which are so eloquently ascribed to the kings are, for the most part, improper. However, if they are ascribed to the sacred personages, since they are of a higher stature, such is possible."

This is the secret of the lies and fabrication of miracles. On the other hand, the followers of a sect that has no foundation need to preserve it with lies. In this regard, Baha'ism, Sufism and Shi'ism are similar. The Baha'is and the Sufis are also impudent in fabricating lies. A wall that has no foundation must be supported with pillars from all directions.

If you converse with Shi'ites (those who are not commoners), you will see that they make every effort not to be defeated and lose an argument. That is why they constantly lie. For instance, if you say, Ali cooperated with Abu Bakr and Omar and did not oppose them, they will say, "He practiced dissimulation." If you say, "He became a relative of Omar and gave his daughter in marriage to him," they will respond, "It was for appeasement." If you say Abu Bakr and Ali converted to Islam even when Islam was weak, and that this is proof that they were sincere Moslems, they will respond that they had gone to a soothsayer, had heard that Islam would advance, and that is why they converted to Islam. If you say: Hasan ebn Ali, despite having the power, lost the office of calif, and Hoseyn ebn Ali, despite having no power, tried to gain it, they will respond: "Each one of the imams was sent a tablet from heaven, to act accordingly." No matter what you say, they have an answer, and they will never give in. A Shi'ite must be persistent and not allow his faith to be shaken. He must be persistent and protect his sect.

Once I told one of them that the story about Omar going to Ali's home and trapping the daughter of the prophet between the door and the wall, which is told by preachers to bring the people to tears, is an out-and-out lie, and I provided proof. I said: What need of a name does a child who is in the belly of the mother have? And then, who would know that it was a boy, so that they would call him "Mohsen"? I had not finished my statement when he responded, "The Prophet had predicted it and had named him Mohsen." I said: This is not found in any book; how can you say that? He said, "It does not need to be in a book, I say so based on my own intellect."

IV: The issue of weeping and religious mournings must be dealt with separately. This, too, has harmful results.

As we said, initially they used to make political gains in this way. People felt sorry for a person who had suffered injustice and, wittingly or unwittingly, would support him. This is how the Shi'ite leaders advanced their purpose, through the injustice suffered by Hoseyn ebn Ali.

The difference is that in those days, "reciting verses and weeping" was practiced only once or twice a year. We know of no more than this during the times of the imams themselves. Then we see in history books that during the reign of the Buyed Dynasty, the Shi'ites in Baghdad would become very moved on the days of Ashura, and would engage in mourning performances.

Later, we see no mention of it in the books until the time of the Safavids, when it started again. Molla Hoseyn Kashefi wrote a book called *Rowzat al-Shohada*, on the story of Karbala, passages of which would be read in meetings, which is how the term *rowzeh-khan* [reciter of religious mourning] was coined.

It seems that simple gatherings had been held by the people, but the shah and his cohorts also became involved, and one can assume that on the days of Ashura, certain dramatic performances were carried out.

We know little about that time. But, during the time of the Qajars, when we have the writings of the European travelers, we see that great ceremonies were held. And in Iran, India, Caucasia, and other places, twelve days in Moharram were observed with many religious mourning ceremonies, and chest beatings, *qamehzani* and *Shah-Hoseyni* were practiced in those days.[29]

In any case, in our time, religious mournings and Moharram plays had created a great problem for Iranians and had become so widespread that in larger cities, the number of religious mourning ceremonies exceeded two and three hundred. They had become a source of income for many people, and many had become rich from them. Some of these people were affiliated with the royal court, for whom titles such as "Soltan ol-Zakerin" and "Malek ol-Zakerin" were given. People would go to religious mournings all year round. When someone died, or returned from a trip, or had a wedding, or bought a house, or had a child, a religious mourning ceremony would be held at his home. Every rich person would hold sessions for ten days or more every year, and would open his house to the people. There were few gatherings in which religious mourning ceremonies were not per-

169

formed.

An intelligent and believing Shi'ite is a person who weeps for Hoseyn; if his father dies, he remembers Abbas, the brother of Hoseyn; if he loses a young son, he thinks of Ali Akbar; if he has a wedding, he holds a religious mourning ceremony to sing about the wedding of Qasem. A Shi'ite woman must always remember Zeynab and Omm-e Kolsum. Whenever something sorrowful occurs, she must try to suppress her own sorrow and weep for the sorrow of the sisters and wives of Hoseyn. This was the instruction given by their leaders, "Let them weep and lament for Hoseyn."

On the other hand, when Moharram arrived, many people wore black, and from the very first day, mourning ceremonies were held in the business arcades and caravanserais, and in the homes of religious jurists and prominent people. Religious mourning ceremonies were held everywhere. The business of professional mourners was thriving. Each, riding a horse or a donkey, would leave one place and hasten to the next session. Everywhere, when one professional mourner would come down from the pulpit, another would climb up.

At the same time, processions would start from every street. Groups of *sinehzan*, "Arabs" and *zanjirzan* paraded together.[30] Many standards were carried in front of them, and they proceeded with drums and bugles (or without them), moaning and weeping. They would go to the bazaars, to the business arcades, and to the homes of religious jurists and prominent people, all day long.

In the evening, Shah Hoseyn processions would start from every alley and street, and then there were religious mourning ceremonies in every mosque.

From the eighth or the ninth, *shabihs*--people dressed as Shemr, Yazid, Hoseyn, Abbas, Ali Akbar, Qasem, Zeyn ol-Abedin the Sick, Zeynab, Omm-e Kolsum, and Sakineh--appear and parade through the bazaars. In Tabriz, on the ninth, they would bring out a lion, which is another story in itself.

On the tenth, Ashura, the madness would increase. From the start of the day, a hundred Shah Hoseyn processions would start. From every alley and street, they would come out, hitting themselves on the head with sabers, with cracked skulls and bloody white shrouds. The people of Qareh Bagh in Tabriz and Tehran would bring persons with "locks and chains on their bodies" [*qofl be-tan*]. On this day, the clerics, the merchants and the rich could no longer contain themselves and, with bare feet and heads, would rub mud on their faces and lead the processions. They would pour ashes and straw on their heads. Some people wept and hit themselves on the head so much that they would faint. In this manner, various processions would start from every direc-

170

tion and meet in the bazaars. Masses of men and women would stand watching and weeping. Many of those who hit their heads with sabers tried to show off by hitting so hard that they would fall down and faint, and every year several people died doing this.

In many cities, on the day of Ashura, they carried catapults [*nakbl*] around. They would build a very large, heavy contraption of wood, which they called a *nakbl*. Every neighborhood had a *nakbl*, and on that day, twenty or thirty or more people would lift it and carry it through the streets. When two *nakbl*s met each other on the road, they would not let each other pass. People would fight and beat each other up, and even sometimes shed blood.

In the cities, where the rivalries of the Heydari and Ne'mati groups had not been eliminated, on Ashura every year there were fights, and heads were cracked and wounds inflicted.

Such displays of ignorance were so numerous that to recount them and write the story of each would fill a large book. Ignorance of this kind was widespread in Iran until Reza Shah Pahlavi prohibited it. For more than ten years, there was little sign of such displays. But, as we know, since his abdication, the government has not attempted to prevent them, and the clerics are trying to spread them once again. We hear that they have started again in many cities, and during Moharram the same displays take place.

As was said, such acts had many bad consequences, which I will only list briefly.

1. Recounting a story that occurred thirteen hundred years ago and weeping and mourning because of it is to turn one's back on and to trample wisdom. The belief that God will be pleased with such weeping and moaning and will reward them is another manifestation of their ignorance. God is pleased with action that is rational and beneficial. What would be the benefit of crying and weeping about an old story of a thousand years ago? Why should God reward it?

The astonishing thing is that Hoseyn's survivors forgot the incident after one or two years and went on with their lives. As we said, Ali ebn Hoseyn reconciled with Yazid and befriended him. Sakineh, the daughter of Hoseyn, who, according to the professional religious mourners, died at the ruins in Syria, and over whose death the Shi'ites have wept rivers of tears, lived for many years afterward, becoming the wife of Mos'ab ebn Zobeyr and then the wife of Abdolmalek Marvan, living happily to the end of her life.

But the Shi'ites have not forgotten that story after thirteen hundred years. Is this not proof of the empty-headedness and ignorance of a people?

2. Chest beating, beating oneself with chains, rubbing mud on

one's face, pouring dirt on one's head, cracking one's skull, jumping and falling, yelling, and other such actions are merely signs of a violent nature and savagery. The Shi'ites consider this to be a gift, and if there are one or more Europeans among the audience, they show off by beating themselves even more and crying even louder. But the truth is that such ignorant behavior has given an excuse to the Europeans to call Iranians and other Easterners "semi-savages" and to consider them undeserving to live free.

For years, the Europeans have tried to keep the Easterners in their own ignorance and savagery and have expected to benefit in two ways from this behavior: first, to keep the Easterners so incapable and helpless in their ignorance that they would easily submit to the shackles of domination; second, to have an excuse in answer to the "humanitarians of the world," who are found in abundance in Europe.

It is for this purpose that since a hundred years ago, Europeans have once again begun coming to Iran and India, have written stories about these displays of ignorance in their books, and have published pictures of them,[31] not to mention some of the Orientalists who have engaged in praising Shi'ism and such practices.

Two orientalists, Monsieur Marbin, a German, and Dr. Joseph, a Frenchman, have written about Shi'ism in their books and praised these Shi'ite practices. The clerics have thus been given an opportunity to translate these two books into Persian and publish them in a book called *Siyasat al-Hoseyniyyeh*. However, we know well that the writings of these Orientalists and political employees are only for deceptive purposes.

According to Monsieur Marbin, Nasiroddin Tusi did a very good thing at the time of the Mongol invasion, in the midst of that calamity, not to forget the Shi'ite-Sunni hostility. He took the Mongols to Baghdad and took revenge upon the enemies of Ali's family. He wanted the Shi'ites to continue in this manner forever, never to empty their hearts of the enmity for the Sunnis, and to engage in other affairs.

According to Dr. Joseph, Shi'ism has made much progress as a result of religious mourning ceremonies. He hoped the Shi'ites would not stop their progress in this direction and would increase the number of Shi'ites (which would well suit the political aims of the Europeans).

3. Besides the fact that weeping and mourning suppress emotions and extinguish the sense of honor, all those religious mourning ceremonies and processions became a preoccupation for the people, preventing them from attending to the affairs of life. The misfortunes from which the Iranians suffer, and which have resulted in their misery and helplessness, have had many causes, of which, undoubtedly, this is one. Rather than becoming aware of world events and the advancement

in sciences and other areas, or contemplating the condition of the country and the masses, they engage in such futile exhibitions. What we see is the result of that preoccupation. They are the victims of the greed of the Europeans, but complain of the injustice of Yazid.

Iranian women are oblivious to everything and do not have the slightest interest in the country and the nation. The educated, as well, do not display any intelligence or understanding in this regard. As a result, they spend most of their time in religious mourning ceremonies and using their intellect and abilities for such purposes.

4. The practice of weeping and pilgrimage, with all the rewards promised, results in another great harm, which is that the Shi'ites unabashedly engage in evil deeds.

One must realize that ordinary people do not have a proper understanding of good and evil. About something that is evil (theft, for instance), they only know that it is a sin and will anger God, and that the evildoer (or thief) will go to Hell. Fear of Hell is the only thing that prevents them from committing it.

They do not understand that evil deeds harm life and cause disorder in life. Hence, when they hear that a person who weeps for Hoseyn or makes a pilgrimage to his shrine will be absolved of all sins and is bound to go to Heaven, they no longer fear, and they engage in evil.

This was tested from the very beginning, and during the past few years, when, because of the war, there was a shortage of food in Iran and prices increased. It was tested once more, because it was seen that those who engaged in hoarding and price hiking, and who destroyed thousands of families, consisted mostly of "pious" hajis and the prayer-chanting people who had made pilgrimages to Mashhad. It was also observed that they took the same money that they had gained in destroying families to go to Karbala and Najaf on pilgrimages and to give to the clerics.

These dishonest people, who have an excuse, pay no attention to the country and the nation and ridicule the homeland, do not hesitate to commit evil in this manner, and, protected by their baseless beliefs, allow themselves the freedom to do whatever they please.

If you study the ordinary people and their beliefs, you will see that secured by what they have heard from the clerics and professional religious mourners, they imagine that the human being has no choice but to commit sins in this world, and the solution is only to weep for Imam Hoseyn and make pilgrimages to him and others, because God made this agreement with Imam Hoseyn on the day of "creation."

If you ask a Shi'ite going to Karbala, "Why are you going to Karbala?" he will answer: "Well, I am a sinner. I must go to be cleansed of my sins." If you say to him, "It would be better not to commit sins, so that you would not need to be cleansed," he will answer in astonishment, "Is it possible for a human being not to sin?"

There is a saying in Tabriz that I have frequently heard: "A dog which is unclean, when it falls in a salt desert and turns to salt, will be cleansed. We are sinners and unclean, we throw ourselves into the salt desert to become cleansed." When you think about it, in this regard, the beliefs of the Shi'ites are not unlike those of the Christians (concerning sinning and penance).

This point can be stated another way. As we know, a human being is comprised of two essences: first is the essence of life, which desires evil, and then there is the essence of the soul, which desires good. In many people the essence of life is dominant, which is why they cannot stop themselves from committing evil. However, at the same time, the soul is not idle. It reprimands them, and their conscience is always ill at ease. As soon as such people hear that anyone who weeps for Imam Hoseyn or makes a pilgrimage will be absolved of sins, like a thirsty person who reaches water, they accept it happily and joyously, and, taking this as a response to the scolding of their conscience, they are relieved. As the common people say: "For what does a blind man ask God? Two eyes." What do murderers, hoarders, thieves, prostitutes, and deceptive clerics need? An organization that will absolve them of all their sins without any suffering or hard work.

That is why you see Tamerlane, despite his bloodthirstiness and cruelty, who in one day killed seventy-thousand people in Esfahan and in Baghdad made minarets of severed heads, always sought out Sufi elders and as soon as he found one, he would become a devotee. You see, Samad Khan, despite the evil nature that made him an instrument in the hands of Nicholas's policy and who killed many of the courageous lovers of freedom, held religious mourning ceremonies and sent four hundred *tomans* in money for candles to Karbala every year. The reason behind these acts is what we explained.

V: In addition to the polemical objections, the story of the Invisible Imam is harmful. When you speak to any Shi'ite about problems or express your hopes for the betterment of the world, he will immediately respond: "He must come to set things right." In Tabriz, they say: "Let me be a sacrifice for him; he will come and set things right."

I must clarify that what we consider problems are not considered problems to Shi'ites. For instance, the backwardness of the nation, the domination of foreigners, the impotence of the government, the disorder of the country, the baseness of morals and emotions and the like are not issues of concern among Shi'ites, or even considered prob-

174

lems. As long as the road to Karbala is open, religious mourning ceremonies are permitted, and their clothes are not tampered with, nothing else matters. For Shi'ites, foreigners who allow them the freedom to practice their sect are better than an Iranian government which would take away such a freedom. This is what they have said many times.

For them, problems consist of seeing that many of the young people and others have become weak in their beliefs, do not to go to the religious mourning ceremonies, do not wish to go on pilgrimage, and do not regard the clerics highly. These are what they consider to be problems, and their response is the same to any other issue discussed.

Worse still is that even though in the past ten years we have made an effort, by the will of God, to stand against materialism and irreligiosity, have established religion on a very strong foundation, have fought aberrations and ignorance, trying to eliminate each and every one, the Shi'ites are very unhappy with our undertaking, because to their way of thinking, this task must be left to the Invisible Imam. As we said, Shi'ites are personality worshippers. They wish for the Invisible Imam to appear and bring goodness to the world. It is not so much a good world that they want as it is its occurrence at the hand of their Imam. That is why they are unhappy with us.

They are like a child who has fallen into a swamp and refuses the hand of the person who wants to take his hand and pull him out. He says, "I want my mother to come"; but his mother is not available and cannot come.

I will never forget one day when I was speaking with a cleric. I told him: You say that Mahdi will come, and one of his tasks will be to eliminate all sects and religions and guide all people in one direction. I asked: How will he do so? Will he perform a "miracle," and have the people go to sleep one night and wake up in the morning all having become Shi'ites, or will he fight the sects and religions and call the people to one religion through reasoning? Which will be the case? Since he knew nothing, he could not respond, and I continued: If you say, "He will do so through a miracle," it is a lie, because such an action is contrary to God's laws. You see that the Prophet of Islam, who was higher than the imaginary Mahdi, tried to eliminate aberrations through reasoning and fighting alone. If you say, "He will call the people to one direction through reasoning," this is what we have set out to do, and we have made some advancement. It is surprising that it does not please you and you do not cooperate with us. It is astonishing that you do not accept the results that have been gained, and instead pursue a baseless supposition.

Rather than respond to me, the dullard said angrily: "Then, you claim to be Mahdi?"

I said: I do not claim to be Mahdi nor do I have any other claims. Why should I make any claims? Rather than claiming, I have engaged in actions and have done what I must do. You answer my question. Since he could not answer me, he began making nonsensical statements. I stopped him and ended the conversation.

Now, here is an example of the harmfulness of that legend. They submit to any kind of abjectness and to the shackles of foreigners and would not change their minds, or else they might find a solution to their problems, thus disrupting the system of the Invisible Imam.

It is astonishing that Dr. Joseph has written in praise of such ideas and has engaged in deception. According to him, the Shi'ites all await the appearance of the Imam of the Age and expect him every day. Such people are always prepared for fighting and bravery, so that as soon as the imam appears they can hurry to help him. He says the Shi'ites all hope to take over the whole world one day, and people with such a hope "are bound to have the natural means available to them one day."

Dr. Joseph believes that with the efforts of the Shi'ites to spread their sect, and with the hopes that they have for the appearance of their Invisible Imam, they will make "extraordinary progress" in the future and may become the largest nation in the world.

Such fabrications of ideas by Dr. Joseph provided the clerics with a pretext. Several years ago, one of the clerics from Tabriz wrote to me: "You say that there is no proof of the existence of the Imam of the Age. The proof should be asked of a European." In this manner, he resorted to a series of nonsensical statements written for political reasons.

It must be asked, Are the written claims of Dr. Joseph regarding the preparedness and fighting ability of Shi'ites true? Are the religious scholars in Najaf, Karbala, Samaria and Qom; their seminary students; and the Hajj and Mashhad pilgrims from Tehran, Tabriz, Kashan and Qazvin trying thus to prepare themselves? Do our seyyeds not display the opposite of the statements of the French doctor? Do we not see with our own eyes that they submit to any kind of humility and are happy that "he will come and set things right"? We see these with our own eyes; should we still be deceived by the statements of Dr. Joseph?

Besides, supposing that the statements of Dr. Joseph are true and that the Shi'ites are engaged in efforts to be battle ready, with hopes of the coming of the Imam of the Age. Do they not say that the Imam of the Age will fight with a sword and cannons? If so, guns, tanks and all such weapons will become useless. What is their preparedness, given such a supposition?

Indeed, if such legends were the source of the greatness and superiority of a people, the Jews, who have been awaiting the "Messiah" for thousands of years and are the founders of this legend, should have achieved greatness and superiority before all others.

Furthermore, while the Shi'ites hope for the appearance of Mahdi, the Christians hope for the descent of Jesus from heaven, and we do not understand why Dr. Joseph, who compassionately provides this guidance to the people of Iran, does not do so for his own people. Why does he not encourage the priests of France to try to increase the hopes of the people regarding the coming of Christ and to thus open the way for the superiority and greatness of that country? Why should the French people form armies, build weapons and engage in political efforts to gain superiority and greatness while the Iranians advance on the path of legend worship? As the saying goes, death is a good thing, for the neighbor, that is.

The same can be said to Monsieur Marbin. This German charlatan, with his modicum of knowledge about Islam and its history, fabricates such statements as: "Hoseyn knowingly went to be killed. He wanted to submit to the injustice of the Omayyads, thereby to overthrow that dynasty." He considers this to be a great policy of Hoseyn's and advises the Shi'ites not to abandon their religious mourning ceremonies and to continue to advance by showing the injustice suffered by their leaders.

We say: Why has Monsieur Marbin not given the same advice to the Germans? Why has he not taught them the great policy of Hoseyn? Why did the Germans not use this policy when they suffered so much hardship at the hands of Napoleon? Why did their kings not welcome being killed, so that the German nation would make a pretext of their killing and, like Iranians, engage in mourning ceremonies and various displays? In 1918, when they suffered defeat at the hands of the French and the British and unwittingly submitted to the Versailles Treaty, why did they not employ this philosophy? Rather than promoting the rise of Hitler and his actions, why did they not make use of their being oppressed?

It is not yet too late. If they come out of this war defeated and their forces are destroyed, instead of other efforts, they can make use of the philosophy of Monsieur Marbin. And if they need professional mourners, *qamehzan*s, *shamshirzan* and the like, they might ask the Iranians for assistance in supplying them.

As we said, these writings of Marbin and Joseph have been published together in a volume entitled *Siyasat al-Hoseyniyyeh*. This book has a history that I must recount here. In 1327 HQ, when the demand for freedom was strong in Iran, after more than a year of fight-

177

ing Mohammad Ali Mirza and the clerics, the freedom-seekers became victorious and took over Tehran as well. The enemies of freedom, comprised mostly of professional religious mourners, clerics and their followers, were disappointed after much resistance and fighting and began to despair. On the other hand, the autocratic government of Russia sent troops to Iran, took over Azarbaijan and other cities, and attempted to diminish the forces of the freedom-seekers. Suddenly, this book appeared and fueled the fire.[32] The clerics and professional religious mourners and many of the people were moved and began to fight the liberals who were trying to eliminate religious mourning ceremonies. They said, "The Europeans recognize Imam Hoseyn, but you infidels do not!" They said this and began their movement.

In Tabriz, more than anywhere else, chaos ensued, the first results of which were that all the religious mourners, more than two hundred, joined hands and set out to hold religious mourning ceremonies in the bazaars and streets. They did so first in the bazaars. They would take over a bazaar, carpet it from one end to the other, place a pulpit in the middle, stop the traffic of people, and turn the bazaar into a religious gathering. The professional religious mourners and their followers would come and sit down, and they would take the pulpit one after another and make the people weep. Three or four days would pass in this manner, and then they would choose another bazaar, and in doing so, they would not forget their enmity towards the Constitutional movement.

After a while, they started in the streets. In Tabriz, there were about seventeen or eighteen large streets. They toured them one by one, and in each one they gathered, performed religious mourning ceremonies, fabricated lies and attacked the Constitutional movement. The effects of the writings of the two Europeans and what occurred as a result of them was a sight to see.

Another result of *Siyasat al-Hoseyniyyeh* was the appearance of certain groups called the *Entezariyun* [Awaiters]. As we said, Dr. Joseph had written in praise of the belief of the Shi'ites in their Invisible Imam and had said that hoping for and awaiting the appearance of such a person was the source of the life of a nation. Some clerics used this statement as a justification for the creation of Awaiters groups in Mashhad, Tabriz and other places. A hundred, two hundred, even a thousand people would gather to perform *Nodbeh* prayers. They would bemoan the delay in the Imam's appearance, weep, gradually begin to cry aloud, and beat themselves on the head and face, and some would faint. They continued such a spectacle from morning to night. They hoped to force the Invisible Imam to come out of hiding through their moaning and crying.

In Tabriz, another event occurred. When they found that moaning, weeping and hitting themselves on the head and face were to no avail, one seyyed, who was a professional preacher for mourning ceremonies and who was the leader of the Awaiters, said, "Let us all set out for Karbala to beseech that shrine to grant our wishes." This suggestion was applauded and a large group of rich and poor, riding and walking, set out on the pilgrimage. I do not know how many set out on the journey or how many of them died along the road. I do know that a hundred families became beggars. I remember well that year that new beggars appeared in the streets, and in order to panhandle money easier, they would say, "Our father has gone to Karbala."

This is the history of *Siyasat al-Hoseyniyyeh*. This is an example of the Shi'ites' readiness to participate in futile and ignorant displays.

VI: One of the heinous practices of the Shi'ites is taking the bones of the dead (rich dead) to Karbala, Najaf, Qom and Mashhad. This practice is so heinous and irrational that I do not know what to call it, or what language to use to scorn it. The body of a dead person must be burned or buried in the ground in order to prevent the stench from tormenting the people. However, they keep the corpse in a box above ground, build an enclosure around it which is open enough to release the stench, and in this way they torment the people. After a year, more or less, they place the bones in a box and take them to the "holy shrines."

This practice, besides tormenting the people and often spreading disease, reveals the ignorance and the uncivilized nature of the Shi'ites and the clerics. God knows what sorts of disgrace have resulted from this practice. In the old times, when the Ottomans sometimes prevented it, they would often bring the bones, place them in horse feed bags, and smuggle them across the border, the discovery of which would cause disgrace.[33]

Why do they do this? What can taking bones from one city to another accomplish? If you ask them, one will say: One of the gates of Paradise is in Karbala, Najaf, or Qom, and as soon as the bugles are blown, the dead person will rise and go straight to heaven. Another will say: A dead person who is placed in a box and taken to Najaf or Karbala will be safe from the pressures of the grave. Another will say: We are sinners and take refuge in that shrine. Or he will say: We are dogs and throw ourselves into the salt desert.

With such weak reasoning, they engage in such heinous and harmful acts that disgrace a nation. Will this not be strong proof for Europeans who call Iranians savages and uncivilized? The Europeans aside, if we ourselves heard that some people treat the bones of the dead in this manner, would we not consider them savages and inferior?

In short, just as it must be reproached greatly from the perspective of religion and theology, Shi'ism must also be reproached in terms of life. In terms of religion, the Shi'ites have fallen into idolatry, and in terms of living, they are inferior to idol worshippers. Let me clarify this statement. Today, life can be lived in several ways.

First is the life that Europeans pursue: Nations fight each other. They make war, shed blood and destroy cities. Among themselves, too, they do not have rational laws. They live by fighting and conflicts. At the same time, they know the meaning of patriotism. They are devoted to the freedom of their country and the honor of their nation. They all join hands and work to build their country and strengthen their government. They make progress in sciences.

Another is the life that religion teaches and that we want. In that life, rather than fighting, nations cooperate with each other, and, instead of engaging in wars and destruction, they make efforts to build the world. Rational laws govern the nations. Everything--agriculture, trade, commerce, culture, marriage and government--is understood and used properly. Sciences are given more value than they are now.[34]

The life of the Shi'ites is none of the above, but is far inferior to them for several reasons, which I will list here.

1. The Shi'ites consider certain dead people to be the operators of the world and expect their progress to derive from them. Rather than finding a way to carry out every task and to obtain results, they want it to be done by those dead people. This world operates on a set of laws, and everything is the result of something else. For instance, a nation that is devoted to its country and people and to protecting that country will prepare an army with cannons, tanks, airplanes and other means and will become strong and superior, and that country will be safe from falling into the hands of foreigners. But the Shi'ites have not understood this and have no interest in such actions. They believe that this country is protected by Imam Reza, or the Master of the Age. In other affairs, they do the same. A woman prevents her son from doing his military service or learning to become a pilot, thinking that if there is a war and the enemy bombers fly over the city, she will protect herself and her family by "pleading with His Holiness Abbas" or "making a vow of sacrifice" and such. A green grocer or a shoe repairman closes his shop, takes his capital, and sets out for Karbala, believing that Imam Hoseyn will give capital. There are countless examples of this kind.

2. Since they [the Shi'ites] recognize those dead people as God's "chosen" ones, those who operate the world of creation, they all devote themselves to the time of those people and do not value their own age. In the minds of the Shi'ites, the best period in the history of

the world has passed, and what remains is worthless. God has done with the world what He set out to do: He has appointed His prophets; he has brought to the world Ali, Hasan, Hoseyn and Ja'far, who are the cream of the crop of creation; He has established His operations in Karbala; He has in reserve His mediators for the Day of Resurrection; He has kept his Imam of the Age ready in Jabalqa and Jabalsa, and there is nothing else He needs to do. The periods that will now pass are the futile times of the world that are not of value. The only thing to do is to go on pilgrimages, weep, not forget the story of Fadak, and not leave Abu Bakr and Omar alone in order to please the imams, so as not to be without their mediation on the Day of Resurrection. Consequently, no misfortune that comes to the nation or the country and no problem that occurs interests the Shi'ites. In fact, they make use of it to create a miracle for their imams and say: "These are the signs of the End of Time, which they have already predicted."

The world is always advancing and the future is better than the past. They believe the contrary to be true. In their opinion, the past is better than the present and the future, unless the Imam of the Age should appear, in which case it will be a new age.

3. In accordance with their beliefs, the Shi'ites hold ill wishes toward the government, engage in hostilities against it, and refuse to pay taxes or serve in the military. Since this issue will be discussed in the next chapter, we will not deal with it here.

These are the causes that greatly demean the lives of the Shi'ites. There are several reasons for the fact that Iran today, with a population of twenty million, is given no importance in world politics, the greatest and the most prominent of which is Shi'ism. Sufism, Kharabatism, Batenism, Aliyollahism, Bahai'ism and the like each have brought much harm to the country. However, the most harm has come from Shi'ism, which is the religion of the majority of the nation.

We know many stories about the misguidance of the Shi'ites and their ignorance. Here we will mention only a few.

1. As mentioned, in 1216 HQ, the Wahabis, headed by So'ud ebn Abdolaziz, conquered Karbala and engaged in six hours of slaughter. They went into homes and killed infants and children and raped women and girls. They destroyed the shrines, broke the silver and iron chests, and did not hesitate to engage in any violence. According to the writings of the Shi'ites themselves, seven thousand people were slaughtered, among them several prominent religious jurists.

The Shi'ites should have learned a lesson from such a sinister story and known that those domes could accomplish nothing. They should have realized that dead people who cannot protect their own shrines are also unable to protect others. But, instead, the Shi'ites went further in their misguidance and have made of this incident another excuse for moaning and weeping and composing poems and eulogies:

> I do not know which tragedy to mourn
> The killing of the young ones or the dishonoring of women
> . . . .
> Ebn So'ud followed the path of Ebn Sa'ad
> Both are most vicious and hardhearted.[35]

On the other hand, they engage in fabricating lies and miracles: "When the Wahabis excavated the tomb of Imam Hoseyn, they saw His Holiness with a torn body and a straw mat upon his head. Suddenly, there was a climatic disturbance and a strong wind began to blow. The Wahabis were frightened and fled."[36]

In addition, the "servants to the shrine," who are unique in their greed and love of money, took advantage of the situation to profiteer, manufacturing wooden prayer beads and purporting that they were made of the broken wood of the tombs. They took them to Iran and other places to sell to the rich at high prices. The author of *Qesas al-'Olama*, who was a well-known clergyman, writes: "A number of them, of which I have a few, came to my father. I hope they place them with me in my shroud, to save me from Hell, because that tomb had been touched by the Prophets; the imams had blessed it; and the angels had rubbed their wings on it so it would last forever."

See to what extent this group has sunk into ignorance. You can see that nothing can shake them. See to what extent they are the enemies of God and his religion. Observe how bold they are in their fabrication of lies and how insistent they are in their ignorance.

2. As we said, in 1320 HQ, the Russians fired cannons at the dome in Mashhad, and soldiers entered the shrine, arresting Seyyed Mohammad Yazdi and others. Meanwhile, several hundred people were killed and much was plundered. This act brought the Shi'ites much suffering. Nevertheless, in Iran, they kept silent and practiced "dissimulation," fearing the Russians, especially since the czar of Russia had destroyed the Iranian Constitution, and the clerics and their followers were very pleased with him. However, in India, the Shi'ites engaged in demonstrations, formed societies, and demanded that the British government retaliate against the Russians for this action.

The owner of *Habl al-Matin*, who was one of the standard-bearers of Shi'ism, wrote many editorials on this issue. In one of them, he writes: "The situation in Khorasan cannot be compared to that of Tabriz." See how stupid a newspaperman is: Tabriz is where the Russians committed unbelievable atrocities, hanging more than seventy valuable men, including Seqat ol-Eslam, Sheykh Salim, Mirza Ali Va'ez, Mir Karim and others, and destroying the very roots of freedom in that city, yet, this stupid writer in Iran considers a few holes made in a dome more important, even incomparable.

In this manner, the Shi'ites tolerated their suffering until two years later, when the 1914 World War started. Because the Germans were victorious initially, the Russians suffered many defeats and the Shi'ites found the opportunity to consider them miracles of Imam Reza and to predict the destruction of Russia. The poets found a "subject matter," took advantage of the rhymes "Tus" [old name for Mashhad] and "Rus" [Russia] and "Porus" [Prussia] to write couplets: With the cannon of Prussia, the King of Tus responded to the ultimatum of Russia, after two years.

Later, when there was an uprising in Russia, Czar Nicholas was overthrown and killed, along with his family, and for years chaos reigned among the Russians, the Shi'ites became more bold and told everyone about Nicholas and his family being killed: "Did you see how Imam Reza defeated him? Anyone who fights the family of Ali will be destroyed!"

See how ignorant they are: The European governments had grouped since forty years prior in preparation for such a war. They had made hundreds of kinds of weapons to use in that war. The Russian social democrats, who had suffered for years, had gathered forces, and as soon as they found the opportunity, they engaged in that rebellion. They disregarded all of this and all that occurred as a result, and gave full credit to Imam Reza.

Should the whole world struggle and suffer, and the results of their efforts and suffering be ascribed to the imams of this group?

More astonishing is that they have not abandoned their ideas about Russia. In the beginning of this war, again they predicted the destruction of Russia. The others aside, in Tabriz, one day there was a discussion among some officers. One colonel said, "I am certain that Russia will be defeated and destroyed; Imam Reza will defeat her."

3. The year before last, when the armies of the two governments came to Iran and took control of the country, they brought supplies for themselves and prevented the transportation of food supplies from one city to another. As a result, prices suddenly increased and, also because the harvest had been so poor, famine started in Tehran and other cities. In Tehran, the streets became full of beggars. Hundreds and even thousands of people died of starvation or were devastated by disease.

At such a time, rather than waking up and realizing that the hunger and misfortune were the result of the chaotic situation of the country and the impotence of the government, and that the chaotic situation of the country and the impotence of the government were the result of their false teaching, thus realizing their guilt and repenting, the clerics ignorantly took advantage of the events, went on pulpits everywhere, and said: "You see what happened, oh unbelievers. You abandoned praying; you refused to fast; you discontinued religious mournings; pilgrimages were prohibited; and women were unveiled. God has been angered and has sent you this calamity." Such statements were repeated everywhere. A large group of men and women were forced to wear turbans, caps or veils, and once again religious mourning ceremonies increased.

One day, I told someone: What such statements mean is that God is sitting in Heaven, has abandoned all else, and only watches Iran, so that as soon as He sees any disobedience, He becomes angry and sends a calamity. Later, when they repent, He is pleased and removes the calamity. This reveals that you do not understand God.

You say that because Iranian women have removed their veils, God has sent this famine. I ask: What has God done to indicate that He has sent a famine? Did it fail to rain? Did nothing grow out of the ground? Did locusts and pests destroy the wheat? When there is none of these, how can you say God has sent a famine? You see with your own eyes that foreigners are taking the food supplies. You see that it is the result of the impotence of the government, and the cause of the government impotence is your ignorant, false teaching. Nevertheless, you blame God for it. Woe to you; woe to you!

Oh ignorant people! Will God take revenge on the women and children of Bushehr and Bandar Abbas for the women of Tehran having unveiled? One group unveils and God becomes angry with the other? Then, why has God not become angry with the European and American women, who are always unveiled? Does He only become angry when Iranian women unveil? You should be ashamed, you ignorant people!

His response to these statements was: "After all, is God not in control of all affairs?" I said: Is this an answer to my questions? Why have you not yet realized that in this world nothing can occur without a cause or motive? Why do you lead the people, despite your ignorance and stupidity?

4. For several years now, there has been a man in Tehran called "Seyyed Mohammad Ali," who, claiming that he used to be blind and has been granted sight by "His Holiness Abbas," goes to offices and homes and gets money from the people. He is so shameless that he says: "Fill a tea glass full of water and bring it to me to bless. Then drink it and you will be safe from illness." When they bring him the glass, he spits in it, and people drink it! No one has yet questioned

whether his claim is true or false. No one has asked: Where do you come from and who knows that you were blind? Who witnessed that "His Holiness Abbas" gave you sight? Why don't you go to work? Why don't you go and find a job? Why do you beg when you are in perfectly good health? Should a person who has received sight through a "miracle" become a beggar? From every office that he goes, he leaves with a great deal of money.

Worse still, many of the heads of departments support him and write him commendations. One day, I saw him in the Ministry of Education. He was standing before the desk of an employee, who was giving him money. I protested and said: "Why do you give money to this parasite?" He sighed and responded: "What can we do? The director general has written him a commendation."

You see, in the Ministry of Education, which is supposed to fight baseless beliefs and motivate the young people to work hard, its Shi'ite "director general" supports a perfectly healthy, beggarly, lying parasite and writes him a commendation.

Once I heard that he had gone to the military academy. One of the officers guided him to various rooms where he could tell his fabricated stories and receive money from the young people. He received 1,500 rials from one room alone!

You see, the Ministry of War, which should cleanse the young people's minds of baseless, futile ideas and make of them honorable officers, strengthens the roots of superstition in their minds in this manner and diminishes the ugliness of panhandling and freeloading in their views. This is all the result of the sect which the officers and others follow, and which is complete superstition and misguidance.

More interesting than all of these is the story of teaching religion to the dead (or as they call it, *talqin*). When you realize that when a person dies and is put in the grave, a cleric must stand over him and say in Arabic, "Listen and understand, oh slave of God. When two angels come to you and ask you who is your creator, answer that God is your creator; Mohammad is your Prophet; and Ali, Hasan, Hoseyn, and so on are your imams. Say that Paradise is true; fire is true; the weighing scale is true; and Sarat Bridge is true," you see how much ignorance is revealed in this act alone.

Firstly, when a person dies, his body is nothing more than a corpse, which will disintegrate after several days, and which is no longer to be dealt with, as all further dealings are with the soul. The body is buried in the ground so that it will disintegrate in the ground and not pose a threat to the living.

It seems that they do not understand something so obvious, and out of ignorance they imagine that all matters are concerned with the body, the grave being a home for it. So, when they put the body in the grave, two angels by the name of "Nakir" and "Monkar" come to him with blazing clubs and ask him questions. If he is unable to answer, they hit him over the head with the blazing clubs and fill the grave with fire.

Secondly, religion consists of instructions for life, which a person must follow while he is alive, not when he is dead. A person who follows religion in his lifetime does not need to be taught. And if he has not followed religion, trying to teach him after his death is useless. What, then, do they imagine religion to be that causes them to behave as they do?

Obviously, they are far removed from the true meaning of religion. As we have said, religion to them means love and worshipping of the "Fourteen Infallible Ones." They imagine that God wants nothing more than love of them. That is why they think that God will be pleased if someone expresses that love after his death, which will ensure his going to heaven.

Thirdly, they imagine that the language used by God is Arabic; therefore, the questions asked by the two angels are in Arabic, and the dead person must answer them in Arabic. The question arises, When a Turk or someone else dies, how does he immediately acquire a knowledge of Arabic?

CHAPTER 4

The Bullying Of The Clerics

Shi'ism has been covered as much as is it need be. Now, we would like to speak about the clerics and their bullying ways. The clerics have formed another organization on top of Shi'ism, which itself is an organization.

With the turns it has taken and the taints that it has acquired, Shi'ism has come to the conclusion that leadership or government at this time belongs to the Invisible Imam. The clerics have taken this statement and say: We are the successors of that Imam, and the government today belongs to us.

Under this pretext, they consider the people to be their subjects and collect religious taxes and "imam's share" from them. On the other hand, they consider the government to be "unjust" and a usurper, and they teach that the people should refuse to pay taxes if they can; they should not allow their children to do their military service; and, if government money comes into their hands, they should steal it, "with the permission of religious scholars."

Now that Iran has accepted a Constitutional system and lives by laws, the clerics even display hostility toward this, forcing the people to dislike and disrupt the government.

This is a very strong claim that the clerics make, the consequences of which are very harmful. On the one hand is Shi'ism and its detriments, and on the other, the claim of the clerics and their detriments.

Government is the main artery of social life. For this reason, since two hundred years ago, when a movement arose among the masses in Europe and America, this subject has been discussed, rebellions have taken place, and much blood has been spilled. It is not lightly that I state that the claim of the clerics is a strong one.

In addition, this claim is creating uncertainty and doubt among the people, because the clerics, who consider government to be theirs, refuse to take charge (and are unable to do so). Hence, a government by others is required, about which the people are skeptical. The result is a government that the people consider "unjust," one which they do not hesitate to wish ill for or the affairs of which they do not hesitate to disrupt. As one of our supporters says: "Internally, they believe in things that they do not utilize, and externally, they engage in actions they do not believe in."

The clerics treat the government in the same manner that their imams did the Islamic caliphate. For instance, Imam Ja'far Sadeq would not try to become calif, and could not have achieved it, but would not submit to others who had tried and attained it. Rather, he encouraged his followers towards enmity and disruption. The same is true of the clerics who do not assume responsibility for affairs but do not submit to others who have done so and instigate the people towards ill will and enmity. In fact, it can be said that their bullying statements exceed those of the imams, because if Ja'far ebn Mohammad had been given the office of calif, he would certainly have accepted it (as his grandson Ali ebn Musa accepted being heir apparent to Ma'mun). However, if government is conferred on the clerics, they will not accept it and they will not come forward to do so, because besides their being an unorganized group incapable of governing, they prefer to sit by in Najaf, Qom or any other city and rule without a crown or throne, collecting money without giving anything in return and living a life of idleness and comfort.

A government requires an army. It requires a police department, a municipal office, and other offices. A ruler must be responsible for calm in the cities, the welfare of the people, and the prosperity of the country. The clerics do not want to accept any of these responsibilities. They prefer to collect tributes without any effort and rule without any responsibility.

As they see it, their interests lie in the existence of a government, as is the case today, which runs the country and carries out the affairs of the government, but one which at the same time is considered "unjust" by the people, so that, in their hearts, the people consider the religious scholars to be their leaders and rulers and pay them their money. The government must do the hard work and they reap the rewards. Any money going to a government that forms an army, maintains a police force and gendarmerie, and establishes departments is religiously illegal. However, any money that they receive without engaging in any effort or accepting any responsibility is considered legal. Those in the government will all go to Hell and the clerics will go straight to Heaven. A policeman who keeps vigil in hot and cold weather all night and protects homes is a sinner, but the offspring of the clerics and the idle, parasitic children of the seyyeds are doers of good deeds. In short, there should be an ill-reputed "civil government" and an honored, reputable "religious government." One should toil and the other reap the rewards.

This is the wish of the clerics, who have so far had the advantage. Yet it goes without saying that this wish is all to the detriment of the people. As we said, this will end in creating doubt among the people, which would have no other consequences than the helplessness and misfortune of a nation.

People who have created a nation with twenty million individuals, more or less, and who live in one place must all value social tasks. Each individual must consider himself responsible for the advancement of such tasks and not hesitate to do his best. The country is their home, it is the source of their life. They must try to protect it and consider it their duty to serve it as soldiers. This is how a nation can be victorious and live proudly and freely.

People who have no love for their country and do not value national affairs will undoubtedly be dominated by foreigners, who will put the shackles of slavery around their necks.

This is the result of the behavior of the clerics. They bring misfortune to a nation of twenty million inhabitants. That is why we say: The claim of the clerics is a very strong one, the detriments of which are also very strong.

One example of the behavior of the clerics and the consequences of their actions is the story of the Constitutional movement. Constitutionalism (or government by the people) is the best form of government. While the caliphate may have been the proper form of government in the world in the Islamic era, today, Constitutionalism is the proper form of government. The progress of the world is evident when the masses take over the affairs of their nation.

Constitutionalism was created in ancient Greece and Rome, but did not survive long. Later, it appeared in Europe, and most countries accepted it. In Iran, too, honorable people wanted it and tried to establish it for years. Then, the late Seyyed Abdollah Behbahani and Seyyed Mohammad Tabataba'i pioneered a movement, and, as has been written in history books, they obtained the decree for a Constitutional government from Mozaffar al-Din Shah and opened the Consultative Assembly in Tehran.

189

Even though the leaders of this movement were two seyyeds and three prominent religious scholars in Najaf, namely Akhund Khorasani, Haji Mirza Hoseyn Tehrani and Haji Sheykh Mazandarani, bravely supported it, a serious rift developed between them and the clerics.

In the beginning, since they did not know the meaning of Constitutionalism and thought that the people had rebelled to take the government from the court and entrust it to them, they cooperated. But no more than seven or eight months had passed before they realized that Constitutionalism was not in their best interests, but to their disadvantage. That is why they began to oppose it, form groups, and become allies of the royal court. In the meantime, battles were fought and much blood was shed. In the end, the Constitutionalists became victorious, took over Tehran, and overthrew Mohammad Ali Mirza. This time, the clerics pleaded with the tyrannical Russian government and gained the support of Nicholas. And for the ten years the Russian army was in Iranian cities, they did not stop at any atrocity or cowardly act.

Later, when Nicholas was overthrown, once again they remained silent, became isolationists, gradually making compromises and establishing relations with the Constitutional movement, and tried to take advantage of it. They sent their children to school, found employment for their relatives in the government offices, and did not stop at anything in terms of profiteering. A group of them became "modernists" and compromised between Constitutionalism and Shi'ism: "The imams always fought the tyrants and dictators. Did Imam Hoseyn not get killed for justice?" They made many such statements and began a thriving business. Many of them sought employment in the government offices or accepted government employment, opening notary public offices.

However, at the same time, they did not forget their hostility towards Constitutionalism, and they did not abandon their claim to the government. Once again, they called the government "unjust" and declared paying taxes and doing military service religiously illegal. Once again, they promised Paradise, and once again they sold the idea of *hurs* and *ghelmans*.[37] They resorted to any means to make the people disappointed in Constitutionalism. They did not stop at protesting any step that was taken towards progress. On the one hand, they shamelessly and impudently took advantage of the legal offices. On the other hand, they collected *zakat*, "imam's share" and *radd-e Mazalem* from the hajis and pilgrims to Mashhad. As the saying goes: "They ate both out of the feed bag and the trough."

Now that there is a movement in Tehran, and representatives are being elected for the Fourteenth Parliamentary Assembly, several clerics are trying to have their sons or brothers elected and most shamelessly print out "communiques" and encourage the people to pay "tariffs" and to "vote." While doing this, they secretly say: "Now that those heathens have the upper hand, religious scholars must be elected in order to prevent such unorthodox innovations."

There are enough stories about these clerics to fill a book. Their behavior is a clear indication that they are a group of irreligious people who pursue nothing but a life of leisure. They have found this profession to be the best way to maintain such a life style. The truth is that before the Constitutional movement, there were both good and bad among the clerics, but when the Constitutional uprising began and the enmity of the clerical establishment towards it became apparent, those with a pure heart and good will resigned, and what was left of the clerical profession consisted of ignorant individuals who know nothing of life but the worship of their stomachs and leisure, who are completely lacking in good will and compassion for the people.

One of the clerics of Azarbaijan was sent to the Consultative Assembly in the first year of the Constitutional movement as the representative of the clerics. The Constitution was being discussed in that session and there was much dispute about it. This man, supported by two seyyeds and others, strongly supported the Constitution, and, for this reason, he gained status among the Constitutionalists, becoming quite prominent. He slyly took advantage of that opportunity, received a huge "salary" from the government treasury, sent his children, who were numerous, to Europe (except for one) or sent them to schools in Iran, and when they returned or graduated from the schools, each took a position in government departments and received huge salaries (as they still do).

Furthermore, he did not abandon the business of being a "Hojjat ol-Eslam." And in these thirty-eight years, he has taken advantage of both Constitutionalism and being a cleric. On the one hand, he had a hand in legislating the Constitution, and, on the other, he taught "religious jurisprudence" in his home. He has never thought: If there is a Constitution, then what is the use of this clerical establishment? If the operation of the country is based on the Constitution, then what is the use of this "Ja'fari jurisprudence"? What is my business, and what title can I hold in accordance with the Constitution? He has merely wanted to have a hand in both markets, to profit from both. And despite being more than eighty years old, he still lives hypocritically and slyly.

There is another story about the same cleric. A native of Azarbaijan said, "In the early years of the Constitution, I had traveled to Tehran with a few other people. I thought one day to visit the cleric. When we went there, we saw a large hall where a 'teaching session' was being held. Theological students had filled the hall and the cleric was

191

engaged in discussion and research." The discussion was about "whether or not it is permissible to draw human faces."

When we sat down, the cleric greeted us and returned to his discussion. We sat down and listened. The cleric spoke and so did the theological students. They recited *hadith*s [reported sayings] and presented evidence. Finally, the cleric said in Arabic: "It is better to be avoided."

Upon our departure, outside we were told: "The son of the cleric, who had gone to Europe to study, has returned." We decided to visit him as well. There we found another kind of setting, in the European style, with chairs and tables. The cleric's son, without a head cover and in Western clothes, shook hands with us and said "merci" several times. When we sat down and began to talk, we asked: "Well, sir, what was your field of study?" Among the courses that the cleric's son mentioned were drawing and painting!

We were surprised, given that the father had argued as he did while the son said something quite different. The father told the theological students, "Drawing faces is not permissible"; the son said that he had studied it and that he was a good "painter."

These are examples of the actions and behavior of the clerics. The clerics in Najaf and Karbala behave differently.

First of all, most of them are sons of some vegetable vendor, gardener or rural farmer. Early in their youth, in order to escape working, they went to school, lived a life of freeloading, happily and lazily, and after some years, went to Najaf or Karbala with the money of some "religious" haji, where they continued freeloading and living until they could be considered "religious jurists" and be called "Hojjat ol-Eslam." Some are clerics's sons, whose fathers had lived the life of a *Hojjat ol-Eslam*, and the sons have known nothing but that kind of life from the time they opened their eyes to the world.

In any case, they are ignorant people who do not know as much about the world and its affairs as a ten-year-old child. And since their minds are filled with religious jurisprudence, reported sayings and long, involved fabrications of principles and philosophy, there is no room left for knowledge or information. So much has happened in the world, sciences have appeared and changes have occurred, which they have either not known or understood or have understood but have not paid any attention to. They live in the present, but cannot look at the world except from the perspective of thirteen hundred years ago.

The good-for-nothings study for six months "whether or not the introduction for a compulsory action is compulsory." They endure hardship for thirty or forty years in order to one day be called a "Hojjat ol-Eslam." Their greatest wish is to get a share of the money from India and gather "emulators" from the "pious" merchants of Iran.

Secondly, they have alienated themselves altogether from Constitutionalism and retain the same organization that existed before the Constitutional era. So many movements have appeared in Iran, wars have occurred, the Constitution has been written, and now a Constitutional government has been in place for thirty-eight years, yet they ignore all of this in Najaf and Karbala and expect nothing of the people but obedience in everything, payment to them of *zakat* and the "imam's share," and, should the government go to war, seeking a "decree" from them. They still seriously pursue lessons in religious jurisprudence and principles, and no one knows what they are good for. They are still engaged in "practical religious dissertations."

During the time of Akhund Khorasani and the other two, the rays of Constitutionalism also shone on Najaf and Karbala, and certain movements appeared there too. But when these three died, one by one, the light stopped shining and was destroyed, leaving not a trace behind. It is interesting that Mirza Hoseyn Na'ini, who was a student of Akhund Khorasani, had written and published a pamphlet during his lifetime about Constitutionalism and its advantages. He later regretted it, gathered up all the copies, took them back, and, as it is reported, instead wrote and published a book about religious mourning, self-flagellation and other such displays.

This is an example of their interest in their own well being and their lack of attention to the interests of the country and the people. One statement must be made: In their ignorance, in trying to preserve their own organization, they are content with the misery of twenty million people.

They make a living from two sources: first, off money which "Hojjat ol-Eslams" receive from India every year through the British representatives, each of whom take a share for themselves, distributing the remainder among the theological students around them; second, off money which is sent or delivered in person by the "pious" merchants and wealthy people in Iran.

We will not speak about the money from India, since we do not know much about it. But we will talk about the money that comes from Iranian merchants and wealthy people.

These pious merchants, wealthy people, and hajis of Iran are a group opposing Constitutionalism and a hostile towards the nation and the country. As soon as they hear such terms as patriotism or law, they boldly ridicule them. They call the Constitutionalists "irreligious" and would not consider any uncivilized action beneath them. They live in this country but oppose anything that is in the interests of this country.

They first found Constitutionalism to be irreconcilable to their

193

sect and opposed it. And this is where the hostilities had their roots. Furthermore, they selfishly enjoy being apart from the people, feeling superior to them, ridiculing and insulting them. When they gather, you see how they constantly speak ill of and ridicule the government, the people of the country, Constitutionalism and law, and how they laugh and relish such behavior.

It pleases them that they have created a group of people among the masses that rebels and disobeys the laws. It pleases them to speak impudently to everyone.

On the other hand, it is in their interests to refuse to pay taxes. And in order to conceal their huge incomes, they keep two sets of books. It pleases them that they keep their sons from doing military service by giving bribes. It pleases them that they enjoy everything in the country, they live for the most part happily, and they do not submit to any of its regulations.

They are so impudent. Their excuse is the Shi'ite sect, and they feel secure in the support of the clerics, particularly the organizations in Najaf and Karbala.

As we said, not only are they enemies of the Constitution and the country, who disobey the laws, but they also avoid good deeds and engage in every evil. As we said, for this reason, they need the Shi'ite sect.

Most of them accumulate wealth through buying and selling goods, hoarding and overpricing. They are people, as we have seen, who look beyond the destruction of families and increase prices every day at the slightest excuse. That is why they need that sect. The Shi'ite sect does not object to such actions of theirs. Rather, it promises Paradise to them after one pilgrimage. This is to them like water is to the thirsty.

For this reason, they value the Shi'ite sect and by giving money to the clerics, they preserve it. They must not allow the organizations in Karbala and Najaf to be eliminated. This is the secret of the interdependence of the rich and the clerics of Najaf and Karbala. Indeed, they support each other. This group protects that one and that one protects this one.

There are also many stories in this connection. I will only record one of them here: In Zanjan, there is a factory which is owned by people from Tabriz. The manager of the factory is one of the very "pious" hajis. This man, despite being a merchant, has become the "deputy" of one of the *mojtaheds* [religious jurists] in Najaf, assigned to collect the "Imam's share," "*radd-e Mazalem*" and other such monies that must be given to the clerics. And every two or three years he goes to Najaf to deliver the money. This man keeps two sets of books for the

194

factory: one for the government, which shows only a small income, and another for themselves, which shows a huge income. And, as we have discovered, every year he separates a huge amount of money as "*khoms* and imam's share" and sets it aside for Najaf.

This is an example of the practices of the "pious" hajis. It is an indication of their ill will towards the government. You can find tens of thousands like this haji among the businessmen and bazaar merchants.

Let us not digress too far. The claims of the clerics about the government and their teaching the people to be hostile towards the government is very harmful. Let me repeat, it is very harmful. This alone can cause the misfortune of the masses, so that as a result of the same claim, large segments of the population wish the government, the country and the nation ill. Not only do they fail to carry out their obligations, but they would not stop at any disruption. Others aside, in government offices, there are many people who consider working for the government to be religiously prohibited, who consider obeying and implementing the laws to be sinful, and who "purge" the money they receive "with the permission of religious scholars." If the same people have government money in their hands, they would not hesitate to steal it as "retribution," and would not stop at breaking any law out of revenge.

A few years ago, I saw an interrogator in Qazvin who openly stated: "This law is imposed on us by the unjust government. I must avoid implementing it, as best I can." You can see what poisonous fruits are created in Iran by the political games of those who wish to rule in Arabia after twelve hundred years in Iran. Can people with such sinister beliefs ever achieve salvation? Where else in the world can you find such ignorance?

There are many reasons for the fact that Constitutionalism did not achieve any results in Iran and today it has fallen into such a disgraceful state, the fact that a population of twenty million has fallen into such misfortune and helplessness, and the fact that the offsprings of the Anglo-Saxons have set out from across the oceans to come and run this country. But the greatest of them all is Shi'ism itself, as well as the claims of the clerics.

One of the great tasks that must be accomplished in Iran is to reveal how baseless this claim is and to cleanse the minds of the people of such sinister and poisonous ideas. We must have many verbal battles about this matter, and we must not stop at any effort. Here, I would like to discuss this claim and bring the clerics to judgment. I would like to respond to a series of their questions.

As we said, the pretext of the clerics in this claim is a statement (a reported saying) from the Invisible Imam: "In events, turn to the repeaters of our statements, because theirs are my proof to you, and I am God's proof to them."[38] There are many such statements quoted from the imams. Such a great claim is based on statements such as this.

Now, I ask the clerics:

I: What positions did those who made these statements hold, and what made them competent to do so? I know they will answer: "They were imams, who must be obeyed." My answer is: This is a name that you have given them yourselves and God dislikes it. According to the Koran: "They are names that you and your forefathers have chosen. God did not bestow upon them such authority."

Then why are these "imams who must be obeyed" not mentioned in the Koran? And why did Imam Ali Abitaleb write Mo'aviyeh: "If the council of the migrants and the companions of the Prophet gather around a man and consider him their imam, God shall be pleased."[39] He did not write: God has chosen me, and the Prophet has foretold it. Did Ali, with his drawn sword, practice "dissimulation"?

Then how do you respond to the criticism that we have made about the "Invisible Imam," as stated in this book? What answer do you have? Firstly, the existence of such a thing must be proven, with evidence, for you to make such a claim. But what evidence exists about it? Which one of those reported sayings that you have recorded in your books is acceptable?

II: The "reported saying" does not indicate the meaning that you intend.

It states: If you find yourself in a situation (which you do not know how to handle and do not know what has been decreed about it), ask those who know our words and can repeat them to you. There is a lot of difference between this statement and the claim made to the government. They are two quite different matters.

I know they will say: "The imam has himself made us proof [hojjat]." I respond: "Hojjat is a term for which we have no equivalent in Persian." A hojjat is a person whose words must be accepted.[40] The imam has said that in events, your words should be accepted. There is a lot of difference between this statement and your taking over the governing of the affairs of the country and having the people under your command. It is quite clear that there is no word about government or ruling in that reported saying.

III: How can you rule or govern a large number of destitute people? You are made up of thousands and tens of thousands of people scattered among the cities, and none of you obeys another. Given this situation, what can you accomplish? If governing is to be autocratic, it should be done with one person who is obeyed by all others, and if it is to take the form of consultation, there must be an assembly in which all

196

gather, consult each other and accept what the majority chooses. With your disunity and disorganization, what can government mean to you?

IV: Let us put all this aside. Suppose government belongs to you and you are capable of running it, then why do you not want to take it over? Why do you not want to "implement religious laws"? What is to prevent you? If you are afraid of the government, given all the followers that you have, if you rise up to the task, undoubtedly, the government will not stand in your way. When did you even show a desire to do so, that we can say you could not do it? When did you ever rise up, so that we could say you did not succeed? Then why, rather than planting doubt in people and abandoning them, do you not rise up to the task?

Supposing that you are incapable of it. What fault is it of the people that you have abandoned? "I neither try myself nor allow others to do so. The people must be trampled. Foreigners must come and suppress them." Who was the teacher who taught you to make the people suffer the way you do?

We know that because you have no answer, you will say: "Let it be a civil government; but it must obtain permission from us." I say: What for? If governing is your right, why do you not rise up to the task? If it is not your right, what need is there of permission? Besides, if the "civil government" is "unjust," why should you grant it "permission"? You say: "The people must implement the Ja'fari jurisprudence, and these laws are contrary to the religious laws." What results can you gain by only granting "permission"? If you want to retain the status quo and allow a large nation to be sacrificed for your freeloading, you should say it out in the open and end these lengthy arguments.

Besides, you are not only one or two persons. From which one of you should the government obtain permission? Is it not true that if one of you gives permission, others will not submit to it and no results will be obtained?

In conclusion, let us suppose that the government obtains permission from all well-known religious scholars. Will you then give up collecting *zakat* and the "Imam's share" and instruct the people to pay the government? If the government is no longer "unjust" with your "permission," will you step aside and leave the people alone? Will you stop instigating doubt in the people?

V: In Islam, *zakat* was like taxation. Islam intended to create a large country governed by one calif, who was to be responsible for the welfare of the people, advancing Islam, creating a strong and able government that would place fighters on the borders, sending "judges" to cities for the peace and security of the people, and establishing a police department. Such tasks require revenues. Today, governments collect taxes, and in those days, Islam established *zakat*. In any case, *zakat* did not belong to the calif personally; it was not his "pocket money."

The Koran has indicated where the revenues from *zakat* must be spent: They must be given to the poor and destitute, used to pay the debts of debtors and to hire mercenaries from among the "heathens" (those of good will) for "religious wars". And of the remainder, a large portion is to be used for such activities as fighting enemies, organizing the army, and purchasing weapons.

Also, the "imam's share" is in the name of the imam himself, one who would be deserving of leadership [*imamat*] or who holds the office of calif. This is considered wages for the person who spends his days and nights trying to maintain the tranquility of the Islamic country. In short, both *zakat* and the "imam's share" were compensations for work and effort, and not for the nurturing of freeloaders and parasites.

Now, my fifth question is: You clerics who do not rise up to the task of administering the country and altogether stand aside and do not take a step forward, under what pretext do you collect *zakat* and the "imam's share," assuming "Islamic rule" or government or whatever you want to call it does belong to you? While you are not engaged in working, how could you collect *zakat* and the "imam's share"? For what purpose do you use the revenues collected as *zakat* and the "imam's share"? Do you administer the country? Do you engage in holy war? Do you mobilize "*mo'alef al-qolub*"? Do you send "judges" and "police" to the cities? *Zakat* and the "imam's share" are designed for these tasks, none of which you do. I do not know for what reason you collect money from the people. I ask you: Is this not "taking what is prohibited"?

I know you will say: We teach religion to the people. My answer is: It is a lie. You teach them nothing. You try to preserve the beliefs people already have. An organization has been built, which you guard. You are so engrossed in profit seeking that you have not yet told the people that "self-infliction of wounds is prohibited." You have not told them, "Do not transport the bones of the dead from one city to another." You have not told them, lest you offend a few and cause them to turn away from you.

Furthermore, supposing that your statements are true. Who said that the revenues from *zakat* and the "imam's share" are for teaching religion to the people? Where is such a statement recorded?

VI: Given your claim about government and that whatever you say concerns Islam, what can your claim mean, since Islam no longer exists?

It will be difficult for you to hear me say that there is no more

198

Islam, and you will not understand what I mean. With your lack of awareness, how could you understand? That is why I direct you to read the book, *Dar Piramun-e Eslam* [On Islam], which has been published. Read it so that you will know that Islam has been completely eliminated and what remains is nothing but an aberration, which must be eliminated.

Today, there remains no country called Islam for you to rule. Today, Moslems of every ethnic group have separated, and each has created a country in the name of that ethnic group. In Iran, people live as Iranians, not as Moslems. That is why they consider the Iraqis, Egyptians, Jews, and Zoroastrians who live in Iran to be one of them. Besides, for many years, Western laws have been practiced in Iran, and Islamic laws have been set aside. Is this not proof that Islam has been eliminated?

If you are able to bring Islam back and establish a country under that name, you can also make a claim to rule it.

VII: After all this, from two hundred years ago, Constitutionalism (or government of the people, which is the best kind of government) began in Europe and America. Here, I do not want to praise Constitutionalism or even try to explain to you the meaning of it, which you do not know. I will only say that this kind of government is known throughout the world, and Iran too, after much bloodshed because of you and the royal court, has accepted it. Now, how can you reconcile your claim to it? What are your thoughts about it? Do you expect the Iranians to abandon the rule of the people that they have gained after so much effort because of your futile and nonsensical claims and once again submit to dictatorial government? Does such an expectation not rise out of ignorance?

These are the questions that I ask of the clerics. These are the criticisms that I make of their claim.

In short, the claim of the clerics about government:

Firstly, is absolutely without foundation and is based on nothing but bullying;

Secondly, is something that cannot be and will not happen;

Thirdly, is merely a claim made by the clerics, and they want nothing else. On the one hand, they collect the *zakat* and the "imam's share" revenues to ensure that their freeloading organization will thrive, and, on the other hand, they always weaken the government and prevent it from becoming powerful.

Many of them, too, blindly and ignorantly follow some path. They are so uninformed and ignorant that they do not understand how clearly harmful it is.

I will make one statement: Your claim is based on bullying and shamelessness, one which will result in harming and ill wishes towards the people.

I do not know how the clerics will respond to these criticisms. I do not know whether they will realize the heinousness of their actions. I do not know if they will remember God and be ashamed.

I have frequently seen that under such circumstances, they begin to make a ruckus, instigate the common people and ignorant old women to rebel, or turn to the government for justice, or keep absolutely silent and ignore all they have seen or heard, all the while continuing to practice such behavior.

That is why I say that the noise you make is no more important than the crowing of crows. And turning to the government is improper and futile. The government can neither do nor say anything about this. The law does not allow it. We have not cursed or "insulted" anyone. We have raised certain objections and demanded answers. What business is it of the government's?

Suppose you make a lot of noise, suppose you get the government involved, and suppose you make visits, hold discussions, and engage in pretenses, will the criticism then be invalidated? Will there be an answer to our questions? Will such behavior be considered another proof that your sect and your claim are baseless? Will this not be another indication of your bullying? Why do you not hold sessions in which you can read, understand and think about our statements and judge them rationally? If they are true, accept them, and if they are not, write a response to us.

In any case, we have warned you.

Such open imposition of ideas cannot be accepted. One cannot see twenty million people sacrificed for your whims and fancies. We have called you to judgment. If you have any answers, tell us, and if you do not, confess your misguided ways and ask God for forgiveness. For you to say, "We neither have any answers nor will we agree with you," is clearly bullying, and it is clear what the response to bullying will be.

What I must write in conclusion is that some of these clerics would like to "excommunicate" us and "implement" their "religious laws." You are like "the man who was banned from entering the village, so he asked to go to the home of the village head."

We make hundreds of fundamental criticisms of the sect, not one which they can respond to, and still they continue so impudently. We say: Your sect has been destroyed from the root, and they want to call us "heathen," according to that sect. This should reveal to everyone how ignorant they are.

They must be told: You miss the point completely. You do not even know the meaning of "heathen" or irreligious. An irreligious person is one who ignores the living God and worships those who have been dead for a thousand years. An irreligious person is one who has not known God, the Creator, and puts the affairs of the world into the hands of "His Holiness Abbas," "His Excellency Ali Akbar," and "Imamzadeh Davud." An irreligious person is one who bows his head before a dome, one who turns to a woman who is a nobody in her own life and who left nothing behind after her death but a name, crying out, "Oh Fatemeh, be a mediator before God on my behalf." An irreligious person is one who mentions the name of God without any reservation, but when the name of an imaginary Invisible Imam is mentioned, he stands up out of respect. An irreligious person is one whose leaders say, "God created us from the highest clay, and created the Shi'ites from the remainder of our clay," and believe in and teach such exaggerations to the people as well. In short, since you do not understand the meaning of religion, you neither understand the meaning of irreligion.

* * *

At the time of the publication of this book, we had printed the letter of Imam Ali ebn Abitaleb to Mo'aviyeh in *Parcham* newspaper, asking the clerics for a response, to which two of them responded. One response came from a person by the name of Towhidi, from Tabriz, and another from Mr. Mohammad Khalesizadeh, from Kashan.

Towhidi writes: "In that letter, his holiness, the Commander of the Faithful, argues on the basis of what the enemy had admitted and understood (*mosallamat-e khasm*). In other words, he says, 'Oh, Mo'aviyeh, you believe that choosing a calif is the responsibility of the Mohajers and Ansar [companions of the Prophet] and with whomever they choose, God will be pleased. Hence, I was chosen by those same people, and in the same manner as they swore allegiance to Abu Bakr and Omar, they also swore allegiance to me. Oh Mo'aviyeh, you cannot refuse to accept this.' His holiness did not want to say what was proper or improper about the method of selection; he wanted to respond to Mo'aviyeh on the basis of Mo'aviyeh's own beliefs."

Mr. Khalesizadeh writes: "His holiness, the Commander of the Faithful, tries to convince Mo'aviyeh, because Mo'aviyeh has no evidence for the legitimacy of the rule of Abu Bakr, Omar and Osman except the assembly and consultation of the Mohajers and Ansar, and he uses this evidence in his correspondence with his holiness, the Commander of the Faithful. The Commander of the Faithful necessarily says that the same procedure that was carried out in regards to the choosing of Abu Bakr, Omar and Osman was also carried out in his case. Therefore, according to his own statement, Mo'aviyeh does not have the right to oppose him, if he confesses to the correctness of the selection of Abu Bakr and Osman."

This is an example of the responses that clerics make to our writing. We ask: For what reason do you change the clear meaning of a statement; why do you change it? Why do you not accept a statement which is so clear? In order not to give up your misguided beliefs, why do you change its meaning?

One of the misguided practices of the Shi'ite leaders is this very practice of reporting (or *ta'vil*). Whenever they find a statement irreconcilable with their wishes, they abandon the clear meaning and twist into it other meanings. This is one of their old methods, which in itself warrants strong criticism.

This is one of the ideas that they have taken from the Batenis. Since we have not spoken about the Batenis in this book, we ignored this criticism in regards to the Shi'ites as well.

After all, for what reason would you change the meaning of a statement by Imam Ali ebn Abitaleb? Imam Ali ebn Abitaleb was not a Seyyed Bab or Baha'ollah, not knowing Arabic well and incapable of communicating what he meant. Could Imam Ali ebn Abitaleb not have made the statements himself that Towhidi fabricated, like an intruder?

If that was what the Imam intended, he should have written, "Oh, Mo'aviyeh, you claim that Abu Bakr, Omar and Osman were justified, and those who gave them allegiance also gave their allegiance to me on the same grounds, and you claim that the Mohajers and Ansar consulted and they too pledged allegiance to me and supported me." For what reason, then, did he write as he did?

It is a strange story. An imam achieves the office of calif, writes a letter to a commander under him, who is contemplating refusing to accept his command, and, in a simple language, he writes: "The same people who took the hand of Abu Bakr, Omar and Osman in allegiance also took may hand."[41] Then he concludes from his own statement and writes: "Therefore, the one present cannot choose another, and the one absent cannot refuse to accept it."[42] He then tries to support that statement and writes: "Consultation is the right of the Mohajers and Ansar; 'God will be pleased with whomever they gather around and call imam.'"[43] He then turns to another issue and writes: "If the one chosen violates what the Mohajers and Ansar dictate and creates a religious 'innovation,' he must be guided, and if he refuses, he must be fought."[44] Since they do not find such simple and clear statements in keeping with their own wishes, they close their eyes completely and say, "He has argued on the basis of what the enemy accepts and understands." We

202

ask again, "For what reason do you change the meaning of such clear statements?"

When Mr. Khalesizadeh writes, "Because Mo'aviyeh has no evidence for the legitimacy of the rule of Abu Bakr, Omar and Osman except for the assembling and consultation of the Mohajers and Ansar, and he uses this evidence in his own correspondence with his holiness, the Commander of the Faithful . . .," he implies that Imam Ali ebn Abitaleb wrote these statements in response to the letters of Mo'aviyeh, which is a figment of his own imagination.

This letter, which is found in *Nahj al-Balagheh*, entitled "Letter to Mo'aviyeh," indicates that the Imam initiated the correspondence and wrote this letter, which is also supported by the letter itself. The same letter is also recorded in history books, and, as I far as I can recall, the same conclusion is reached from them. In any case, Mr. Khalesizadeh speaks from his imagination, as do others. Whatever the case may be, whether this was the first letter or it was a response to Mo'aviyeh's letter, it cannot and does not mean what these two persons have interpreted it to mean.

Both of these respondents have used the Shaqshaqieh sermon and consider it as evidence. They say that in that sermon, Imam Ali ebn Abitaleb expressed his displeasure with Abu Bakr and others as califs.

I say: That sermon is not found in the history books and cannot be accepted as authentic. Supposing that we believe it, it would indicate no more than a complaint and does not reveal anything more than that Imam Ali ebn Abitaleb privately considered himself to be more competent to be calif than others, which is different from what the Shi'ites say.

Then, if you try to interpret that letter and say that it was written as *elzam-e khasm* [convincing the enemy], others can also interpret the sermon and say that the Imam had said it for "ta'lif-e qolub" [appeasing the hearts] of the Rafezis, who were in great numbers in Kufeh.

If someone makes such an interpretation of this statement, you will have no answer to it. This is a door that you have opened yourself. As the Arabs say: "What makes your argument more valid than mine?"

In conclusion, we will have to mention once more that these discussions do not belong to religion. There is no room in religion for past and future events. In religion, the names of one person or another are not mentioned. Indeed, this is irreligiosity, when certain people want to abandon their own lives to speak about the events of thirteen hundred years ago, to create factionalists among the dead, and engage in conflicts from all sides. Religion is to prevent human beings from being so ignorant, and to prevent them from engaging in such futile actions.

As we said, religion is "understanding the meaning of the world and life and living in accordance with the dictates of rational faculties." Anyone who would like to be well informed about it should read my book, *Varjavand Bonyad*, and my other books.

What has forced us into such discussions is the fact that, as we said, the clerics have made a claim to the government and they disrupt the life of the nation. And their pretext is that Imam Ali ebn Abitaleb was chosen calif by God, and other such statements. In order to show that their claim is without any foundation, we have been forced to engage in such discussions.

NOTES

1. This letter is found in *Nahj ol-Balagheh* and is also mentioned in history books.(Kasravi)

The Arabic originals given by Kasravi in this footnote and other footnotes throughout the text are omitted. Translations of Arabic phrases throughout the text are based on Kasravi's Persian renditions wherever the original text provides them. (tr)

2. As in the letter of Imam Ali ebn Abitaleb to Mo'aviyeh, the calif was called the "imam." (Kasravi)

3 - 4. Arabic original in footnote omitted here. (tr)

5. In his *Islamic Messianism* (Albany: SUNY Press, 1981), p. 96, Abdulaziz Sachedina mentions the fourth deputy as Abu al-Hasan Ali b. Muhamad al-Sammarri. (tr)

6. Arabic original in footnote omitted here. (tr)

7. The book *Mahdi* has been translated into and published in Persian. (Kasravi)

James Darmesteter: French Iranologist, 1849-1894. (tr)

8. *Baha'ism*, already published. (Kasravi)

9 - 12. Arabic original in footnote omitted here. (tr)

13. On two occasions, it has been stated in the Koran: "I do not know of the unknown." On another occasion, it is stated: "If I knew of the unknown, I would have multiplied the good and no harm would touch me." (Kasravi)

14. In the Koran, on one occasion, several miracles are demanded. "They said: Either make a spring spout out of the ground, create a garden full of date palms and vines with springs of water passing through them, create a house made of gold, ascend to the sky, write a book and bring it back descending from the heavens, make the sky fall on our heads, or bring before us God and the angels." In response, it is stated: "Am I but an individual human being whom God has sent to you?" On another occasion, it is stated: "We do not send miracles, because when we did so in the past, they were considered lies." On still another occasion, the Koran states: "They said, Then why is a sign (miracle) not given to him? Tell them: All signs are in the possession of God, and I am only a warner." (Kasravi)

15 - 25. Arabic original in footnote omitted here. (tr)

26. *The Moslem World*. (Kasravi)

27. The photograph of the surah in question in omitted here. (tr)

28. A prayer recited to ward off danger. (tr)

29. *Qamehzani*: inflicting wounds on one's shaved head with a saber. *Shah-Hoseyni*: also referring to the same practice, which is accompanied by chanting "Shah Hoseyn," a reference to the third Shi'ite imam. A practice in commemoration of the martyrdom of the third Shi'ite imam. (tr)

30. *Sinehzan*: literally, "person beating oneself on the chest." *Zanjirzan*: literally, "person beating oneself with chains," forms of self-flagellation in the commemoration of the martyrdom of the third Shi'ite imam, Hoseyn. (tr)

31. The pictures of the *qamehzan*, *qofl be-tan*, the corpse of Qasem, and the bride of Qasem included in this volume are from the monthly publication *Tour du Monde*, which was founded eighty years ago in Paris and published for many years. These pictures were in turn taken from a book by a Russian world traveler, who toured Caucasia and, in order to show the savagery of the Caucasians, took these pictures and published them in his book. (Kasravi)

The pictures referred to in this note are not included in this volume. (tr)

32. It had first been published in *Habl ol-Matin* and then in a separate book in Tabriz. (Kasravi)

33. This story is so well known that Molla Mohammad Ali Nakhchavani, a religious jurist who died more than a decade ago, was asked about it. He responded: "It does not matter. The body of Ali Akbar was also torn to pieces." (Kasravi)

34. Anyone who wants to learn about the true meaning of religion and religious life should read *Varjavand Bonyad*. (Kasravi)

35. This is from a long poem composed by a poet named Arzi. (Kasravi) One couplet is omitted here. (tr)

36. These statements are recorded in the book *Qesas al-'Olama'*. (Kasravi)

37. *Hur* and *ghelman*s: Although *hur* and *ghelman* are plural in Arabic, they are used as singular forms in Persian and refer to beautiful females and males in Paradise who, according to popular beliefs, are given as reward in the next world to the faithful. (tr)

38 - 39. Arabic original in the footnote omitted here. (tr)

40. The discrepancy between this and other statements made earlier in this section by Kasravi's opponents is unclear. (tr)

41 - 44. Arabic original in the footnote omitted here. (tr)

SELECTED BIBLIOGRAPHY
OF THE WRITINGS OF AHMAD KASRAVI

Afsaran-e Ma [Our Officers]. Tehran: 1323 [1944/45].

A'in [Creed]. Tehran: 1311 [1932/33].

Az Sazman-e Melal-e Mottafeq Cheh Natijeh Tavanad Bud? [What Will Be the Result of the United Nations?]. Tehran: 1324 [1945/46].

Baha'igari [Baha'ism]. Tehran: 1322 [1943/44].

Bahmanmah-e 1323 [Bahman, 1323]. Tehran: np, nd.

Chand Tarikhcheh [Some Histories]. Tehran: 1314 [1935/36].

Dadgah [Court of Justice]. Tehran: 1323 [1944/45].

Dah Sal dar Adliyyeh [Ten Years in the Justice Department]. Tehran:np, nd.

Dar Pasokh-e Bad-Khahan [Response to Ill Wishers]. Tehran: np, nd.

Dar Piramun-e Adabiyyat [On Literature]. Tehran: 1323 [1944/45].

Dar Piramun-e Islam [On Islam]. Tehran: 1322 [1943/44].

Dar Piramun-e Falsafeh-ye Yunan [On Greek History]. Tehran: 1344[1965/66].

Dar Piramun-e Janevaran [On Animals]. Tehran: 1324 [1945/46].

Dar Piramun-e Kherad [On Rational Faculties]. Tehran: 1322[1943/44].

Dar Piramun-e Ravan [On the Soul]. Tehran: 1324 [1945/46].

Dar Piramun-e Roman [On Fiction]. Tehran: 1322 [1943/44].

Dar Piramun-e She'r va Sha'eri [On Poetry and Poetry Writing]. np,nd.

Dar Rah-e Siyasat [On the Path of Politics]. Tehran: 1324 [1945/46].

Din va Danesh [Religion and Science]. Tehran: 1319 [1940/41].

Din va Jahan [Religion and the World]. Tehran: 1323 [1944/45].

Dowlat be Ma Pasokh Dehad [Let the Government Respond to Us]. Tehran:1323 [1944/45].

Emruz Char-e Chist? [What Is the Cure Today?]. Tehran: 1324 [2945/46].

Emruz Cheh Bayad Kard? [What Must Be Done Today?]. Tehran: 1320 [1941/42].

Enkizisiyon dar Iran [Inquisition in Iran] (incomplete). Tehran: 1322 [1943/44].

Farhang Ast Ya Neyrang? [Is It Culture or Deception?]. Tehran: 1323:[1944/45].

Farhang Chist? [What Is Culture?]. Tehran: 1322 [1943/44].

Goft va Shenid [Conversation]. Tehran: 1323 [2944/45].

Hafez Cheh Miguyad? [What Does Hafez Say?]. Tehran: 1322

[1943/44].

Kafnameh [The Book of Kaf]. np, nd.

Kar va Pisheh va Pul [Work, Profession and Money]. Tehran: 1323 [1944/45].

Khaharan va Dokhtaran-e Ma [Our Sisters and Daughters]. Tehran: 1323[1944/45].

Khoda Ba Mast [God Is With Us]. Tehran.

Ma Cheh Mikhahim? [What Do We Want?]. Tehran: 1319 [1940/41].

Mardom-e Yahud [The Jewish People] (incomplete). Tehran: np, nd.

Mashrut-e Behtarin Shekl va Akherin Natijeh-ye Andisheha-ye Nezhad-e Adami Ast [Constitutionalism Is the Best Form and the Best Result of Human Thought]. np, nd.

Mosha'sha'iyan [The Mosha'sha'is]. Tehran: 1324 [1945/46].

Namha-ye Shahrha va Deyhha[The Names of Cities and Villages]. Tehran:1308 [1929/30].

Nik va Bad [Good and Evil]. Tehran: 1323 [1944/45].

Pendarha [Superstitions]. Tehran: 1322 [1943/44].

Peydayesh-e Amrika [The Creation of America]. Tehran: 1324 [1945/46].

Porsesh va Pasokh [Question and Answer]. Tehran: 1325 [1946/47].

Qanun-e Dadgari [The Law of Adjudication]. Tehran: 1312 [1933/34].

Rah-e Rastegari [Path to Salvation]. Tehran: 1316 [1937/38].

Sarnevesht-e Iran Cheh Khakhad Bud? [What Will Be the Fate of Iran?]. Tehran: 1324 [1945/46].

Shahriyaran-e Gomnam [The Unknown Monarchs]. Tehran: 1307-1309 [1928-31].

Sheykh Safi va Tabarash [Sheykh Safi and His Ancestry]. Tehran: 1323 [1944/45].

Shi'igari [Shi'ism]. Tehran: 1322 [1943/44].

Sizdahom-e Mordad [Thirteenth of Mordad]. Tehran: 1323 [1944/45].

Sufigari [Sufism]. Tehran: 1322 [1943/44].

Tarikhcheh-ye Chopoq va Ghalyan [The History of Clay Pipes and Water Pipes]. Tehran: 1323 [1944/45].

Tarikhcheh-ye Shir va Khorshid [The History of the "Lion and Sun"]. Tehran: 1309 [1930/31].

Tarikh-e Hijdah Soleh-ye Azarbayjan [The Eighteen-Year History of Azarbaijan]. Tehran: 1313-1319 [1934-41].

Tarikh-e Mashruteh-ye Iran [The History of the Iranian Constitutional Movement. Tehran: 1319-21 [1940-43].

Tarikh-e Nader Shah [The History of Nader Shah]. Tehran: np, nd.

Tarikh-e Pansad Saleh-ye Khuzestan [The Five-Hundred-Year History of Khuzestan. Tehran: 1312 [1933/34].

Varjavand Bonyad [Sacred Foundation]. Tehran: 1322 [1943/44].

Yekom-e Azar-e 1322 [The First of Azar, 1322]. Tehran: 1323 [1944/45].

Yekom-e Azar-e 1323 [The First of Azar, 1323]. Tehran: np, nd.

Yekom-e Deymah-e 1322 [The First of Dey, 1322]. Tehran: 1323 [1944/45].

Yekom-e Deymah-e 1323 [The First of Dey, 1323]. Tehran: np, nd.

Yekom-e Deymah va Dastanash [The First of Dey and It's Story]. np,nd.

Zaban-e Azari [The Azari Language]. Tehran: np, nd.

Zaban-e Farsi [The Persian Language]. Tehran: 1316 [1937/38].

Zaban-e Pak [Pure Language]. Tehran: 1322 [1943/44].

Zendegani-ye Man [My Life]. Tehran: 1323 [1944/45].